POETRY
FOR A
LIFETIME

POETRY FOR A

LIFETIME

All-time favorite poems to delight and inspire all ages

❖

When the trials and tribulations of present day society,
Lead me to think I may soon need psychiatry,
I step outside beneath a friendly tree,
And lose myself in song or poetry.
Then my heart with rapture fills,
And dances with Wordsworth's daffodils.
The Editor

SELECTED AND ANNOTATED BY

SAMUEL NORFLEET ETHEREDGE

M
MIRAVISTA

POETRY FOR A LIFETIME
Copyright © 1999 by MiraVista Press

PUBLISHED BY MIRAVISTA PRESS

ISBN 0-9665804-0-0

Library of Congress Catalog Card Number: 98-86906

Cover design by Steve Kirschner.
Book design and layout by Scott Fitzgerell and Robert C. Etheredge
Some of the images used herein were obtained from IMSI's MasterClips
Collection, 1895 Francisco Blvd. East, San Rafael, CA 94901-5506 USA
Some images copyright www.arttoday.com

Cover image *Riverbank, Autumn* by Maxfield Parrish
Image courtesy the Archives of the American Illustrators Gallery,
New York City (c) Copyright 1998, by ASaP of Holderness, NH, 03245, USA
Authorized by The Maxfield Parrish Family Trust

MiraVista Press
P.O. Box 961
Orinda, CA 94563
888-811-0746 (toll free)
925-253-9472
Fax: 925-940-9516
Email: poetry@miravista.com
Web: http://www.miravista.com

ACKNOWLEDGEMENTS

For the privilege of reprinting poems in this book, I would like to thank the many wonderful books of poetry I reviewed. I made every effort to get permission for any copyrighted poems contained herein. If I have not given proper permission for any poem, please notify me so I can include that permission in the next printing.

For *Repentance, I Believe, Brother Jim, Inspiration, The Ordinary Man,* and *Moderation,* reprinted by permission of The Putman Publishing Group from THE BEST OF ROBERT SERVICE by Robert Service. Copyright (c) 1907, 1909, 1912, 1916, 1921, 1949, 1950, 1951, 1952, 1953 by Dodd, Mead and Company, Inc.; Copyright (c) 1940 by Robert Service.

William Bennett, for his wonderful *Book of Virtues*, a superb combination of poetry and inspiring prose.

Wally Riddell, for permitting me to include the select group of his *Bits of Wit and Wisdom*.

Eloise Lang for her World of Poetry award winning *Talents*.

I also want to thank my friends who encouraged me verbally and by lending me their treasured books. My wife, for the hours I spent in the libraries, book stores and over the stack of books at home. And most specially my co-editor son, Robert C. Etheredge, for the many hours of help in finding, printing, correcting, assembling, alphabetizing and putting this whole collection into book form. Also my daughter, Suzanne Ramseyer, for help in assembling the material.

INTRODUCTION BY THE EDITOR

When I happened to mention to a group of friends that I was compiling an anthology of poetry, one of them spoke up, "Why do you want to put together a bunch of poems by other people?" This made me do a little soul searching for a good answer. I realized that I had loved poetry since I was a child, learning all the old standards that my folks taught me, and quite a few besides. I did a lot of reading while still in grammar school and particularly loved poems. The poetry enjoyment continued through an excellent high school and college curriculum. While serving as a Navy doctor with the Marine 3rd Division in the Pacific during World War II, I encountered many poems written by the boys during the long days of boredom, awaiting movement to the field of action. During this time I scribbled out two of the enclosed poems, *Bougainville* and *Hate Comes to Paradise*. (Please pardon me for including them.)

In recent years it has bothered me considerably that, first, my four children, and then later my grandchildren seem to have had minimum exposure to most of the old "goodies" that I had always greatly enjoyed, such as *Old Ironsides, Paul Revere's Ride*, and *Annabel Lee*, just to scratch the surface. When I discovered that my grandkids had not even heard of *Casey at the Bat* or *The Wreck of the Hesperus*, I felt I would surely like to do something about it.

To that end I have reviewed thousands of poems in the past two to three years. Naturally the ones selected here represent my personal choices.

On a recent popular game show, the three very sharp adults could not answer the important last question, "What poem, written in 1913, contains the line 'A nest of robins in her hair'?" I was shocked and I am sure Joyce Kilmer wanted to throw down an 'enlightning' bolt.

My leanings closely resemble those of Longfellow which he expressed so well in *The Day is Done*.

"Come, read to me some poem,
Some simple and heartfelt lay,
That shall soothe this restless feeling,
And banish the thoughts of day.

Not from the grand old masters,
Not from the bards sublime,
Whose distant footsteps echo
Through the corridors of Time.

For, like strains of martial music,
Their mighty thoughts suggest
Life's endless toil and endeavor,
And tonight I long for rest."

Thanks, Mr. Longfellow, for expressing it so beautifully. So that explains the presence of very little from the "Greats," such as Byron, Keats and Shelly, while heavy on Kipling, Service and Guest. That's how I like it; I hope you do too. And I hope my grandkids, and yours, will learn to read and enjoy poetry.

If I have helped turn just a few from their *Calfpath*; made one or two take the *If* test; maybe led a couple to memorize *Annabel Lee*; and a boy or two to love *Casey at the Bat*; and brought solace to even one blind person with Milton's beautiful ode on his blindness; then I feel I have helped a bit to accomplish what I set out to do.

I have bolded (highlighted) many very special passages for emphasis. Also, I have added quite a bit of accessory information, where indicated, and other comments to help stir up interest, especially in the younger group. I wish I could add songs, too, because I truly feel

Music is the Poetry of Expression
Poetry is the Music of Literature.

Thank you—relax and enjoy,
Samuel Norfleet Etheredge

DEDICATION

❖

This book is dedicated to the youth of America in the hope
that it will stir up interest and enjoyment in the very
rewarding field of poetry. If it does, then I guarantee those
feelings will last a lifetime.

❧ TABLE OF CONTENTS ❧

NURSERY

Now I Lay Me Down to Sleep
by Unknown

Certainly my first prayer, and I would bet it was yours too.

Now I lay me down to sleep;
    I pray the Lord my soul to keep.
If I should die before I wake,
    I pray the Lord my soul to take.

Twinkle, Twinkle, Little Star
by Unknown

Has any kid missed this one?

Twinkle, twinkle, little star!
    How I wonder what you are,
Up above the world so high,
    Like a diamond in the sky.

When the glorious sun is set,
    When the grass with dew is wet,
Then you show your little light,
    Twinkle, twinkle all the night.

In the dark-blue sky you keep,
    And often through my curtains peep,
For you never shut your eye,
    Till the sun is in the sky.

As your bright and tiny spark
    Guides the traveler in the dark,
Though I know not what you are,
    Twinkle, twinkle, little star!

Lullaby Town

by John Irving Diller

Pleasant dreams; Eden in Dreamland. Now don't
you fall asleep reading it to the little ones.

There's a quaint little place they call Lullaby Town—
It's just back of those hills where the sunsets go down.
Its streets are of silver, its buildings of gold,
And its palaces dazzling things to behold;
There are dozens of spires, housing musical chimes;
Its people are folk from the Nursery Rimes,
And at night it's alight, like a garden of gleams,
With fairies, who bring the most wonderful dreams.

The Sandman is Mayor, and he rules like a King.
The climate's so balmy that, always, it's spring,
And it's never too cold, and it's never too hot,
And I'm told that there's nowhere a prettier spot;
All in and about it are giant old trees,
Filled with radiant birds that will sing when you please;
But the strange thing about it—this secret, pray, keep—
Is, it never awakes till the world is asleep.

So when night settles down, all its lights snap aglow,
And its streets fill with people who dance to and fro.
Mother Goose, Old King Cole and his fiddlers three,
Miss Muffet, Jack Sprat and his wife, scamper free,
With a whole host of others, a boisterous crew,
Not forgetting the Old Lady Who Lived in a Shoe
And her troublesome brood who, with brownie and sprite,
Go trooping the streets, a bewildering sight.

There's a peddler who carries, strapped high on his back,
A bundle. Now, guess what he has in that pack.
There's a crowd all about him a-buying his wares,
And they're grabbing his goods up in threes and in pairs.
No, he's not peddling jams nor delectable creams.
Would you know what he's selling? Just wonderful dreams!

There are dreams for a penny and dreams that cost two;
And there's no two alike, and they're sure to come true;
And the buyers fare off with a toss of the head,
And they visit the Sandman, then hie them to bed;
For there's nothing to do in this land of Bo-Peep,
But to frolic and sing and then go off to sleep!

Twenty Froggies

by George Cooper

Our public schools could surely use some Master Bullfrogs.

Twenty froggies went to school
    Down beside a rushy pool.
Twenty little coats of green,
    Twenty vests all white and clean.

"We must be on time," said they,
    "First we study, then we play;
That is how we keep the rule,
    When we froggies go to school."

Master Bull-frog, brave and stern,
    Called his classes in their turn,
Taught them how to nobly strive,
    Also how to leap and dive;

Taught them how to dodge a blow,
    From the sticks that bad boys throw.
Twenty froggies grew up fast,
    Bull-frogs they became at last;

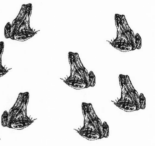

Polished in a high degree,
    As each froggie ought to be,
Now they sit on other logs,
    Teaching other little frogs.

Sweet and Low
by Alfred Tennyson (1809-1892)

A great lullaby. Sing it for me again, Mom.

Sweet and low, sweet and low.
    Wind of the western sea,
Low, low, breathe and blow,
    Wind of the western sea!
Over the rolling waters go,
    Come from the dropping moon and blow,
Blow him again to me;
    While my little one, while my pretty one sleeps.

Sleep and rest, sleep and rest,
    Father will come to thee soon;
Rest, rest, on mother's breast,
    Father will come to thee soon;
Father will come to his babe in the nest,
    Silver sails all out of the west
Under the silver moon:
    Sleep, my little one, sleep, my pretty one, sleep.

There Was a Little Girl
by Henry Wadsworth Longfellow (1807-1892)

Oh! There were some like that in Longfellow's time too!

There was a little girl, she had a little curl
    Right in the middle of her forehead;
And when she was good, she was very, very good,
    And when she was bad, she was horrid.

Wynken, Blynken, and Nod
by *Eugene Field (1850-1895)*

The author identifies these three characters in the
last stanza, so you may want to read it over
again so that the youngsters will really enjoy it.

Wynken, Blynken and Nod one night
    Sailed off in a wooden shoe,—
Sailed on a river of crystal light
    Into a sea of dew.
"Where are you going, and what do you wish?"
    The old moon asked the three.
"We have come to fish for the herring-fish
    That live in this beautiful sea;
    Nets of silver and gold have we,"
        Said Wynken,
        Blynken,
        And Nod.

The old moon laughed and sang a song,
    As they rocked in the wooden shoe;
And the wind that sped them all night long
    Ruffled the waves of dew;
The little stars were the herring-fish
    That lived in the beautiful sea.
"Now cast your nets wherever you wish,—
    Never afeard are we!"
    So cried the stars to the fishermen three,
        Wynken,
        Blynken,
        And Nod.

All night long their nets they threw
    To the stars in the twinkling foam,—
Then down from the skies came the wooden shoe,
    Bringing the fishermen home:
'Twas all so pretty a sail, it seemed
    As if it could not be;
And some folk thought 'twas a dream they'd dreamed
    Of sailing that beautiful sea;

But I shall name you the fishermen three:
 Wynken,
 Blynken,
 And Nod.

Wynken and Blynken are two little eyes,
 And Nod is a little head,
And the wooden shoe that sailed the skies
 Is a wee one's trundle-bed;
So shut your eyes while Mother sings
 Of wonderful sights that be,
And you shall see the beautiful things
 As you rock on the misty sea
 Where the old shoe rocked the fishermen three,–
 Wynken,
 Blynken,
 And Nod.

The Three Little Kittens

by Eliza Lee Follen (1787-1859)

Always good for a chuckle!

Three little kittens lost their mittens,
And they began to cry,
"Oh, mother dear,
We very much fear
That we have lost our mittens."
"Lost your mittens!
You naughty kittens!
Then you shall have no pie!"
"Mee-ow, mee-ow, mee-ow."
"No, you shall have no pie."

The three little kittens found their mittens,
And they began to cry,
"Oh, mother dear,
See here, see here!
See, we have found our mittens!"
"Put on your mittens,
You silly kittens,

And you may have some pie."
"Purr-r, purr-r, purr-r,
Oh, let us have the pie!
Purr-r, purr-r, purr-r."

The three little kittens put on their mittens,
And soon ate up the pie;
"Oh, mother dear,
We greatly fear
That we have soiled our mittens!"
"Soiled your mittens!
You naughty kittens!"
Then they began to sigh,
"Mee-ow, mee-ow, mee-ow."
Then they began to sigh,
"Mee-ow, mee-ow, mee-ow."

The three little kittens washed their mittens,
And hung them out to dry;
"Oh, mother dear,
Do not you hear
That we have washed our mittens?"
"Washed your mittens!
Oh, you're good kittens!
But I smell a rat close by,
Hush, hush! Mee-ow, mee-ow."
"We smell a rat close by,
Mee-ow, mee-ow, mee-ow."

Animal Fair

by Unknown

A little monkey business.

I went to the animal fair,
The birds and beasts were there.
The big baboon, by the light of the moon,
Was combing his auburn hair.
The monkey, he got drunk,
And sat on the elephant's trunk.
The elephant sneezed and fell on his knees,
And that was the end of the monk.

Nursery Rhymes

by Unknown

> One, two,
>> Buckle my shoe;
> Three, four,
>> Shut the door;
> Five, six,
>> Pick up sticks;
> Seven, eight,
>> Lay them straight;
> Nine, ten,
>> A good fat hen;
> Eleven, twelve,
>> Who will delve?

❖ ❖ ❖ ❖ ❖

> This little pig went to market.
>> This little pig stayed at home.
> This little pig had roast beef.
>> This little pig had none.
> And this little pig cried wee, wee, wee,
>> All the way home.

❖   ❖ ❖ ❖ ❖

> Sing a song of sixpence,
>> A pocket full of rye;
> Four and twenty blackbirds
>> Baked in a pie;

> When the pie was opened
>> The birds began to sing;
> Was not that a dainty dish
>> To set before the king?

> The king was in his counting-house
>> Counting out his money;
> The queen was in the parlour
>> Eating bread and honey;

The maid was in the garden
    Hanging out the clothes,
Then came a little blackbird
    And snapt off her nose.

❖ ❖ ❖ ❖ ❖

Old King Cole
    Was a merry old soul,
And a merry old soul was he;
    He called for his pipe,
And he called for his bowl,
    And he called for his fiddlers three.

❖ ❖ ❖ ❖ ❖

Ba, ba, black sheep,
    Have you any wool?
Yes, sir, yes sir,
    Three bags full.
One for my master,
    And one for my dame,
But none for the little boy
    Who cries in the lane.

❖ ❖ ❖ ❖ ❖

Pease-porridge hot,
    Pease-porridge cold,
Pease-porridge in the pot,
    Nine days old.
Some like it hot,
    Some like it cold,
Some like it in the pot,
    Nine days old.

❖ ❖ ❖ ❖ ❖

    Hi! diddle, diddle,
    The cat and the fiddle,
The cow jumped over the moon;
    The little dog laughed
    To see such sport,
While the dish ran after the spoon.

❖ ❖ ❖ ❖ ❖

Old Mother Hubbard
Went to the cupboard,
To get her poor dog a bone;
But when she came there
The cupboard was bare,
And so the poor dog had none.

❖ ❖ ❖ ❖ ❖

What are little boys made of,
What are little boys made of?
Snaps and snails, and puppy-dogs' tails;
That's what little boys are made of.

What are little girls made of,
What are little girls made of?
Sugar and spice, and everything nice;
That's what little girls are made of.

❖ ❖ ❖ ❖ ❖

Ride a cock-horse to Banbury Cross,
To see an old lady upon a white horse,
Rings on her fingers, and bells on her toes,
And so she makes music wherever she goes.

❖ ❖ ❖ ❖ ❖

Little Miss Muffit,
Sat on a tuffit,
Eating of curds and whey;
There came a great spider
That sat down beside her,
And frightened Miss Muffit away.

❖ ❖ ❖ ❖ ❖

Little Bo-peep has lost her sheep,
And can't tell where to find them;
Leave them alone, and they'll come home,
Wagging their tails behind them.

❖ ❖ ❖ ❖ ❖

Mary, Mary, quite contrary,
How does your garden grow?
With cockle-shells and silver bells
And columbines all in a row.

❖ ❖ ❖ ❖ ❖

Little Polly Flinders,
Sat among the cinders,
Warming her pretty little toes;
Her mother came and caught her,
And whipped her little daughter
For spoiling her nice new clothes.

❖ ❖ ❖ ❖ ❖

Little boy blue, come blow your horn,
The sheep's in the meadow, the cow's in the corn;
Where's the little boy that looks after the sheep?
He's under the hay-stack fast asleep.

❖ ❖ ❖ ❖ ❖

Humpty Dumpty sat on a wall,
Humpty Dumpty had a great fall;
All the king's horses and all the king's men
Cannot put Humpty Dumpty together again.

❖ ❖ ❖ ❖ ❖

Little Jack Horner sat in the corner eating a Christmas pie;
He put in his thumb, and he took out a plum,
And said, "What a good boy am I!"

❖ ❖ ❖ ❖ ❖

Jack Sprat could eat no fat,
His wife could eat no lean;
And so betwixt them both, you see,
They lick'd the platter clean.

❖ ❖ ❖ ❖ ❖

Jack and Jill went up the hill,
To fetch a pail of water;
Jack fell down and broke his crown
And Jill came tumbling after.

❖ ❖ ❖ ❖ ❖

Peter, Peter, pumpkin eater,
    Had a wife and couldn't keep her;
He put her in a pumpkin shell
    And there he kept her very well.

❖ ❖ ❖ ❖ ❖

Rub-a-dub-dub,
Three men in a tub,
And who do you think they be?
    The butcher, the baker,
    The candlestick-maker;
Turn 'em out, knaves all three!

❖ ❖ ❖ ❖ ❖

Hickory, dickory, dock,
The mouse ran up the clock;
    The clock struck one,
    The mouse ran down,
Hickory, dickory, dock.

❖ ❖ ❖ ❖ ❖

A dillar, a dollar,
A ten o'clock scholar,
    What makes you come so soon?
    You used to come at ten o'clock
But now you come at noon.

❖ ❖ ❖ ❖ ❖

The Queen of Hearts
She made some tarts,
All on a summer's day;
    The Knave of Hearts
    He stole those tarts,
And with them ran away.

The King of Hearts
Called for the tarts,
And beat the Knave full sore;
    The Knave of Hearts
    Brought back the tarts,
And vowed he'd steal no more!

❖ ❖ ❖ ❖ ❖

Mary had a little lamb,
    Its fleece was white as snow;
And everywhere that Mary went,
    The lamb was sure to go.

He followed her to school one day,
    Which was against the rule;
It made the children laugh and play
    To see a lamb at school.

And so the teacher turned him out,
    But still he lingered near,
And waited patiently about
    Till Mary did appear.

Then he ran to her, and laid
    His head upon her arm,
As if he said, "I'm not afraid—
    You'll keep me from all harm."

"What makes the lamb love Mary so?"
    The eager children cried.
"Oh, Mary loves the lamb, you know,"
    The teacher quick replied.

And you each gentle animal
    In confidence may bind,
And make them follow at your will,
    If you are only kind.

The Children's Hour

by Henry Wadsworth Longfellow (1807-1892)

Delightful. A father's treasure. A granddad's heaven.
I bet you read it twice. Oh, how quickly they grow
and go.

> Between the dark and the daylight,
>   When the light is beginning to lower,
> Comes a pause in the day's occupations
>   That is known as the Children's Hour.

> I hear in the chamber above me
>   The patter of little feet,
> The sound of a door that is opened,
>   And voices soft and sweet.

> From my study I see in the lamplight,
>   Descending the broad hall stair,
> Grave Alice and laughing Allegra,
>   And Edith with golden hair.

> A whisper, and then a silence;
>   Yet I know by their merry eyes,
> They are plotting and planning together
>   To take me by surprise.

> A sudden rush from the stairway,
>   A sudden raid from the hall!
> By three doors left unguarded
>   They enter my castle wall!

> They climb up into my turret,
>   O'er the arms and back of my chair ;
> If I try to escape, they surround me;
>   They seem to be everywhere.

They almost devour me with kisses,
    Their arms about me entwine,
Till I think of the Bishop of Bingen
    In his Mouse-Tower on the Rhine.

Do you think, O blue-eyed banditti,
    Because you have scaled the wall,
Such an old mustache as I am
    Is not a match for you all?

I have you fast in my fortress,
    And will not let you depart,
But put you down into the dungeon
    In the round-tower of my heart.

And there will I keep you forever,
    Yes, forever and a day,
Till the wall shall crumble to ruin,
    And moulder in dust away.

The Arrow and the Song

by Henry Wadsworth Longfellow (1807-1892)

They tell their own story in a charming way.

I shot an arrow into the air,
    It fell to earth, I knew not where;
For, so swiftly it flew, the sight
    Could not follow it in its flight.

I breathed a song into the air,
    It fell to earth, I knew not where;
For who has sight so keen and strong,
    That it can follow the flight of song?

Long, long afterward, in an oak
    I found the arrow, still unbroke;
And the song, from beginning to end,
    I found again in the heart of a friend.

My Shadow

by Robert Louis Stevenson (1850-1894)

Surely brings to mind that great song, *Me and My Shadow.*

I have a little shadow that goes in and out with me,
And what can be the use of him is more than I can see.
He is very, very like me from the heels up to the head;
And I see him jump before me, when I jump into my bed.

The funniest thing about him is the way he likes to grow—
Not at all like proper children, which is always very slow;
For he sometimes shoots up taller like an India-rubber ball,
And he sometimes gets so little that there's none of him at all.

He hasn't got a notion of how children ought to play,
And can only make a fool of me in every sort of way.
He stays so close beside me, he's a coward, you can see;
I'd think shame to stick to nursie as that shadow sticks to me!

One morning, very early, before the sun was up,
I rose and found the shining dew on every buttercup;
But my lazy little shadow, like an arrant sleepy-head,
Had stayed at home behind me and was fast asleep in bed.

Days of Birth

by Unknown

An old familiar.

Monday's child is fair of face,
     Tuesday's child is full of grace,
Wednesday's child is full of woe,
     Thursday's child has far to go,
Friday's child is loving and giving,
     Saturday's child works hard for its living,
But the child that's born on the Sabbath day
     Is fair and wise and good and gay.

A Boy's Song

by James Hogg (1770-1835)

The best of country living, and it sure beats drugs and street warfare.

Where the pools are bright and deep,
Where the gray trout lies asleep,
Up the river and o'er the lea,
That's the way for Billy and me.

Where the blackbird sings the latest,
Where the hawthorn blooms the sweetest,
Where the nestlings chirp and flee,
That's the way for Billy and me.

Where the mowers mow the cleanest,
Where the hay lies thick and greenest,
There to trace the homeward bee,
That's the way for Billy and me.

Where the hazel bank is steepest,
Where the shadow falls the deepest,
Where the clustering nuts fall free,
That's the way for Billy and me.

Why the boys should drive away
Little sweet maidens from the play,
Or love to banter and fight so well,
That's the thing I never could tell.

But this I know, I love to play,
Through the meadow, among the hay;
Up the water and o'er the lea,
That's the way for Billy and me.

The Boy Who Never Told a Lie

by Unknown

A very laudable goal for any youngster, boy or girl, or even a President.

Once there was a little boy,
    With curly hair and pleasant eye—
A boy who always told the truth,
    And never, never told a lie.

And when he trotted off to school,
    The children all about would cry,
"There goes the curly-headed boy—
    The boy that never tells a lie."

And everybody loved him so,
    Because he always told the truth,
That every day, as he grew up,
    Twas said, "There goes the honest youth."

And when the people that stood near
    Would turn to ask the reason why,
The answer would be always this:
    "Because he never tells a lie."

The Days of the Month

by Unknown

A standard memory enhancer for the calendar.

Thirty days hath September,
    April, June, and November;
February has twenty-eight alone.
    All the rest have thirty-one,
Excepting leap-year—that's the time
    When February's days are twenty-nine.

The Boy Reciter

by David Everett (1769-1813)

Musings of a first time young orator. Sounds as if
this little Yankee's knees weren't even knocking.

You'd scarce expect one of my age
To speak in public on the stage,
And if I chance to fall below
Demosthenes or Cicero,
Don't view me with a critic's eye,
But pass my imperfections by.
Large streams from little fountains flow,
Tall oaks from little acorns grow;
And though now I am small and young,
Of judgment weak and feeble tongue,
Yet all great, learned men, like me
Once learned to read their ABC.
But why may not Columbia's soil
Rear men as great as Britain's Isle,
Exceed what Greece and Rome have done
Or any land beneath the sun?
Mayn't Massachusetts boast as great
As any other sister state?
Or where's the town, go far or near,
That does not find a rival here?
Or where's the boy but three feet high
Who's made improvement more than I?
These thoughts inspire my youthful mind
To be the greatest of mankind:
Great, not like Caesar, stained with blood,
But only great as I am good.

If I Only Was the Fellow

by Will S. Adkin

It doesn't have to be the Impossible Dream,
the unreachable star. Mom will always be
happy with less, if it's your best.

While walking down a crowded
　　　City street the other day,
I heard a little urchin
　　　To a comrade turn and say,
"Say, Chimmey, lemme tell youse,
　　　I'd be happy as a clam
If I only was de feller dat
　　　Me mudder t'inks I am.

"She t'inks I am a wonder,
　　　An' she know her little lad
Could never mix wit' nuttin
　　　Dat was ugly, mean or bad.
Oh, lot o' times I sit and t'ink
　　　How nice, 'twould be, gee whiz!
If a feller was de feller
　　　Dat his mudder t'inks he is."

My friends, be yours a life of toil
　　　Or undiluted joy,
You can learn a wholesome lesson
　　　From that small, untutored boy.
Don't aim to be an earthly saint,
　　　With eyes fixed on a star:
Just try to be the fellow that
　　　Your mother thinks you are.

Hiawatha's Childhood
by Henry Wadsworth Longfellow (1807-1892)

A little long, but very worthwhile and
especially good to read to children with
explanations along the way. If you don't
remember it, they will. A real lesson in,
and of nature, through the eyes of our
Native Americans.

By the shores of Gitche Gumee,
By the shining Big-Sea-Water,
Stood the wigwam of Nokomis,
Daughter of the Moon, Nokomis.
Dark behind it rose the forest,
Rose the black and gloomy pine-trees,
Rose the firs with cones upon them;
Bright before it beat the water,
Beat the clear and sunny water,
Beat the shining Big-Sea-Water.

There the wrinkled old Nokomis
Nursed the little Hiawatha,
Rocked him in his linden cradle,
Bedded soft in moss and rushes,
Safely bound with reindeer sinews;
Stilled his fretful wail by saying,
"Hush! the Naked Bear will hear thee!"
Lulled him into slumber, singing,
"Ewa-yea! my little owlet!"
Who is this, that lights the wigwam?
With his great eyes lights the wigwam?
Ewa-yea! my little owlet!"

Many things Nokomis taught him
Of the stars that shine in heaven;
Showed him Ishkoodah, the comet,
Ishkoodah, with fiery tresses;
Showed the Death-Dance of the spirits,
Warriors with their plumes and war-clubs,
Flaring far away to northward

In the frosty nights of winter;
Showed the broad white road in heaven,
Pathway of the ghosts, the shadows,
Running straight across the heavens,
Crowded with the ghosts, the shadows.

At the door on summer evenings,
Sat the little Hiawatha;
Heard the whispering of the pine-trees,
Heard the lapping of the waters,
Sounds of music, words of wonder;
"Minne-wawa!" said the pine-trees,
"Mudway-aushka!" said the water.
Saw the fire-fly Wah-wah-taysee,
Flitting through the dusk of evening,
With the twinkle of its candle
Lighting up the brakes and bushes,

And he sang the song of children,
Sang the song Nokomis taught him.
"Wah-wah-taysee, little fire-fly,
Little, flitting, white-fire insect,
Little, dancing, white-fire creature,
Light me with your little candle,
Ere upon my bed I lay me,
Ere in sleep I close my eyelids!"

Saw the moon rise from the water,
Rippling, rounding from the water,
Saw the flecks and shadows on it,
Whispered, "What is that, Nokomis?"
And the good Nokomis answered:
"Once a warrior, very angry,
Seized his grandmother, and threw her
Up into the sky at midnight;
Right against the moon he threw her;
'Tis her body that you see there."

Saw the rainbow in the heaven,
In the eastern sky the rainbow,
Whispered, "What is that, Nokomis?"
And the good Nokomis answered:
"'Tis the heaven of flowers you see there;
All the wild-flowers of the forest,
All the lilies of the prairie,
When on earth they fade and perish,
Blossom in that heaven above us."

When he heard the owls at midnight,
Hooting, laughing in the forest,
"What is that?" be cried in terror;
"What is that," he said, "Nokomis?"
And the good Nokomis answered:
"That is but the owl and owlet,
Talking in their native language,
Talking, scolding at each other."

Then the little Hiawatha
Learned of every bird its language,
Learned their names and all their secrets,
How they built their nests in summer,
Where they hid themselves in winter,
Talked with them whene'er he met them,
Called them "Hiawatha's Chickens."

Of all beasts he learned the language,
Learned their names and all their secrets,
How the beavers built their lodges,
Where the squirrels hid their acorns,
How the reindeer ran so swiftly,
Why the rabbit was so timid,
Talked with them whene'er he met them,
Called them "Hiawatha's Brothers."

The Owl and the Pussy-Cat

by Edward Lear (1812-1888)

A unique old standard. What an odd combination.

The Owl and the Pussy-Cat went to sea
    In a beautiful pea-green boat;
They took some honey, and plenty of money
    Wrapped up in a five-pound note.
The Owl looked up to the moon above,
    And sang to a small guitar,
"O lovely Pussy! O Pussy, my love!
    What a beautiful Pussy you are,—
        You are,
    What a beautiful Pussy you are!"

Pussy said to the Owl, "You elegant fowl!
    How wonderful sweet you sing!
Oh, let us be married,—too long we have tarried,—
    But what shall we do for a ring?"
They sailed away for a year and a day
    To the land where the Bong-tree grows,
And there in a wood a piggy-wig stood
    With a ring in the end of his nose,—
        His nose,
    With a ring in the end of his nose.

"Dear Pig, are you willing to sell for one shilling
    Your ring?" Said the piggy, "I will."
So they took it away, and were married next day
    By the turkey who lives on the hill.
They dined upon mince and slices of quince,
    Which they ate with a runcible spoon[1],
And hand in hand on the edge of the sand
    They danced by the light of the moon,—
        The moon,
    They danced by the light of the moon.

[1] *Runcible Spoon - a utensil that has two straight and one curved prong.*

Suppose

by Phoebe Cary (1824-1871)

Fond wishes for every Mom and Dad, with
great hopes that the lessons will sink in.

Suppose, my little lady,
    Your doll should break her head;
Could you make it whole by crying
    Till your eyes and nose were red?
And wouldn't it be pleasanter
    To treat it as a joke,
And say you're glad 'twas dolly's
    And not your own that broke?

Suppose you're dressed for walking,
    And the rain comes pouring down;
Will it clear off any sooner
    Because you scold and frown?
And wouldn't it be nicer
    For you to smile than pout,
And so make sunshine in the house
    When there is none without?

Suppose your task, my little man,
    Is very hard to get;
Will it make it any easier
    For you to sit and fret?
And wouldn't it be wiser,
    Than waiting like a dunce,
To go to work in earnest
    And learn the thing at once?

Suppose that some boys have a horse,
    And some a coach and pair;
Will it tire you less while walking
    To say, "It isn't fair"
And wouldn't it be nobler
    To keep your temper sweet,
And in your heart be thankful
    You can walk upon your feet?

Suppose the world don't please you.
      Nor the way some people do;
Do you think the whole creation
      Will be altered just for you?
And isn't it, my boy or girl,
      the wisest, bravest plan,
Whatever comes, or doesn't come,
      To do the best you can?

Whistling Boy

by Nixon Waterman

I bet you whistlers didn't know your whistle cheered up someone besides yourself. So please don't stop.

When the curtain of night, 'tween the dark and the light,
      Drops down from the set of the sun,
And the toilers who roam, to the loved ones come home,
      As they pass by my window is one
Whose coming I mark, for the song of the lark
      As it joyously soars in the sky
Is no dearer to me than the notes, glad and free,
      Of the boy who goes whistling by.

If a sense of unrest settles over my breast
      And my spirit is clouded with care,
It all flies away if he happens to stray
      Past my window a-whistling an air.
And I never shall know how much gladness I owe
      To this joy of the ear and the eye,
But I'm sure I'm in debt for much pleasure I get
      From the boy who goes whistling by.

And this music of his, how much better it is
      Than to burden his life with a frown,
For the toiler who sings to his purposes brings
      A hope his endeavor to crown.
And whenever I hear his glad notes, full and clear,
      I say to myself I will try
To make all of life with a joy to be rife,
      Like the boy who goes whistling by.

Jest 'Fore Christmas

by Eugene Field (1850-1895)

Would that the Christmas spirit lasted all year. Here's a good start.

Father calls me William, sister calls me Will,
Mother calls me Willie, but the fellers call me Bill!
Mighty glad I ain't a girl—ruther be a boy,
Without them sashes, curls, an' things that's worn by Fauntleroy!
Love to chawnk green apples and go swimmin' in the lake—
Hate to take the castor-ile they give for bellyache!
'Most all the time, the whole year round, there ain't no flies on me,
But jest 'fore Christmas I'm as good as I kin be!

Got a yeller dog named Sport, sick him on the cat;
First thing she knows she doesn't know where she is at!
Got a clipper sled, an' when us kids goes out to slide,
'Long comes the grocery cart, an' we all hook a ride!
But sometimes when the grocery man is worried an' cross,
He reaches at us with his whip, an' larrups up his hoss,
An' then I laff an' holler, "Oh, ye never teched me!"
But jest 'fore Christmas I'm as good as I kin be!

Gran'ma says she hopes that when I git to be a man,
I'll be a missionarer like her oldest brother, Dan,
As was et up by the cannibals that live in Ceylon's Isle,
Where every prospeck pleases, an' only man is vile!
But gran'ma she has never been to see a Wild West show,
Nor read the life of Daniel Boone, or else I guess she'd know
That Buff'lo Bill an' cowboys is good enough for me!
Excep' jest 'fore Christmas, when I'm as good as I kin be!

And then old Sport he hangs around, so solemn-like an' still,
His eyes they seem a-sayin': "What's the matter, little Bill"?
The old cat sneaks down off her perch an' wonders what's become
Of them two enemies of hern that used to make things hum!
But I am so perlite an' tend so earnestly to biz,
That mother says to father: "How improved our Willie is!"
But father, havin' been a boy hisself, suspicions me
When, jest 'fore Christmas, I'm as good as I kin be!
For Christmas, with its lots an' lots of candies, cakes an' toys),

Was made, they say, for proper kids an' not for naughty boys;
So wash yer face an' bresh yer hair, an' mind yer p's and q's,
And don't bust out yer pantaloons, and don't wear out yer shoes;
Say "Yess-um" to the ladies, and "Yessur" to the men,
An' when they's company, don't pass yer plate for pie again;
But, thinkin' of the things yer'd like to see upon that tree,
Jest 'fore Christmas be as good as yer kin be!

The Night Before Christmas
by Clement Clark Moore (1779-1863)

Although written a century and a half ago, people will
be loving this in 2099 as much as they do now. It should
bring a special prize if memorized by age 8. All of us
kids are forever grateful to Mr. Moore. Bless you!

'Twas the night before Christmas, when all through the house,
Not a creature was stirring, not even a mouse;
The stockings were hung by the chimney with care,
In hopes that St. Nicholas soon would be there.
The children were nestled all snug in their beds,
While visions of sugarplums danced in their heads;
And mamma in her 'kerchief, and I in my cap,
Had just settled our brains for a long winter's nap,
When out on the lawn there arose such a clatter,
I sprang from the bed to see what was the matter.
Away to the window I flew like a flash,
Tore open the shutters and threw up the sash.
The moon on the breast of the new-fallen snow
Gave the luster of mid-day to objects below.
When, what to my wondering eyes should appear,
But a miniature sleigh, and eight tiny reindeer,
With a little old driver, so lively and quick,
I knew in a moment it must be St. Nick.
More rapid than eagles his coursers they came,
And he whistled, and shouted, and called them by name;
"Now, Dasher! now, Dancer! now, Prancer and Vixen!
On, Comet! on, Cupid! on, Donder and Blitzen!
To the top of the porch! to the top of the wall!
Now dash away! dash away! dash away all!"
As dry leaves that before the wild hurricane fly,

When they meet with an obstacle, mount to the sky;
So up to the house-top the coursers they flew,
With the sleigh full of toys, and St. Nicholas, too.
And then, in a twinkling, I heard on the roof
The prancing and pawing of each little hoof.
As I drew in my head, and was turning around,
Down the chimney St. Nicholas came with a bound.
He was dressed all in fur, from his head to his foot,
And his clothes were all tarnished with ashes and soot;
A bundle of toys he had flung on his back,
And he looked like a peddler just opening his pack.
His eyes—how they twinkled! his dimples how merry!
His cheeks were like roses, his nose like a cherry!
His droll little mouth was drawn up like a bow,
And the beard of his chin was as white as the snow;
The stump of a pipe he held tight in his teeth,
And the smoke it encircled his head like a wreath.
He had a broad face and a little round belly,
That shook when he laughed, like a bowlful of jelly.
He was chubby and plump, a right jolly old elf,
And I laughed when I saw him, in spite of myself.
A wink of his eye and a twist of his head,
Soon gave me to know I had nothing to dread;
He spoke not a word, but went straight to his work,
And filled all the stockings; then turned with a jerk,
And laying his finger aside of his nose,
And giving a nod, up the chimney he rose.
He sprang to his sleigh, to his team gave a whistle
And away they all flew like the down on a thistle.
But I heard him exclaim, ere he drove out of sight,
"Happy Christmas to all, and to all a good-night."

The Little Red Hen

Retold by Penryhn W. Coussens

This is a lesson for kids: and I hope they get the point or the lesson is lost. However, the theme applies to adults, too. No work—No Aid.

A little red hen once found a grain of wheat. "Who will plant this wheat?" she said.

"I won't," says the dog.

"I won't," says the cat.

"I won't," says the pig.

"I won't," says the turkey.

"Then I will," says the little red hen. "Cluck! cluck!"

So she planted the grain of wheat.

Very soon the wheat began to grow and the green leaves came out of the ground. The sun shone and the rain fell and the wheat kept on growing until it was tall, strong, and ripe.

"Who will reap this wheat?" says the little red hen.

"I won't," says the dog.

"I won't," says the cat.

"I won't," says the pig.

"I won't," says the turkey.

"I will, then," says the little red hen. "Cluck! cluck!"

So she reaped the wheat.

"Who will thresh this wheat?" says the little red hen.

"I won't," says the dog.

"I won't," says the cat.

"I won't," says the pig.

"I won't," says the turkey.

"I will, then," says the little red hen. "Cluck! cluck!"

So she threshed the wheat.

"Who will take this wheat to mill to have it ground?" says the little red hen.

"I won't," says the dog.

"I won't," says the cat.

"I won't," says the pig.

"I won't," says the turkey.

"I will, then," says the little red hen. "Cluck! cluck!"

So she took the wheat to mill, and by and by she came back with the flour.

"Who will bake this flour?" says the little red hen.
"I won't," says the dog.
"I won't," says the cat.
"I won't," says the pig.
"I won't," says the turkey.
"I will, then," says the little red hen. "Cluck! cluck!"
    So she baked the flour and made a loaf of bread.

"Who will eat this bread?" says the little red hen.
"I will," says the dog.
"I will," says the cat.
"I will," says the pig.
"I will," says the turkey.
"No, I will," says the little red hen. "Cluck! cluck!"
    And she ate up the loaf of bread.

How to Be Happy

by Unknown

What a simple, pleasant way to happiness. Makes
you want to go out and do it now. Let's hope it
becomes contagious. Good for all ages, too.

Are you almost disgusted with life, little man?
    I'll tell you a wonderful trick
That will bring you contentment, if anything can,
    Do something for somebody, quick!

Are you awfully tired with play, little girl?
    Wearied, discouraged, and sick—
I'll tell you the loveliest game in the world,
    Do something for somebody, quick!

Though it rains, like the rain of the flood, little man,
    And the clouds are forbidding and thick,
You can make the sun shine in your soul, little man,
    Do something for somebody, quick!

Though the stars are like brass overhead, little girl,
    And the walks like a well-heated brick,
And our earthly affairs in a terrible whirl,
    Do something for somebody, quick!

Let Dogs Delight to Bark and Bite

by Isaac Watts

Simply stated.

> Let dogs delight to bark and bite,
>   For God hath made them so;
> Let bears and lions growl and fight,
>   For 'tis their nature to.
>
> But, children, You should never let
>   Such angry passions rise;
> Your little hands were never made
>   To tear each other's eyes.

Our Heroes

by Phoebe Cary (1824-1871)

A strong plea to just say "NO!" and a word of praise for those who do. A real battle-cry in our war on drugs and crime today.

> Here's a hand to the boy who has courage
>   To do what he knows to be right;
> When he falls in the way of temptation,
>   He has a hard battle to fight.
> Who strives against self and his comrades
>   Will find a most powerful foe.
> All honor to him if he conquers.
>   A cheer for the boy who says "No!"
>
> There's many a battle fought daily
>   The world knows nothing about;
> There's many a brave little soldier
>   Whose strength puts a legion to rout.
> And he who fights sin single-handed
>   Is more of a hero, I say,
> Than he who leads soldiers to battle
>   And conquers by arms in the fray.

Be steadfast, my boy, when you're tempted,
  To do what you know to be right.
Stand firm by the colors of manhood,
  And you will o'ercome in the fight.
"The right," be your battle cry ever
  In waging the warfare of life,
And God, who knows who are the heroes,
  Will give you the strength for the strife.

Children's Puzzles
by Unknown

Besides being fun poems, these are puzzles for the kids to figure out.

As I was going to St. Ives,
I met a man with seven wives;
    Every wife had seven sacks,
    Every sack had seven cats,
    Every cat had seven kits—
Kits, cats, sacks and wives,
How many were going to St. Ives?

❖ ❖ ❖ ❖ ❖

Two legs sat upon three legs,
    With one leg in his lap;
In comes four legs
    And runs away with one leg;
Up jumps two legs,
    Catches up three legs,
Throws it after four legs,
    And makes him drop one leg.

❖ ❖ ❖ ❖ ❖

Little Nancy Etticoat,
In a white petticoat,
And a red nose;
The longer she stands
The shorter she grows.

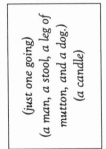

(just one going)
(a man, a stool, a leg of mutton, and a dog.)
(a candle)

Home

by Edgar A. Guest

You'll never again have trouble defining and differentiating between a house and a home. Guest surely does a much better job than Webster in separating the two. Webster's defined a house as a building in which people live, and a home as the place in which one's domestic affections are centered. Rather dull, don't you think?

It takes a heap o' livin' in a house t' make it home,
A heap o' sun an 'shadder, an ye sometimes have t' roam
Afore ye really 'preciate the things ye lef' behind
An' hunger fer 'em somehow, with 'em allus on yer mind.
It don't make any differunce how rich ye get t' be,
How much yer chairs an' tables cost, how great yer luxury;
It ain't home t' ye, though it be the palace of a king,
Until somehow yer soul is sort o' wrapped 'round everything.

Home ain't a place that gold can buy or get up in a minute;
Afore it's home there's got t' be a heap o' livin' in it;
Within the walls there's got t' be some babies born, and then
Right there ye've got t' bring 'em up t' women good, an' men;
And gradjerly, as time goes on, ye find ye wouldn't part
With anything they ever used—they've grown into yer heart:
The old high chairs, the playthings, too, the little shoes they wore
Ye hoard; an' if ye could ye'd keep the thumbmarks on the door.

Ye've got t' weep t' make it home, ye've got t' sit an' sigh
An' watch beside a loved one's bed, an' know that Death is nigh;
An' in the stillness o' the night t' see Death's angel come,
An' close the eyes o' her that smiled, an' leave her sweet voice dumb.
Fer these are scenes that grip the heart, an' when yer tears are dried,
Ye find the home is dearer than it was, an' sanctified
An' tuggin' at ye always are the pleasant memories
O' her that was an' is no more—ye can't escape from these.

Ye've got t' sing an' dance fer years, ye've got t' romp an' play,
An' learn t' love the things ye have by usin' 'em each day;
Even the roses 'round the porch must blossom year by year
Afore they come a part o' ye, suggestin' someone dear
Who used t' love 'em long ago, an' trained 'em jes' t' run
The way they do, so's they would get the early mornin' sun;
Ye've got t' love each brick an' stone from cellar up t' dome:
It takes a heap o' livin' in a house t' make it home.

Home, Sweet Home!

By John Howard Payne (1792-1852)

Let's face it—there's just no place like it,
be it ever so humble.

'Mid pleasures and palaces though we may roam,
Be it ever so humble, there's no place like home;
A charm from the sky seems to hallow us there,
Which, seek through the world, is ne'er met with elsewhere.
    Home! Home! sweet, sweet Home!
There's no place like Home! there's no place like Home!

An exile from Home, Splendour dazzles in vain;
O, give me my lowly thatched cottage again!
The birds singing gaily, that came at my call,—
Give me them,—and the peace of mind, dearer than all!
    Home! Home! sweet, sweet Home!
There's no place like Home! there's no place like Home!

How sweet 'tis to sit 'neath a fond father's smile,
And the cares of a mother to soothe and beguile!
Let others delight 'mid new pleasures to roam,
But give me, oh, give me, the pleasures of Home!
          Home! Home! sweet, sweet Home!
There's no place like Home! there's no place like Home!

To thee I'll return, overburdened with care;
The heart's dearest solace will smile on me there;
No more from that cottage again will I roam;
Be it ever so humble, there's no place like Home.
          Home! Home! sweet, sweet Home!
There's no place like Home! there's no place like Home!

Our Mother

by Unknown

We love ya', Mom.

Hundreds of stars in the pretty sky,
          Hundreds of shells on the shore together.
Hundreds of birds that go singing by,
          Hundreds of birds in the sunny weather;

Hundreds of dewdrops to greet the dawn,
          Hundreds of bees in the purple clover,
Hundreds of butterflies on the lawn,
          But only one mother the wide world over.

Nobody Knows But Mother

by *Mary Morrison*

Another big vote for motherhood. I always
believed it was here to stay. I wonder what
moms do in their spare time?

How many buttons are missing today?
    Nobody knows but Mother.
How many playthings are strewn in her way?
    Nobody knows but Mother.
How many thimbles and spools has she missed?
How many burns on each fat little fist?
How many bumps to be cuddled and kissed?
    Nobody knows but Mother.

How many hats has she hunted today?
    Nobody knows but Mother.
Carelessly hiding themselves in the hay—
    Nobody knows but Mother.
How many handkerchiefs willfully strayed?
How many ribbons for each little maid?
How for her care can a mother be paid?
    Nobody knows but Mother.

How many muddy shoes all in a row?
    Nobody knows but Mother.
How many stockings to darn, do you know?
    Nobody knows but Mother.
How many little torn aprons to mend?
How many hours of toil must she spend?
What is the time when her day's work shall end?
    Nobody knows but Mother.

How many lunches for Tommy and Sam?
    Nobody knows but Mother.
Cookies and apples and blackberry jam—
    Nobody knows but Mother.
Nourishing dainties for every "sweet tooth,"

Toddling Dottie or dignified Ruth—
How much love sweetens the labor, forsooth?
    Nobody knows but Mother.

How many cares does a mother's heart know?
    Nobody knows but Mother.
How many joys from her mother love flow?
    Nobody knows but Mother.
How many prayers for each little white bed?
How many tears for her babes has she shed?
How many kisses for each curly head?
    Nobody knows but Mother.

The Hand that Rocks the Cradle is the Hand that Rules the World

by William Ross Wallace (1819-1891)

And he said it before the days of Elizabeth II, Margaret Thatcher, Indira Ghandi, Eva Peron, Eleanor Roosevelt and Hillary Clinton. If you're not convinced, read this.

Blessing on the hand of women!
    Angels guard its strength and grace,
In the palace, cottage, hovel,
    Oh, no matter where the place;
Would that never storms assailed it,
    Rainbows ever gently curled;
For the hand that rocks the cradle
    Is the hand that rules the world.

Infancy's the tender fountain,
    Power may with beauty flow,
Mother's first to guide the streamlets,
    From them souls unresting grow—
Grow on for the good or evil,
    Sunshine streamed or evil hurled;
For the hand that rocks the cradle
    Is the hand that rules the world.

Woman, how divine your mission
    Here upon our natal sod!
Keep, oh, keep the young heart open
    Always to the breath of God!
All true trophies of the ages
    Are from mother-love impearled;
For the hand that rocks the cradle
    Is the hand that rules the world.

Blessings on the hand of women!
    Fathers, sons, and daughters cry,
And the sacred song is mingled
    With the worship in the sky—
Mingles where no tempest darkens,
    Rainbows evermore are hurled;
For the hand that rocks the cradle
    Is the hand that rules the world.

The Cane-Bottomed Chair

by *William Makepeace Thackeray (1811-1863)*

The only thing I could possibly add here would be a cushion.

In tattered old slippers that toast at the bars,
And a ragged old jacket perfumed with cigars,
Away from the world and its toils and its cares,
I've a snug little kingdom up four pairs of stairs.

To mount to this realm is a toil, to be sure,
But the fire there is bright and the air rather pure;
And the view I behold on a sunshiny day
Is grand, through the chimney-pots over the way.

This snug little chamber is crammed in all nooks
With worthless old knickknacks and silly old books,
And foolish old odds and foolish old ends,
Cracked bargains from brokers, cheap keepsakes from friends.

Old armour, prints, pictures, pipes, china (all cracked),
Old rickety tables, and chairs broken-backed;
A twopenny treasury, wondrous to see;
What matter? 'tis pleasant to you, friend, and me.

No better divan need the Sultan require,
Than the creaking old sofa that basks by the fire,
And 'tis wonderful, surely, what music you get
From the rickety, ramshackle, wheezy spinet.

That praying-rug came from a Tureoman's camp;
By Tiber once twinkled that brazen old lamp;
A Mameluke fierce yonder dagger has drawn;
'Tis a murderous knife to toast muffins upon.

Long, long through the hours, and the night, and the chimes,
Here we talk of old books, and old friends, and old times:
As we sit in a fog made of rich Latakie,
This chamber is pleasant to you, friend, and me.

But of all the cheap treasures that garnish my nest,
There's one that I love and I cherish the best;
For the finest of couches that's padded with hair
I never would change thee, my cane-bottomed chair.

'Tis a bandy-legged, high-shouldered, worm-eaten seat,
With a creaking old back, and twisted old feet;
But since the fair morning when Fanny sat there,
I bless thee and love thee, old cane-bottomed chair.

If chairs have but feeling, in holding such charms,
A thrill must have passed through your withered old arms!
I looked, and I longed, and I wished in despair;
I wished myself turned to a cane-bottomed chair.

It was but a moment she sat in this place,
She'd a scarf on her neck, and a smile on her face!
A smile on her face, and a rose in her hair,
And she sat there, and bloomed in my cane-bottomed chair.

And so I have valued my chair ever since,
Like the shrine of a saint, or the throne of a prince;
Saint Fanny, my patroness sweet I declare,
The queen of my heart and my cane-bottomed chair.

When the candles burn low, and the company's gone,
In the silence of night as I sit here alone—
I sit here alone, but we yet are a pair—
My Fanny I see in my cane-bottomed chair.

She comes from the past, and revisits my room;
She looks as she then did, all beauty and bloom;
So smiling and tender, so fresh and so fair,
And yonder she sits in my cane-bottomed chair.

Send Them to Bed with a Kiss

by Unknown

Probably the best advice in this whole book. How many
blighted lives might be saved if there was much more
of this going on.

O Mothers, so weary, discouraged,
    Worn out with the cares of the day,
You often grow cross and impatient,
    Complain of the noise and the play;
For the day brings so many vexations,
    So many things going amiss;
But, mothers, whatever may vex you,
    Send the children to bed with a kiss!

The dear little feet wander often,
    Perhaps, from the pathway of right,
The dear little hands find new mischief
    To try you from morning till night;
But think of the desolate mothers
    Who'd give all the world for your bliss,
And, as thanks for your infinite blessings,
    Send the children to bed with a kiss!

For some day their noise will not vex you,
    The silence will hurt you far more;
You will long for their sweet childish voices,
    For a sweet childish face at the door;
And to press a child's face to your bosom,
    You'd give all the world for just this!
For the comfort 'twill bring you in sorrow,
    Send the children to bed with a kiss!

The New Arrival

by George Washington Cable

A great ship in a little bundle, safely into harbor. And I
know too well exactly how he felt.

There came to port last Sunday night
    The queerest little craft,
Without an inch of rigging on;
    I looked and looked—and laughed!
It seemed so curious that she
    Should cross the Unknown water,
And moor herself within my room—
    My daughter! O, my daughter!

Yet by these presents witness all
    She's welcome fifty times,
And comes consigned in hope and love—
    And common-metre rhymes.
She has no manifest by this;
    No flag floats o'er the water;
She's too new for the British Lloyds—
    My daughter! O, my daughter!

Ring out, wild bells—and tame ones too;
    Ring out the lover's moon.
Ring in the little worsted socks,
    Ring in the bib and spoon.
Ring out the muse, ring in the nurse,
    Ring in the milk and water.
Away with paper, pen and ink—
    My daughter! O, my daughter!

The Old Arm-Chair

by Eliza Cook

A great tribute to mother by way of the old chair. A great daily reminder to have around. My fondest memories of my own dear mother are of her in her old armed rocking chair; a chair that I still cherish.

I love it—I love it, and who shall dare
        To chide me for loving that old armchair!
I've treasured it long as sainted prize—
        I've bedewed it with tears, I've embalmed it with sighs;
'Tis bound by a thousand bands to my heart,
        Not a tie will break, not a link will start;
Would you learn the spell?—A mother sat there,
        And a sacred thing is that old armchair.

In childhood's hour I lingered near,
        The hallowed seat with listening ear;
And gentle words that mother would give,
        To fit me to die, and teach me to live.
She told me shame would never betide
        With truth for my creed, and God for my Guide;
She taught me to lisp my earliest prayer,
        As I knelt beside that old arm-chair.

I sat and watched her many a day,
        When her eyes were dim and her locks were grey,
And I almost worshipped her when she smiled
        And turned from her Bible to bless her child.
Years rolled on, but the last one sped,
        My idol was shattered—my earth-star fled;
I learnt how much the heart can bear,
        When I saw her die in that old arm-chair.

'Tis past! 'tis past! but I gaze on it now
        With quivering breath and throbbing brow;
'Twas there she nursed me—'twas there she died,
        And memory flows with lava tide!
Say it is folly, and deem me weak,
        While the scalding tears run down my cheek;
But I love it—I love it, and cannot tear
        My soul from my mother's old armchair.

Mother's Boys

by Unknown

You know what? I'll bet
there was not an instant delay in this mother's stating her choice.

Yes, I know there are stains on my carpet,
     The traces of small muddy boots;
And I see your fair tapestry glowing,
     All spotless with flowers and fruits.

And I know that my walls are disfigured
     With prints of small fingers and hands;
And that your own household most truly
     In immaculate purity stands.

And I know that my parlor is littered
     With many odd treasures and toys,
While your own is in daintiest order,
     Unharmed by the presence of boys.

And I know that my room is invaded
     Quite boldly all hours of the day;
While you sit in yours unmolested
     And dream the soft quiet away.

Yes, I know there are four little bedsides
     Where I must stand watchful each night,
While you may go out in your carriage,
     And flash in your dresses so bright.

Now, I think I'm a neat little woman;
     And I like my house orderly, too;
And I'm fond of all dainty belongings,
     Yet, I would not change places with you.

No! keep your fair home with its order,
     Its freedom from bother and noise;
And keep your own fanciful leisure,
     But give me my four splendid boys.

Little Boy Blue

by Eugene Field (1850-1895)

A touching story told in a charming
way. How those memories remain.

The little toy dog is covered with dust,
But sturdy and stanch he stands;
And the little toy soldier is red with rust,
And his musket moulds in his hands.
Time was when the little toy dog was new,
And the soldier was passing fair,
And that was the time when our Little Boy Blue
Kissed them and put them there.

"Now, don't you go till I come," he said,
"And don't you make any noise!"
So toddling off to his trundle-bed
He dreamt of the pretty toys.
And as he was dreaming, an angel song
Awakened our Little Boy Blue,—
Oh, the years are many, the years are long,
But the little toy friends are true!

Ay, faithful to Little Boy Blue they stand,
Each in the same old place,
Awaiting the touch of a little hand,
The smile of a little face.
And they wonder, as waiting these long years through,
In the dust of that little chair,
What has become of our Little Boy Blue
Since he kissed them and put them there.

Thanksgiving Day

by Lydia Maria Child (1802-1880)

Great nostalgia. Today it would be "jump in the Jeep and we'll zip over to Granddad's to watch the football classic."

Over the river and through the wood,
  To grandfather's house we go;
    The horse knows the way
    To carry the sleigh
  Through the white and drifted snow.

Over the river and through the wood—
  Oh, how the wind does blow!
    It stings the toes
    And bites the nose,
  As over the ground we go.

Over the river and through the wood,
  To have a first-rate play.
    Hear the bells ring,
    "Ting-a-ting-ding!"
  Hurrah for Thanksgiving Day!

Over the river and through the wood
  Trot fast, my dapple-gray!
    Spring over the ground,
    Like a hunting-hound!
  For this is Thanksgiving Day.

Over the river and through the wood,
  And straight through the barn-yard gate,
    We seem to go
    Extremely slow,—
  It is so hard to wait!

Over the river and through the wood—
  Now grandmother's cap I spy!
    Hurrah for the fun!
    Is the pudding done!
  Hurrah for the pumpkin-pie!

Brother Jim

by Robert Service (1874-1958)

Jim may remind you of a number of your friends and relatives. I hope you
are not Jim. He's got it all, including the ulcers.

My brother Jim's a millionaire,
　　While I have scarce a penny;
His face is creased with lines of care,
　　While my mug hasn't any.
With inwardness his eyes are dim,
　　While mine laugh out in glee,
And though I ought to envy him,
　　I think he envies me.

He has a chateau, I a shack,
　　And humble I should be
To see his stately Cadillac
　　Beside my jalopy.
With chain of gold his belly's girt,
　　His beard is barber trim;
Yet bristle-chinned with ragged shirt,
　　I do not envy Jim.

My brother is a man of weight;
　　For every civic plum
He grabs within the pie of state,
　　While I am just a bum.
Last Winter he was near to croak
　　With gastric ulcers grim...
Ah no! although I'm stony broke
　　I will not envy Jim.

He gets the work, I get the fun;
　　He has no time for play;
Whereas with paddle, rod and gun
　　My life's a holiday.
As over crabbed script he pores
　　I scan the sky's blue rim...
Oh boy! While I have God's outdoors
　　I'll never envy Jim.

Out to Old Aunt Mary's

by James Whitcomb Riley (1852-1926)

Are those days gone forever? "Where are you,
Aunt Mary? And all those special treats?"

> Wasn't it pleasant, O brother mine,
> In those old days of the lost sunshine
> Of youth—when the Saturday's chores were through,
> And the "Sunday's wood" in the kitchen, too,
> And we went visiting "me and you,"
>> Out to Old Aunt Mary's?

> It all comes back so clear today!
> Though I am as bald as you are gray—
> Out by the barn-lot, and down the lane,
> We patter along in the dust again,
> As light as the tips of the drops of the rain,
>> Out to Old Aunt Mary's!

> We cross the pasture, and through the wood
> Where the old gray snag of the poplar stood,
> Where the hammering red-heads hopped awry,
> And the buzzard "raised" in the clearing sky,
> And lolled and circled, as we went by,
>> Out to Old Aunt Mary's.

> And then in the dust of the road again;
> And the teams we met, and the countrymen;
> And the long highway, with sunshine spread
> As thick as butter on country bread,
> Our cares behind, and our hearts ahead
>> Out to Old Aunt Mary's.

> Why, I see her now in the open door,
> Where the little gourds grew up the sides, and o'er
> The clapboard roof!—And her face—ah, me!
> Wasn't it good for a boy to see—
> And wasn't it good for a boy to be
>> Out to Old Aunt Mary's?

The jelly, the jam and the marmalade,
    And the cherry and quince "preserves" she made!
And the sweet-sour pickles of peach and pear,
With cinnamon in 'em, and all things rare
And the more we ate was the more to spare,
    Out to Old Aunt Mary's!

And the old spring-house in the cool green gloom
    Of the willow-trees, and the cooler room
Where the swinging-shelves and the crocks were kept—
Where the cream in a golden languor slept
While the waters gurgled and laughed and wept
    Out to Old Aunt Mary's!

And as many a time have you and I—
    Barefoot boys in the days gone by—
Knelt, and in tremulous ecstasies
Dipped our lips into sweets like these,—
Memory now is on her knees
    Out to Old Aunt Mary's!

And O, my brother, so far away,
    This is to tell you she waits today
To welcome us:—Aunt Mary fell
Asleep this morning, whispering, "Tell
The boys to come!" And all is well
    Out to Old Aunt Mary's!

The House with Nobody in It

by Joyce Kilmer (1886-1918)

Kilmer stresses how much nicer it is to make a
house into a home, rather that the other way
around. I wonder why he didn't mention trees.

Whenever I walk to Suffern along the Erie track
I go by a poor old farmhouse with its shingles broken and black.
I suppose I've passed it a hundred times, but I always stop for a minute
And look at the house, the tragic house, the house with nobody in it.

I never have seen a haunted house, but I hear there are such things;
That they hold the talk of spirits, their mirth and sorrowings.
I know this house isn't haunted, and I wish it were, I do;
For it wouldn't be so lonely if it had a ghost or two.

This house on the road to Suffern needs a dozen panes of glass,
And somebody ought to weed the walk and take a scythe to the grass,
It needs new paint and shingles, and the vines should be trimmed
    and tied;
But what it needs the most of all is some people living inside.

If I had a lot of money and all my debts were paid,
I'd put a gang of men to work with brush and saw and spade.
I'd buy that place and fix it up the way it used to be,
And I'd find some people who wanted a home and give it to them free.

Now a new house standing empty, with staring window and door,
Looks idle, perhaps, and foolish, like a hat on its block in the store.
But there's nothing mournful about it; it cannot be sad and lone
For the lack of something within it that it has never known.

But a house that has done what a house should do, a house that has
    sheltered life,
That has put its loving wooden arms around a man and his wife,
A house that has echoed a baby's laugh and held up his stumbling
    feet,
Is the saddest sight, when it's left alone, that ever your eyes could meet.

So whenever I go to Suffern along the Erie track
I never go by the empty house without stopping and looking back;
Yet it hurts me to look at the crumbling roof and the shutters fallen
    apart,
For I can't help thinking the poor old house is a house with a
    broken heart.

Talents

by Eloise Lang

This poem won **Golden Poet of 1992** at the World of Poetry Awards..

God gives everybody talents
Some have many, some have few,
But just how much you make of yours
Is strictly up to you.

For why possess a golden voice,
Yet keep it ever mute?
Or long to write a symphony,
Content to play a flute.

Why long to be an artist
With a palette and a brush
Yet let that talent lose itself
In life's chaotic rush?

Why not be like the gardener,
Who with patient, tender care
Exerts his every effort
To produce a plant that's rare.

Yet some neglect their talents
Till like forgotten seeds,
They are lost amidst the rush of life
And smothered by the weeds.

So search yourself for talents
If they're buried in the sod
Take the time to cultivate them
Make your garden grow—for God.

For this is true of talents,
Though they're only God's to give,
After He has done the planting
It's up to you to make them live!

The Spider and the Fly: A Fable

by Mary Howitt (1799-1888)

A great lesson on flattery and conceit. Don't just enjoy the poetry—be sure to get the lesson. I recommend it especially to rich widows. There are a lot of slick, two-legged spiders out there!

"Will you walk into my parlor?" said the spider to the fly;
"'Tis the prettiest little parlor that ever you did spy.
The way into my parlor is up a winding stair,
And I have many pretty things to show when you are there."
"O no, no," said the little fly, "to ask me is in vain,
For who goes up your winding stair can ne'er come down again."

"I'm sure you must be weary, dear, with soaring up so high;
Will you rest upon my little bed?" said the spider to the fly.
"There are pretty curtains drawn around, the sheets are fine and thin,
And if you like to rest awhile, I'll snugly tuck you in."
"O no, no," said the little fly, "for I've often heard it said,
They never, never wake again, who sleep upon your bed."

Said the cunning spider to the fly, "Dear friend, what shall I do,
To prove the warm affection I've always felt for you?
I have within my pantry good store of all that's nice;
I'm sure you're very welcome; will you please to take a slice?"
"O no, no," said the little fly, "kind sir, that cannot be;
I've heard what's in your pantry, and I do not wish to see."

"Sweet creature!" said the spider, "you're witty and you're wise,
How handsome are your gauzy wings, how brilliant are your eyes!
I have a little looking-glass upon my parlor shelf,
If you'll step in one moment, dear, you shall behold yourself.
"I thank you, gentle sir," she said, "for what you're pleased to say,
And bidding you good-morning now, I'll call another day."

The spider turned him round about, and went into his den,
For well he knew the silly fly would soon be back again:
So he wove a subtle web, in a little corner sly,
And set his table ready to dine upon the fly.
Then he came out to his door again, and merrily did sing,
"Come hither, hither, pretty fly, with the pearl and silver wing:
Your robes are green and purple; there's a crest upon your head;
Your eyes are like the diamond bright, but mine are dull as lead."

Alas, alas! how very soon this silly little fly,
Hearing his wily flattering words, came slowly flitting by.
With buzzing wings she hung aloft, then near and nearer drew,
Thinking only of her brilliant eyes, and green and purple hue;
Thinking only of her crested head-poor foolish thing
At last, up jumped the cunning spider, and fiercely held her fast.
He dragged her up his winding stair, into his dismal den,
Within his little parlor; but she ne'er came out again!

And now, dear little children, who may this story read,
To idle, silly, flattering words, I pray you ne'er give heed;
Unto an evil counselor close heart, and ear, and eye,
And take a lesson from this tale of the Spider and the Fly.

A Smile

by Unknown

This you will have to read again, and smile, darn ya', smile, winning or losing.

> Let others cheer the winning man,
>   There's one I hold worth while;
> 'Tis he who does the best he can,
>   Then loses with a smile.
> Beaten he is, but not to stay
>   Down with the rank and file;
> That man will win some other day,
>   Who loses with a smile.

Taken at the Flood

by William Shakespeare (1564-1616) in "Julius Caesar"

A good, short lecture for all college grads forging their futures. When the right times come, make your moves.

> There is a tide in the affairs of men
> Which, taken at the flood, leads on to fortune;
> Omitted, all the voyage of their life
> Is bound in shallows and in miseries.
> On such a full sea are we now afloat,
> And we must take the current when it serves,
> Or lose our ventures.

A Wise Old Owl

by Edward Hersey Richards

Wise advice from a wise old bird.

> A wise old owl lived in an oak;
>   The more he saw the less he spoke;
> The less he spoke the more he heard:
>   Why can't we all be like that bird?

Yes, why can't we?

Hustle and Grin

by Unknown

Good advice. Don't let it go to waste.

Smile and the world smiles with you;
  "Knock," and you go it alone;
    For the cheerful grin
    Will let you in
  Where the kicker is never known.

Growl, and the way looks dreary;
  Laugh, and the path is bright;
    For a welcome smile
    Brings sunshine, while
  A frown shuts out the light.

Sigh, and you "rake in" nothing,
  Work, and the prize is won;
    For the nervy man
    With backbone can
  By nothing be outdone.

Hustle! and fortune awaits you;
  Shirk! and defeat is sure;
    For there's no chance
    Of deliverance
  For the chap who can't endure.

Sing, and the world's harmonious.
  Grumble, and things go wrong;
    And all the time
    You are out of rhyme
  With the busy, bustling throng.

Kick, and there's trouble brewing;
  Whistle, and life is gay;
    And the world's in tune
    Like a day in June,
  And the clouds all melt away.

The Old Man's Comforts
And How He Gained Them
by Robert Southey (1774-1843)

Reflections of a wise old man's lifetime. The
rollicking pleasures of youth are replaced
by the more comfortable blessings of old
age. All of us super-seniors know just what he means.

"You are old, Father William," the young man cried;
    "The few locks which are left you are gray;
You are hale, Father William,—a hearty old man:
    Now tell me the reason, I pray."

"In the days of my youth," Father William replied,
    "I remembered that youth would fly fast,
And abused not my health and my vigor at first,
    That I never might need them at last."

"You are old, Father William," the young man cried,
    "And pleasures with youth pass away;
And yet you lament not the days that are gone:
    Now tell me the reason, I pray."

"In the days of my youth," Father William replied,
    "I remembered that youth could not last;
I thought of the future, whatever I did,
    That I never might grieve for the past."

"You are old, Father William," the young man cried,
    "And life must be hastening away;
You are cheerful, and love to converse upon death:
    Now tell me the reason, I pray."

"I am cheerful, young man," Father William replied;
    "Let the cause thy attention engage;
In the days of my youth, I remembered my God,
    And He hath not forgotten my age."

Hullo!

by Sam Walter Foss (1858-1911)

Doesn't that have a friendly warm sound to it?
Doesn't cost a cent, either.

When you see a man in woe,
Walk straight up and say, "Hullo!"
Say "Hullo!" and "How d'ye do?
How's the world been using you?"
Slap the fellow on his back,
Bring your hand down with a whack;
Waltz straight up and don't go slow,
Shake his hand and say, "Hullo!"

Is he clothed in rags? Oh, ho!
Walk straight up and say, "Hullo!"
Rags are but a cotton roll
Just for wrapping up a soul;
And a soul is worth a true
Hale and hearty "How d'ye do?"
Don't wait for the crowd to go;
Walk straight up and say, "Hullo!"

When big vessels meet, they say,
They salute and sail away:
Just the same as you and me,
Lonely ships upon the sea,
Each one sailing his own jog
For a port beyond the fog;
Let your speaking-trumpet blow,
Lift your horn and cry, "Hullo!"

Say "Hullo!" and "How d'ye do?"
Other folks are good as you,
When you leave your house of clay,
Wandering in the far away;
When you travel through the strange
Country far beyond the range,
Then the souls you've cheered will know
Who you be, and say, "Hullo!"

Be the Best of Whatever You Are

by Douglas Malloch

We all dream of great deeds and high
positions, away from the pettiness and
humdrum of ordinary life. Yet success is not
necessarily occupying a lofty place or doing
conspicuous work; it is being the best that is
in you. Rattling around in too big a job is
worse than filling a small one to overflowing.
Dream, aspire by all means; but do not ruin
the life you must lead by dreaming pipe dreams of the one you would like
to lead. Make the most of what you have and are. Perhaps your trivial,
immediate accomplishment is your one sure way of proving your mettle.
Above all, "Do it well or not at all."

> If you can't be a pine on the top of the hill,
>   Be a scrub in the valley—but be
> The best little scrub by the side of the rill;
>   Be a bush if you can't be a tree.
>
> If you can't be a bush, be a bit of the grass,
>   And some highway happier make;
> If you can't be a muskie, then just be a bass—
>   But the liveliest bass in the lake!
>
> We can't all be captains, we've got to be crew,
>   There's something for all of us here,
> There's big work to do, and there's lesser to do,
>   And the task you must do is the near.
>
> If you can't be a highway then just be a trail,
>   If you can't be the sun be a star;
> **It isn't by size that you win or you fail—**
>   **Be the best of whatever you are!**

Can't

by Edgar Guest

Thank goodness that Edison, Marconi, the Wright
Brothers, Fulton and others didn't know this word.
CAN is not only easier to say, it is also easier to
write, and the results are limitless.

Can't is the worst word that's written or spoken;
    Doing more harm here than slander and lies;
On it is many a strong spirit broken,
    And with it many a good purpose dies.
It springs from the lips of the thoughtless each morning
    And robs us of courage we need through the day:
It rings in our ears like a timely sent warning
    And laughs when we falter and fall by the way.

Can't is the father of feeble endeavor,
    The parent of terror and halfhearted work;
It weakens the efforts of artisans clever,
    And makes of the toiler an indolent shirk.
It poisons the soul of the man with a vision,
    It stifles in infancy many a plan;
It greets honest toiling with open derision
    And mocks at the hopes and the dreams of a man.

Can't is a word none should speak without blushing;
    To utter it should be a symbol of shame;
Ambition and courage it daily is crushing;
    It blights a man's purpose and shortens his aim.
Despise it with all of your hatred of error;
    Refuse it the lodgment it seeks in your brain;
Arm against it as a creature of terror,
    And all that you dream of, you someday shall gain.

John Wesley's Rule

Concise—and nice.

> Do all the good you can,
> By all the means you can,
> In all the ways you can
> In all the places you can,
> At all the times you can,
> To all the people you can,
> As long as ever you can.

Count That Day Lost

by George Eliot (1819-1880)

When you count up, what is your batting average in both categories? That is, what good things you did, and what you didn't, but could have.

> If you sit down at set of sun
> And count the acts that you have done,
> And, counting, find
> One self-denying deed, one word
> That eased the heart of him who heard,
> One glance most kind
> Then you may count that day well spent.
>
> But if, through all the livelong day,
> You've cheered no heart, by yea or nay—
> If, through it all
> You've nothing done that you can trace
> That brought the sunshine to one face—
> No act most small
> That helped some soul and nothing cost—
> Then count that day as worse than lost.

Do It Now
by Berton Braley

This is a great shorty. All I can say is, read the highlighted part again and remember to act accordingly. This is another one you will want to read again many times.

If with pleasure you are viewing any work a man is doing,
    If you like him or you love him, tell him now;
Don't withhold your approbation till the parson makes oration
    And he lies with snowy lilies on his brow.
No matter how you shout it, he won't really care about it.
    He won't know how many teardrops you have shed;
If you think some praise is due him, now's the time to slip it to him,
    For he cannot read his tombstone when he's dead.

More than fame, and more than money, is the comment kind and
    sunny,
    And the hearty, warm approval of a friend.
For it gives to life a savor, and it makes you stronger, braver,
    And it gives you heart and spirit to the end.
If he earns your praise—bestow it; if you like him let him know it;
    Let the words of true encouragement be said;
Do not wait till life is over and he's underneath the clover,
    For he cannot read his tombstone when he's dead.

Amen!

Charity
by Unknown

Good advice in a nut shell.

There is so much good in the worst of us,
    And so much bad in the best of us,
That it ill behooves any of us
    To find fault with the rest of us.

Do It Now!
by Unknown

If things haven't been going too well on the job, or you've been hemming and hawing, be sure to read and remember this, and act accordingly.

>If you've got a job to do,
>>**Do it now!**
>If it's one you wish were through,
>>**Do it now!**
>If you're sure the job's your own,
>Do not hem and haw and groan—
>>**Do it now!**
>Don't put off a bit of work,
>>**Do it now!**
>It doesn't pay to shirk,
>>**Do it now!**
>If you want to fill a place
>And be useful to the race,
>Just get up and take a brace—
>>**Do it now!**
>Don't linger by the way,
>>**Do it now!**
>You'll lose if you delay,
>>**Do it now!**
>If the other fellows wait
>Or postpone until it's late,
>You hit up a faster gait—
>>**Do it now!**

Don't Quit

by Unknown

Feel like cashing in your chips? Read on...

> When things go wrong, as they sometimes will,
> When the road you're trudging seems all up hill,
> When the funds are low and the debts are high,
> And you want to smile, but you have to sigh,
> When care is pressing you down a bit,
> Rest, if you must—but don't you quit.
>
> Life is queer with its twists and turns,
> As everyone of us sometimes learns.
> And many a failure turns about
> When he might have won had he stuck it out;
> Don't give up, though the pace seems slow,
> You might succeed with another blow.
>
> Often the goal is nearer than
> It seems to a faint and faltering man.
> Often the struggler has given up
> When he might have captured the victor's cup.
> And he learned too late, when the night slipped down,
> How close he was to the golden crown.
>
> Success is failure turned inside out—
> The silver tint of the clouds of doubt—
> And you never can tell how close you are,
> It may be near when it seems afar;
> So stick to the fight when you're hardest hit—
> It's when things seem worst that you mustn't quit.

There—feel better? Thank you, Unknown.

Drop a Pebble in the Water
by James W. Foley

A very clever comparison of spreading waves of
water, waves of ugly rumors, and of complimentary
words of praise. Be sure the waves you start are
cheerful and kind, because they surely do spread.

Drop a pebble in the water: just a splash, and it is gone;
But there's half-a-hundred ripples circling on and on and on,
Spreading, spreading from the center, flowing on out to the sea.
And there is no way of telling where the end is going to be.

Drop a pebble in the water: in a minute you forget,
But there's little waves a-flowing, and there's ripples circling yet,
And those little waves a-flowing to a great big wave have grown;
You've disturbed a mighty river just by dropping in a stone.

Drop an unkind word, or careless: in a minute it is gone;
But there's half-a-hundred ripples circling on and on and on.
They keep spreading, spreading, spreading from the center as they
     go,
And there is no way to stop them, once you've started them to flow.

Drop an unkind word, or careless: in a minute you forget;
But there's little waves a-flowing, and there's ripples circling yet,
And perhaps in some sad heart a mighty wave of tears you've stirred,
And disturbed a life was happy, ere you dropped that unkind word.

Drop a word of cheer and kindness: just a flash and it is gone;
But there's half-a-hundred ripples circling on and on and on,
Bearing hope and joy and comfort on each splashing, dashing wave
Till you wouldn't believe the volume of the one kind word you gave.

Drop a word of cheer and kindness: in a minute you forget;
But there's gladness still a-swelling, and there's joy a-circling yet,
And you've rolled a wave of comfort whose sweet music can be
     heard
Over miles and miles of water just by dropping one kind word.

Get a Transfer

by Unknown

If you are on the wrong line of life, here is an easy way out—get a transfer. You, and your world, will be better off.

If you are on the Gloomy Line,
     Get a transfer.
If you're inclined to fret and pine,
     Get a transfer.
Get off the track of doubt and gloom,
Get on the Sunshine Track—there's room—
     Get a transfer.

If you're on the Worry Train,
     Get a transfer.
You must not stay there and complain,
     Get a transfer.
The Cheerful Cars are passing through,
And there's lots of room for you—
     Get a transfer.

If you're on the Grouchy Track,
     Get a transfer.
Just take a Happy Special back,
     Get a transfer.
Jump on the train and pull the rope,
That lands you at the station Hope—
     Get a transfer.

He Who Knows
Persian Proverb

A little wisdom, well put.

> He who knows not, and knows not that he knows not, is a fool,
> > Shun him;
> He who knows not, and knows that he knows not, is a child,
> > Teach him.
> He who knows, and knows not that he knows, is asleep,
> > Wake him.
> He who knows, and knows that he knows, is wise,
> > Follow him.

Horse Sense
by Unknown

Come on, let's quit kicking, and pull hard.

> A horse can't pull while kicking,
> > This fact I merely mention.
> And he can't kick while pulling,
> > Which is my chief contention.
>
> Let's imitate the good old horse
> > And lead a life that's fitting;
> Just pull an honest load, and then
> > There'll be no time for kicking.

How Old Are You

by H. S. Fritsch

There's hope beyond "three score and ten," and besides, you're only as old as you feel or act. After reading this, I feel younger.

Age is a quality of mind.
If you have left your dreams behind,
If hope is cold,
If you no longer look ahead,
If your ambitions' fires are dead—
Then you are old.
But if from life you take the best,
If in life you keep the jest,
If love you hold;
No matter how the years go by,
No matter how the birthdays fly—
You are not old.

I Know Something Good About You

by Louis C. Shimon

Why wait? Let's be the first to say it.

Wouldn't this old world be better
        If the folks we meet would say—
"I know something good about you!"
        And treat us just that way?

Wouldn't it be fine and dandy
        If each handclasp, fond and true,
Carried with it this assurance—
        "I know something good about you!"

Wouldn't life be lots more happy
        If the good that's in us all
Were the only thing about us
        That folks bothered to recall?

Wouldn't life be lots more happy
    If we praised the good we see?
For there's such a lot of goodness
    In the worst of you and me!

Wouldn't it be nice to practice
    That fine way of thinking, too?
You know something good about me,
    I know something good about you?

It Isn't the Town, It's You

by R. W. Glover (1712-1785)

Come on! Quit complaining and pull your
load. The town will seem better, even if it isn't.
And you could even help it get better.

If you want to live in the kind of a town
    That's the kind of a town you like,
You needn't slip your clothes in a grip
    And start on a long, long hike.

You'll find elsewhere what you left behind,
    For there's nothing that's really new.
It's a knock at yourself when you knock your town;
    It isn't your town—it's you.

Real towns are not made by men afraid
    Lest somebody else gets ahead.
When everybody works and nobody shirks
    You can raise a town from the dead.

And if while you make your stake
    Your neighbor can make one, too,
Your town will be what you want to see,
    It isn't your town—it's you.

Life's Scars

by Ella Wheeler Wilcox (1855-1919)

A great message on the theme, we always hurt the ones we love most.
And the wounds are always the deepest. There's a tremendous lesson
here, and it seems aimed primarily at married couples. You really should
think hard about this one. And remember.

They say the world is round, and yet
    I often think it square,
So many little hurts we get
    From corners here and there.
But one great truth in life I've found,
    While journeying to the West—
The only folks who really wound
    Are those we love the best.

The man you thoroughly despise
    Can rouse your wrath, 'tis true;
Annoyance in your heart will rise
    At things mere strangers do;
But those are only passing ills;
    This rule all lives will prove;
The rankling wound which aches and thrills,
    Is dealt by hands we love.

The choicest garb, the sweetest grace,
    Are oft to strangers shown;
The careless mien, the frowning face,
    Are given to our own.
We flatter those we scarcely know,
    We please the fleeting guest,
And deal full many a thoughtless blow
    To those who love us best.

Love does not grow on every tree,
    Nor true hearts yearly bloom.
Alas for those who only see
    This cut across a tomb!
But, soon or late, the fact grows plain
    To all through sorrow's test:
The only folks who give us pain
    Are those we love the best.

Lifting and Leaning
by Ella Wheeler Wilcox (1855-1919)

Was she thinking about Social Security in stanza eight, about "one lifter to twenty who lean"? Come on now. Are you a lifter or a leaner?

There are two kinds of people on earth today,
Just two kinds of people, no more, I say.

Not the good and the bad, for 'tis well understood
The good are half bad and the bad are half good.

Not the happy and sad, for the swift-flying years
Bring each man his laughter and each man his tears.

Not the rich and the poor, for to count a man's wealth
You must first know the state of his conscience and health.

Not the humble and proud, for in life's busy span
Who puts on vain airs is not counted a man.

No! the two kinds of people on earth I mean
Are the people who lift and the people who lean.

Wherever you go you will find the world's masses
Are ever divided in just these two classes.

And, strangely enough, you will find, too, I ween,
There is only one lifter to twenty who lean.

In which class are you? are you easing the load
Of overtaxed lifters who toil down the road?

Or, are you a leaner who lets others bear
Your portion of worry and labor and care?

(Note: Social Security used to have about 30 lifters for each leaner. It's now down to low single digits. Think about it. They've got to change the ratio.)

Mr. Meant-To

by Unknown

Probably a cousin of Mr. Around-To-It

> Mr. Meant-To has a comrade,
>   And his name is Didn't-Do;
> Have you ever chanced to meet them?
>   Did they ever call on you?
>
> These two fellows live together
>   In the house of Never-Win,
> And I'm told that it is haunted
>   By the ghost of Might-Have-Been.

My Creed

by Howard Arnold Walter

Sounds like Ms. Perfect, but if you grade yourself
B+ on this test, you're super.

> I would be true, for there are those who trust me;
>   I would be pure, for there are those who care;
> I would be strong, for there is much to suffer;
>   I would be brave, for there is much to dare.
> I would be friend of all—the foe, the friendless;
>   I would be giving, and forget the gift.
> I would be humble, for I know my weakness;
>   I would look up—and laugh—and love—and lift.

Optimism
by Ella Wheeler Wilcox (1855-1919)

Sure beats pessimism every time. Feel it and show it. Put on a happy face; you'll like it and so will your friends.

> Talk happiness. The world is sad enough
> Without your woes. No path is wholly rough;
> Look for the places that are smooth and clear,
> And speak of those, to rest the weary ear
> Of Earth, so hurt by one continuous strain
> Of human discontent and grief and pain.
>
> Talk faith. The world is better off without
> Your uttered ignorance and morbid doubt.
> If you have faith in God, or man, or self,
> Say so. If not, push back upon the shelf
> Of silence all your thoughts, till faith shall come;
> No one will grieve because your lips are dumb.
>
> Talk health. The dreary, never-changing tale
> Of mortal maladies is worn and stale.
> You cannot charm, or interest, or please
> By harping on that minor chord, disease.
> Say you are well, or all is well with you,
> And God shall hear your words and make them true.

Outwitted
by Edwin Markham

Why does this seem so hard for us to do?

> He drew a circle that shut me out—
> Heretic, rebel, a thing to flout.
> But Love and I had the wit to win:
> We drew a circle that took him in!

Perseverance

by Johann Wolfgang von Goethe (1789-1832)

To each his own. Or as the old saying goes, "As you sow, so shall you reap." And that's the way it shall be, and should be.

> We must not hope to be mowers,
>   And to gather the ripe gold ears,
> Unless we have first been sowers
>   And watered the furrows with tears.
>
> It is not just as we take it,
>   This mystical world of ours,
> Life's field will yield as we make it
>   A harvest of thorns or of flowers.

Polonius' Advice to Laertes

from "Hamlet"
by William Shakespeare (1564-1616)

Not quite poetry, but too good not to include, especially the last six lines. There's some mighty good advice by the Bard in these last lines—you'd better read them again slowly. I wonder if Kipling read this advice when he wrote *If*. Certainly his poem has much the same theme.

> "There,—my blessing with you!
> And these few precepts in thy memory
> See thou character—Give thy thoughts no tongue,
> Nor any unproportion'd thought his act.
> Be thou familiar, but by no means vulgar.
> The friends thou hast, and their adoption tried,
> Grapple them to thy soul with hoops of steel;
> But do not dull thy palm with entertainment
> Of each new-hatched, unfledged comrade. Beware
> Of entrance to a quarrel; but being in,
> Bear't that the opposed may beware of thee.
> Give every man thine ear, but few thy voice:
> Take each man's censure, but reserve thy judgment.
> Costly thy habit as thy purse can buy,
> But not expressed in fancy; rich, not gaudy:

For the apparel oft proclaims the man.
Neither a borrower nor a lender be,
For loan oft loses both itself and friend,
And borrowing dulls the edge of husbandry.
This above all: to thine own self be true,
And it must follow, as the night the day,
Thou canst not then be false to any man."

Solitude
by Ella Wheeler Wilcox (1855-1919)

Advice well worth heeding. I really like this one.
Very special! The title is deceiving.

> **Laugh, and the world laughs with you;**
> **Weep, and you weep alone.**
> **For the sad old earth must borrow its mirth,**
> **But has trouble enough of its own.**
> Sing, and the hills will answer;
> Sigh, it is lost on the air.
> The echoes bound to a joyful sound,
> But shrink from voicing care.
>
> **Rejoice, and men will seek you;**
> **Grieve, and they turn and go.**
> **They want full measure of all your pleasure,**
> **But they do not need your woe.**
> Be glad, and your friends are many;
> Be sad, and you lose them all.
> There are none to decline your nectared wine,
> But alone you must drink life's gall.
>
> Feast, and your halls are crowded;
> Fast, and the world goes by.
> Succeed and give, and it helps you live,
> But no man can help you die.
> There is room in the halls of pleasure
> For a long and lordly train,
> But one by one we must all file on
> Through the narrow aisles of pain.

Smile

by Unknown

Remember from that other poem, *Solitude*:
"Laugh and the world laughs with you. Weep
and you weep alone." Remember also that a
smile is a special gift of God to mankind. So
smile! Gee, you look better.

Like a bread without the spreadin',
    Like a puddin' without sauce,
Like a mattress without beddin',
    Like a cart without a hoss,
Like a door without a latchstring,
    Like a fence without a stile,
Like a dry an' barren creek bed—
    Is the face without a smile

Like a house without a dooryard,
    Like a yard without a flower,
Like a clock without a mainspring,
    That will never tell the hour;
A thing that sort o' makes yo' feel
    A hunger all the while—
Oh, the saddest sight that ever was
    Is a face without a smile!

The face of man was but for smiles,
    An' thereby he is blest
Above the critters of the field,
    The birds an' all the rest;
He's just a little lower
    Than the angels in the skies,
An' the reason is that he can smile;
    Therein his glory lies!

So smile an' don't forgit to smile,
    An' smile, an' smile ag'in;
'Twill help you all along the way,
    An' cheer you mile by mile;
An' so, whatever is your lot,
    Jes' smile, an' smile, an' smile.

The Gate At the End of Things

by Unknown

Do what is recommended and yours won't be a
toll gate, or a locked gate, and certainly
not a Watergate or a Travelgate.

Some people say the world's all a stage
        Where each plays a part in life;
While others proclaim that life is quite real,
        Its joys, its battles, its strife.
Some say it's a joke, we should laugh it along,
        Should smile at the knocks and stings;
Whatever is true just take this from me,
        There's a gate at the end of things.

Don't try to kid yourself with the thought,
        You can do as you please all the while;
Don't think you can kick the poor fellow who's down,
        While you climb to the top of the pile.
Don't go back on your pal, just because he won't know,
        Oh, in his eyes you may be a king;
Some day he will see you just as you are,
        At the gate at the end of things.

Don't think you fool all the folks all the while,
        You may do it sometimes, that is true;
They will find you out in the end every time,
        The only one you fool is you.
If you see a man down, why, give him a hand,
        And find how much pleasure it brings,
To know you are ready to meet all mankind,
        At the gate at the end of things.

Don't let your head swell 'cause your bank roll is large
        And your clothes are the latest style;
There is many a prince walking round in rags,
        May have you beaten a mile.
Just try to remember as through life you go,
        If you're square you're as good as a king,
And you won't have to crawl through a hole in the wall,
        At the gate at the end of things.

If you've got a wife, as most fellows have,
　　Remember what she's been to you,
When prosperity smiles, treat her like a pal,
　　She's the one that has stuck to you;
Don't look for the girl from the Great White Way,
　　Who wears diamonds, fine clothes and those things;
Think how you'd feel to meet your little girl,
　　At the gate at the end of things.

Live like a man, it don't cost any more,
　　To act on the square and be right.
It's reward enough to know you're a man,
　　To hear people say, "He's a knight."
You can look everybody straight in the eye,
　　And your voice has sincerity's ring;
Then you're ready to go and pass through with the bunch,
　　At the gate at the end of things.

Work While You Work

Poem from McGuffey's Primer (19-20 cen)
Basic ergonomics, for a winner.

Work while you work,
　　Play while you play;
One thing each time,
　　That is the way.

All that you do,
　　Do with your might;
Things done by halves
　　Are not done right.

The Sin of Omission

by Margaret E. Sangster (1838-1912)

"Do you ever sit at the setting of the sun, and dream of the things that you might have done." (From the song *When You Come to the End of the Day*.) Let's turn these dreams to actions.

It isn't the thing you do, dear,
    It's the thing you leave undone
That gives you a bit of a heartache
    At setting of the sun.
The tender word forgotten,
    The letter you did not write,
The flowers you did not send, dear,
    Are your haunting ghosts at night.

The stone you might have lifted
    Out of a brother's way;
The bit of heartsome counsel
    You were hurried too much to say;
The loving touch of the hand, dear,
    The gentle, winning tone
Which you had no time nor thought for
    With troubles enough of you own.
Those little acts of kindness
    So easily out of mind,
Those chances to be angels
    Which we poor mortals find—
They come in night and silence,
    Each sad, reproachful wraith,
When hope is faint and flagging,
    And a chill has fallen on faith.

For life is all too short, dear,
    And sorrow is all too great,
To suffer our slow compassion
    That tarries until too late;
And it isn't the thing you do, dear,
    It's the thing you leave undone,
Which gives you a bit of a heartache
    At the setting of the sun.

The Thinker

by Berton Braley

A well deserved and beautifully stated tribute to the brains behind the brawn. Not to the ones who make things, but to the ones that conceive them and make them run.

Back of the beating hammer
　　By which the steel is wrought,
Back of the workshop's clamor
　　The seeker may find the Thought—
The Thought that is ever master
　　Of iron and steam and steel,
That rises above disaster
　　And tramples it under heel!

The drudge may fret and tinker
　　Or labor with lusty blows,
But back of him stands the Thinker,
　　The clear-eyed man who knows;
For into each plow or saber,
　　Each piece and part and whole,
Must go the Brains of Labor,
　　Which gives the work a soul!

Back of the motors humming,
　　Back of the bells that sing,
Back of the hammers drumming,
　　Back of the cranes that swing,
There is the eye which scans them,
　　Watching through stress and strain,
There is the Mind which plans them—
　　Back of the brawn, the Brain!

Might of the roaring boiler,
　　Force of the engine's thrust,
Strength of the sweating toiler—
　　Greatly in these we trust.
But back of them stands the Schemer,
　　The Thinker who drives things through;
Back of the Job—the Dreamer
　　Who's making the dream come true!

The Winds of Fate

by Ella Wheeler Wilcox (1855-1919)

Set your sails. Don't just follow the wind. And don't
blame a head-wind if you don't reach your goal.

One ship drives east and another drives west
With the selfsame winds that blow.
'Tis the set of the sails
And not the gales
Which tells us the way to go.

Like the winds of the sea are the ways of fate,
As we voyage along through life:
'Tis the set of a soul
That decides its goal,
And not the calm or the strife.

Then Laugh

by Bertha Adams Backus

Remember to put 'em ALL in—then keep sitting and
laughing—and no peeking. I guarantee you'll like this
one.

Build for yourself a strong box,
Fashion each part with care;
When it's strong as your hand can make it
Put all your troubles there;
Hide there all thought of your failures,
And each bitter cup that you quaff;
Lock all your heartaches within it,
Then sit on the lid and laugh.

Tell no one else its contents,
Never its secrets share;
When you've dropped in your care and worry
Keep them forever there;
Hide them from sight so completely
That the world will never dream half;
Fasten the strong box securely—
Then sit on the lid and laugh.

Try Smiling

by Unknown

I agree, wholeheartedly, and do my best to follow suit.

> When the weather suits you not,
>   Try smiling.
> When your coffee isn't hot,
>   Try smiling.
> When your neighbors don't do right,
> Or your relatives all fight,
> Sure 'tis hard, but then you might
>   Try smiling.
>
> Doesn't change the things, of course—
>   Just smiling.
> But it cannot make them worse—
>   Just smiling.
> And it seems to help your case,
> Brightens up a gloomy place,
> Then, it sort o' rests your face—
>   Just smiling.

Your Mission

by Ellen M. H. Gates (1835-1920)

Every soldier can't be a General; nor each sailor an Admiral. Do, and be, the best you can, and help a lot of people on the way. Then you're doing your share, and fulfilling your mission. Ellen says it beautifully.

> If you cannot on the ocean
>   Sail among the swiftest fleet,
> Rocking on the highest billows,
>   Laughing at the storms you meet,
> You can stand among the sailors,
>   Anchored yet within the bay;
> You can lend a hand to help them,
>   As they launch their boats away.

If you are too weak to journey
    Up the mountain, steep and high,
You can stand within the valley,
    While the multitude go by.
You can chant in happy measure,
    As they slowly pass along;
Though they may forget the singer,
    They will not forget the song.

If you have not gold and silver
    Ever ready to command,
If you cannot toward the needy
    Reach an ever-open hand,
You can visit the afflicted,
    O'er the erring you can weep;
You can be a true disciple,
    Sitting at the Savior's feet.

If you cannot in the conflict
    Prove yourself a soldier true,
If where the fire and smoke are thickest
    There's no work for you to do,
When the battle field is silent,
    You can go with a careful tread;
You can bear away the wounded,
    You can cover up the dead.

Do not then stand idly waiting
    For some greater work to do:
Fortune is a lazy goddess,
    She will never come to you.
Go and toil in any vineyard,
    Do not fear to do or dare;
If you want a field of labor,
    You can find it anywhere.

Which Are You

by *Unknown*

Are you a builder-upper or a tearer-downer?
Remember what Jean Sibelius once said, "No
statue has ever been erected to a critic."

I watched them tearing a building down,
A gang of men in a busy town;
With a ho-heave-ho and a lusty yell
They swung a beam and the sidewalk fell.
I asked the foreman: "Are these men skilled,
And the men you'd hire if you had to build?"
He gave a laugh and said: "No indeed!
Just common labor is all I need.
I can easily wreck in a day or two
What builders have taken a year to do!"

And I thought to myself as I went my way,
Which of these roles have I tried to play?
Am I a builder who works with care,
Measuring life by the rule and square?
Am I shaping my deeds to a well-made plan,
Patiently doing the best I can?
Or am I a wrecker, who walks the town,
Content with the labor of tearing down.

The Man Who Thinks He Can

by *Walter D. Wintle*

A winner. Remember the Little Engine in the children's book—I think I can,
I think I can—and he did.

If you think you are beaten, you are;
    If you think you dare not, you don't;
If you'd like to win, but think you can't,
    It's almost a cinch you won't.
If you think you'll lose, you're lost,
    For out in the world we find
Success begins with a fellow's will;
    It's all in the state of mind.

If you think you're outclassed, you are;
    You've got to think high to rise.
You've got to be sure of yourself before
    You can ever win a prize.
Life's battles don't always go
    To the stronger or faster man;
But soon or late the man who wins
    Is the man who thinks he can.

Tell Him So

by Unknown

Not hard to do, if you do it right away. It will
probably come back, plus interest.

If you hear a kind word spoken
    Of some worthy soul you know,
It may fill his heart with sunshine
    If you only tell him so.

If a deed, however humble,
    Helps you on your way to go,
Seek the one whose hand has helped you,
    Seek him out and tell him so!

If your heart is touched and tender
    Toward a sinner, lost and low,
It might help him to do better
    If you'd only tell him so!

Oh, my sisters, oh, my brothers,
    As o'er life's rough path you go,
If God's love has saved and kept you,
    Do not fail to tell men so!

Results and Roses
by Edgar Guest

My sore back confirms this absolutely. However, still my favorite relaxation, and most rewarding.

The man who wants a garden fair,
    Or small or very big,
With flowers growing here and there,
    Must bend his back and dig.

The things are mighty few on earth
    That wishes can attain.
Whate'er we want of any worth
    We've got to work to gain.

It matters not what goal you seek
    Its secret here reposes:
You've got to dig from week to week
    To get Results or Roses.

Moderation
by Robert Service (1874-1958)

Service thinks the best way is moderation in eating, drinking, spending, saving, and making love. But you will note that in the latter he advises to be moderate in your moderation. Bless him.

What pious people label vice
    I reckon mainly pleasure;
I deem that women, wine and dice
    Are good in modest measure;
Though sanctity and truth receive
    My hearty approbation,
Of all the virtues, I believe
    The best is Moderation.

Be moderate in love and hate,
    Soft pedal on emotion;
And never let your passion get
    The better of your caution.
Should Right or Leftist seek to goad
    You from the course that's level,
Stick to the middle of the road
    And send them to the devil.

Though rich the feast, be moderate
    In eating and in drinking;
An appetite insatiate
    Is evil to my thinking.
Though ladies languidly await
    Your kisses, on your way shun
Their wiles, but—well, be moderate
    Even in moderation.

Avoid extremes: be moderate
    In saving and in spending;
An equable and easy gait
    Will win an easy ending...
So here's to him of open mind,
    Of sense and toleration,
That hope of headlong human-kind,
    The Man of Moderation.

Little Things

by Ebenzer Cobham Brewer

Little things mean a lot; in the long run, a whole lot.
Should I mention the atom?

> Little drops of water,
>   Little grains of sand,
> Make the mighty ocean
>   And the pleasant land.
>
> Thus the little minutes,
>   Humble though they be,
> Make the mighty ages
>   Of eternity.
>
> So our little errors
>   Lead the soul away
> From the path of virtue
>   Far in sin to stray.
>
> Little deeds of kindness
>   Little words of love
> Help to make earth happy
>   Like the heaven above.

Laughter

by Robert Service (1874-1958)

Very good advice to anyone who can really look at
his true self—and laugh. The deeper we look into
ourselves, the harder we may laugh.

> I laugh at Life: its antics make for me a giddy game,
> Where only foolish fellows take themselves with solemn aim.
> I laugh at pomp and vanity, at riches, rank and pride;
> At social inanity, its swagger, swank and side.
> At poets, pastry-cooks and kings, at folk sublime and small,
> Who fuss about a thousand things that matter not at all;
> At those who dream of name and fame, at those who scheme for pelf...
> But best of all the laughing game—is laughing at myself.

Some poet chap has labeled man the noblest work of God:
I see myself a charlatan, a humbug and a fraud.
Yea, 'spite of show and shallow wit, and sentimental drool,
I know myself a hypocrite, a coward and a fool.
And though I kick myself with glee profoundly on the pants,
I'm little worse, it seems to me, than other human ants.
For if you probe your private mind, impervious to shame,
Oh, Gentle Reader, you may find you're much about the same.

Then let us mock with ancient mirth this comic, cosmic plan;
The stars are laughing at the earth; God's greatest joke is man.
For laughter is a buckler bright, and scorn a shining spear;
So let us laugh with all our might at folly, fraud and fear.
Yet on our sorry selves be spent our most sardonic glee.
Oh, don't pay life the compliment to take it *seriously*.
For he who can himself despise, be surgeon to the bone,
May win to worth in others' eyes, to wisdom in his own.

To-Day

by Lydia Avery Coonley Ward

Live today. Tomorrow, good or bad, doesn't always come.

Why fear to-morrow, timid heart?
        Why tread the future's way?
We only need to do our part
        To-day, dear child, to-day.

The past is written! Close the book
        On pages sad and gay;
Within the future do not look,
        But live to-day—to-day.

'Tis this one hour that God has given;
        His Now we must obey;
And it will make our earth his heaven
        To live to-day—to-day.

I Believe
by Robert Service (1874-1958)

A bit socialistic perhaps, but notice that he states first that everyone should do his full share of work. And he ends by stating that he has not followed his own creed. That's where practicality comes into view.

It's my belief that every man
     Should do his share of work,
And in our economic plan
     No citizen should shirk.
That in return each one should get
     His meed of fold and food,
And feel that all his toil and sweat
     Is for the common good.

It's my belief that every chap
     Should have an equal start,
And there should be no handicap
     To hinder his depart;
That there be fairness in the fight,
     And justice in the race,
And every lad should have the right
     To win his proper place.

It's my belief that people should
     Be neither rich nor poor;
That none should suffer servitude,
     And all should be secure.
That wealth is loot, and rank is rot,
     And foul is class and clan;
That to succeed a man may not
     Exploit his brother man.

It's my belief that heritage
     And usury are wrong;
That each should win a worthy wage
     And sing an honest song...
Not one like this—for though I rue
     The wrong of life, I flout it.
Alas! I'm not prepared to do
     A goddam thing about it.

Forget It

by Unknown

How easy to expose a nasty secret whose
expression could do someone a great harm
or cause great anguish. How thoughtful and
compassionate to forget it.

If you see a tall fellow ahead of the crowd,
A leader of music, marching fearless and proud,
And you know of a tale whose mere telling aloud
Would cause his proud head to in anguish be bowed,
    It's a pretty good plan to forget it.

If you know of a skeleton hidden away
In a closet, and guarded and kept from the day
In the dark; whose showing, whose sudden display
Would cause grief and sorrow and lifelong dismay,
    It's a pretty good plan to forget it.

If you know of a spot in the life of a friend
(We all have spots concealed, world without end),
Whose touching his heartstrings would sadden or rend,
Till the shame of its showing no grieving could mend,
    It's a pretty good plan to forget it.

If you know of a thing that will darken the joy
Of a man or a woman, a girl or a boy,
That will wipe out a smile or the least way annoy
A fellow, or cause any gladness to cloy,
    It's a pretty good plan to forget it.

The Calf-Path
by Sam Walter Foss (1858-1911)

This is a great one. I have read and reread this
to my children and grandchildren to stress the
wonderful moral theme: don't follow blindly
every calf path just because it has always been
the way to go. God gave us a constantly
curious mind to outthink all calves and long-
gone ancestors. Still, look around and you will see many "calf paths." This
brings to mind an old saying in one of my text books—"Be not the first by
which the new is tried, Nor yet the last to cast the old aside." In other
words, always look for a new and better way, but make sure it is better. If
you know a better way to do anything, DO IT and the calves will follow,
not lead. That is how all the great inventions and advances of civilization
have been made.

> One day, through the primeval wood,
> A calf walked home, as good calves should;
> But made a trail all bent askew,
> A crooked trail as all calves do.
> Since then two hundred years have fled,
> And, I infer, the calf is dead.
> But still he left behind his trail,
> And thereby hangs my moral tale.
>
> The trail was taken up next day
> By a lone dog that passed that way;
> And then a wise bell-wether sheep
> Pursued the trail o'er vale and steep,
> And drew the flock behind him, too,
> As good bell-wethers always do.
>
> And from that day, o'er hill and glade,
> Through those old woods a path was made;
> And many men wound in and out,
> And dodged and turned, and bent about
> And uttered words of righteous wrath
> Because 'twas such a crooked path.
> But still they followed—do not laugh—
> The first migrations of that calf,
> And through this winding wood-way stalked,
> Because he wobbled when he walked.

This forest path became a lane,
That bent, and turned, and turned again;
This crooked lane became a road,
Where many a poor horse with his load
Toiled on beneath the burning sun,
And traveled some three miles in one.
And thus a century and a half
They trod the footsteps of that calf.

The years passed on in swiftness fleet,
The road became a village street;
And this, before men were aware,
A city's crowded thoroughfare;
And soon the central street was this
Of a renowned metropolis;
And men two centuries and a half
Trod in the footsteps of that calf.

Each day a hundred thousand rout
Followed the zigzag calf about;
And o'er his crooked journey went
The traffic of a continent.
A hundred thousand men were led
By one calf near three centuries dead.
They followed still his crooked way,
And lost one hundred years a day;
For thus such reverence is lent
To well-established precedent.

A moral lesson this might teach,
Were I ordained and called to preach:
For men are prone to go it blind
Along the calf-paths of the mind,
And work away from sun to sun
To do what other men have done.
They follow in the beaten track,
And out and in, and forth and back,
And still their devious course pursue,
To keep the path that others do.

But how the wise old wood-gods laugh,
Who saw the first primeval calf!
Ah! many things this tale might teach,—
But I am not ordained to preach.

Be True

by Horatius Bonar (1808-1889)

Remember what Keats said about the urn. "Beauty is truth, truth beauty. That is all ye know on earth and all ye need to know." And Sir Walter Scott in *Marmion* warned further, "O, What a tangled web we weave when first we practice to deceive."

Thou must be true thyself,
      If thou the truth wouldst teach;
Thy soul must overflow, if thou
      Another's soul wouldst reach!
It needs the overflow of heart
      To give the lips full speech.

Think truly, and thy thoughts
      Shall the world's famine feed;
Speak truly, and each word of thine
      Shall be a fruitful seed;
Live truly, and thy life shall be
      A great and noble creed.

The Cry of a Dreamer

by John Boyle O'Reilly (1844-1890)

Obviously not a city-boy.

I am tired of planning and toiling
    In the crowded hives of men;
Heart-weary of building and spoiling,
    And spoiling and building again.
And I long for the dear old river,
    Where I dreamed my youth away;
For a dreamer lives forever,
    And a toiler dies in a day.

I am sick of the showy seeming
    Of a life that is half a lie;
Of the faces lined with scheming
    In the throng that hurries by.
From the sleepless thoughts' endeavour,
    I would go where the children play;
For a dreamer lives forever,
    And a thinker dies in a day.

I can feel no pride, but pity
    For the burdens the rich endure;
There is nothing sweet in the city
    But the patient lives of the poor.
Oh, the little hands too skillful
    And the child mind choked with weeds!
The daughter's heart grown willful,
    And the father's heart that bleeds!

No, no! from the street's rude bustle,
    From trophies of mart and stage,
I would fly to the woods' low rustle
    And the meadows' kindly page.
Let me dream as of old by the river,
    And be loved for the dream alway;
For a dreamer lives forever,
    And a toiler dies in a day.

Six Feet of Earth

by Unknown

Not a pleasant thought, but all too true. The
idea should bring a few of the high and
mighty down to size, but some egos just can't
be deflated.

I'll sing you a song of the world and its ways,
    And the many strange people we meet—
From the rich man who rolls in his millions of wealth,
    To the struggling wretch on the street.
But a man, tho' he's poor, and in tatters and rags,
    We should never affect to despise;
But think of the adage, remember, my friends,
    That six feet of earth makes us all of one size.

There's the rich man with thousands to spare if he likes,
    But he haughtily holds up his head,
And who thinks he's above the mechanic who toils,
    And is honestly earning his bread;
But his gold and his jewels he can't take away,
    To the world up above, when he dies;
For death levels all, and conclusively shows
    That six feet of earth makes us all of one size.

There's many a coat that is tatter'd and torn,
    That beneath lies a true, honest heart,
But because he's not dress'd like his neighbors in style,
    Why, "Society" keeps them apart.
For on one Fortune smiles while the other one fails,
    Yes, no matter what venture he tries;
But time calls them both to the grave in the end,
    And six feet of earth makes us all of one size.

Then when you once see a poor fellow that tries
    To baffle the world and its frown,
Let us help him along, and perchance he'll succeed—
    Don't crush him because he is down.
For a cup of cold water, in charity given,
    Is remembered with joy in the skies;
We are all but human, we have all got to die,
    And six feet of earth makes us all of one size.

Ode on a Grecian Urn

by John Keats (1795-1821)

Not one of my favorites but the last two lines are classic.
I'll be happy if you just read those two. I told you I like
poetry light and musical.

Thou still unravished bride of quietness,
    Thou foster child of Silence and slow Time,
Sylvan historian, who canst thus express
    A flowery tale more sweetly than our rhyme:
What leaf-fring'd legend haunts about thy shape
    Of deities or mortals, or of both,
        In Tempe or the dales of Arcady?
What men or gods are these? What maidens loath?
    What mad pursuit? What struggle to escape?
        What pipes and timbrels? What wild ecstasy?

Heard melodies are sweet, but those unheard
    Are sweeter; therefore, ye soft pipes, play on;
Not to the sensual ear, but, more endeared,
    Pipe to the spirit ditties of no tone;
Fair youth, beneath the trees, thou canst not leave
    Thy song, nor ever can those trees be bare;
        Bold Lover, never, never canst thou kiss,
Though winning near the goal—yet, do not grieve;
    She cannot fade, though thou hast not thy bliss,
        For ever wilt thou love, and she be fair!

Ah, happy, happy boughs! that cannot shed
    Your leaves, nor ever bid the Spring adieu;
And, happy melodist, unwearied,
    For ever piping songs for ever new;
More happy love! more happy, happy love!
    For ever warm and still to be enjoy'd,
        For ever panting, and for ever young;
All breathing human passion far above,
    That leaves a heart high-sorrowful and cloy'd,
        A burning forehead, and a parching tongue.

Who are these coming to the sacrifice?
     To what green altar, O mysterious priest,
Lead'st thou that heifer lowing at the skies,
     And all her silken flanks with garlands drest?
What little town by river or seashore,
     Or mountain-built with peaceful citadel,
          Is emptied of this folk, this pious morn?
And, little town, thy streets for evermore
     Will silent be; and not a soul to tell
          Why thou are desolate, can e'er return.

O Attic shape! Fair attitude! with brede
     Of marble men and maidens overwrought,
With forest branches and the trodden weed;
     Thou, silent form, dost tease us out of thought
As doth eternity: Cold Pastoral!
     When old age shall this generation waste,
          Thou shalt remain, in midst of other woe
Than ours, a friend to man, to whom thou say'st,
     "Beauty is truth, truth beauty,"—that is all
          Ye know on earth, and all ye need to know.

⊸ FAITH AND REVERENCE ⊷

L'Envoi
by Rudyard Kipling (1865-1936)

Thought provoking. A pleasant picture of life after death, as Kipling paints it. He obviously firmly believed in a life hereafter, and a great one for those that deserve it.

When earth's last picture is painted, and the tubes are twisted and
    dried,
When the oldest colors have faded, and the youngest critic has died,
We shall rest, and, faith, we shall need it—lie down for an aeon or two,
Till the Master of All Good Workmen shall set us to work anew!

And those that were good will be happy: they shall sit in a golden
    chair;
They shall splash at a ten-league canvas with brushes of comets' hair;
They shall find real saints to draw from—Magdalene, Peter, and
    Paul;
They shall work for an age at a sitting and never be tired at all!

And only the Master shall praise us, and only the Master shall
    blame;
And no one shall work for money, and no one shall work for fame;
But each for the joy of the working, and each, in his separate star,
Shall draw the Thing as he sees It for the God of Things as They
    Are!

The Creation

by Cecil Frances Alexander (1818-1895)

A simply stated appreciation of all the good
things created for us by the Almighty.

> All things bright and beautiful,
>> All creatures, great and small,
> All things wise and wonderful,
>> The Lord God made them all.
>
> Each little flower that opens,
>> Each little bird that sings,
> He made their glowing colors,
>> He made their tiny wings;
>
> The rich man in his castle,
>> The poor man at his gate,
> God made them, high or lowly,
>> And order'd their estate.
>
> The purple-headed mountain,
>> The river running by,
> The sunset and the morning
>> That brightens up the sky;
>
> The cold wind in the winter,
>> The pleasant summer sun,
> The ripe fruits in the garden—
>> He made them every one.
>
> The tall trees in the greenwood,
>> The meadows where we play,
> The rushes by the water
>> We gather every day;—
>
> He gave us eyes to see them,
>> And lips that we might tell
> How great is God Almighty
>> Who has made all things well!

The Fool's Prayer

by Edward Rowland Sill (1841-1887)

The king learns a lesson from the cleverly
worded, thoughtful prayer of a "fool." A truly
humbling experience from King to fool by
one shrewd dialogue.

The royal feast was done; the King
    Sought some new sport to banish care,
And to his jester cried: "Sir Fool,
    Kneel now, and make for us a prayer!"

The jester doffed his cap and bells,
    And stood the mocking court before;
They could not see the bitter smile
    Behind the painted grin he wore.

He bowed his head, and bent his knee
    Upon the monarch's silken stool;
His pleading voice arose: "O Lord,
    Be merciful to me, a fool!

"No pity, Lord, could change the heart
    From red with wrong to white as wool;
The rod must heal the sin: but Lord,
    Be merciful to me, a fool!

"'Tis not by guile the onward sweep
    Of truth and right, O Lord, we stay;
'Tis by our follies that so long
    We hold the earth from heaven away.

"These clumsy feet, still in the mire,
    Go crushing blossoms without end;
These hard, well-meaning hands we thrust
    Among the heart-strings of a friend.

"The ill-timed truth we might have kept—
    Who knows how sharp it pierced and stung?
The word we had not sense to say—
    Who knows how grandly it had rung!

"Our faults no tenderness should ask,
　　The chastening stripes must cleanse them all;
But for our blunders—oh, in shame
　　Before the eyes of heaven we fall.

"Earth bears no balsam for mistakes;
　　Men crown the knave, and scourge the tool
That did his will; but Thou, O Lord,
　　Be merciful to me, a fool!"

The room was hushed; in silence rose
　　The King, and sought his gardens cool,
And walked apart, and murmured low,
　　"Be merciful to me, a fool!"

Ring Out Wild Bells

by *Alfred Tennyson (1809-1892)*

A cheerful, moving New Year's greeting. This is
over 100 years old, but as you read each stanza,
you will be sure it is referring to current events.
Striking.

Ring out wild bells to the wild sky,
　　The flying cloud, the frosty light;
　　The year is dying in the night;
Ring out, wild bells, and let him die.

Ring out the old, ring in the new,
　　Ring, happy bells, across the snow;
　　The year is going, let him go;
Ring out the false, ring in the true.

Ring out the grief that saps the mind
　　For those that here we see no more;
　　Ring out the feud of rich and poor,
Ring in redress to all mankind.

Ring out a slowly dying cause,
　　And ancient forms of party strife;
　　Ring in the nobler modes of life,
With sweeter manners, purer laws.

Ring out the want, the care, the sin,
    The faithless coldness of the times;
    Ring out, ring out my mournful rhymes,
But ring the fuller minstrel in.

Ring out false pride in place and blood,
    The civic slander and the spite;
    Ring in the love of truth and right,
Ring in the common love of good.

Ring out old shapes of foul disease,
    Ring out the narrowing lust of gold;
    Ring out the thousand ways of old,
Ring in the thousand years of peace.

Ring in the valiant man and free,
    The larger heart, the kindlier hand;
    Ring out the darkness of the land,
Ring in the Christ that is to be.

The Lord is my Shepherd
Psalms xxiii

To me, and I am sure to almost everyone else, the most beautiful passage in the Bible.

The Lord is my shepherd; I shall not want
He maketh me to lie down in green pastures; he leadeth me beside the still waters,
He restoreth my soul; he leadeth me in the paths of righteousness for his name's sake.
Yea, though I walk through the valley of the shadow of death, I will fear no evil; for thou art with me; thy rod and thy staff they comfort me.
Thou preparest a table before me in the presence of mine enemies; thou anointest my head with oil; my cup runneth over.
Surely goodness and mercy shall follow me all the days of my life; and I will dwell in the house of the Lord forever.

A Prayer

by Berton Braley

A Regular Wish and a Regular Prayer by a
Regular Man. I give him a Regular A+.

Lord, Let me live like a Regular Man,
    With Regular friends and true;
Let me play the game on a Regular plan
    And play it that way all through;
Let me win or lose with a Regular smile
    And never be known to whine,
For that is a Regular Fellow's style
    And I want to make it mine!

Oh, give me a Regular chance in life,
    The same as the rest, I pray,
And give me a Regular girl for wife
    To help me along the way;
Let us know the lot of humanity,
    Its regular woes and joys,
And raise a Regular family
    Of Regular girls and boys!

Let me live to a Regular good old age,
    With Regular snow-white hair,
Having done my labor and earned my wage
    And played my game for fair;
And so at last when the people scan
    My face on its peaceful bier,
They'll say, Well, he was a Regular Man!
    And drop a Regular tear!

Landing of the Pilgrim Fathers

by Felicia D. Hemans (1743-1835)

The Pilgrims, having separated from the Church of England, and seeking a place to worship as they saw fit, first fled to the Netherlands. Then, to avoid further persecution, they sailed on the Mayflower in 1620 to New England, where they landed at Plymouth Rock, on a cold December day. They lost almost half their number the first winter, but the others hung on and the rest is history. But don't forget, Jamestown was settled thirteen years previously.

> The breaking waves dashed high
>   On a stern and rock-bound coast,
> And the woods against a stormy sky
>   Their giant branches tossed;
>
> And the heavy night hung dark
>   The hills and water o'er,
> When a band of exiles moored their bark
>   On the wild New England shore.
>
> Not as the conqueror comes,
>   They, the true-hearted, came;
> Not with the roll of the stirring drums,
>   And the trumpet that sings of fame;
>
> Not as the flying come,
>   In silence and in fear;
> They shook the depths of the desert gloom
>   With their hymns of lofty cheer.
>
> Amidst the storm they sang,
>   And the stars heard, and the sea,
> And the soundless aisles of the dim woods rang
>   To the anthem of the free.
>
> The ocean eagle soared
>   From his nest by the white wave's foam;
> And the rocking pines of the forest roared,—
>   This was their welcome home.

There were men with hoary hair
   Amid that pilgrim band:—
Why had they come to wither there,
   Away from their childhood's land?

There was woman's fearless eye,
   Lit by her deep love's truth;
There was manhood's brow, serenely high,
   And the fiery heart of youth.

What sought they thus afar?
   Bright jewels of the mine,
The wealth of seas, the spoils of war?
   They sought a faith's pure shrine.

Ay, call it holy ground,
   The spot where first they trod;
They have left unstained what there they found—
   Freedom to worship God.

Abou Ben Adhem

by James Henry Leigh Hunt (1784-1859)

Religion in a simple form, but impressive, and very readable.

Abou Ben Adhem (may his tribe increase!)
Awoke one night from a deep dream of peace,
And saw, within the moonlight in his room,
Making it rich, and like a lily in bloom,
An Angel writing in a book of gold:
Exceeding peace had made Ben Adhem bold,
And to the Presence in the room he said,
"What writest thou?" The Vision raised its head,
And with a look made of all sweet accord
Answered, "The names of those who love the Lord."
"And is mine one?" said Abou. "Nay, not so,"
Replied the Angel. Abou spoke more low,
But cheerly still; and said, "I pray thee, then,
Write me as one that loves his fellow-men."
The Angel wrote, and vanished. The next night
It came again with a great wakening light,
And showed the names whom love of God had blessed,
And, lo! Ben Adhem's name led all the rest!

Battle-Hymn of the Republic
by Julia Ward Howe (1819-1910)

The story is that, during the Civil War, Julia was very stirred by the soldiers in Washington singing with vigor the popular song of the day, *John Brown's Body*. Being a strong unionist, she sat down and penned this stirring battle song to the same tune. It became the Union's answer to the South's *Dixie*. If you have never heard this powerful song done by a large choral group, you have missed a heart-stirring thrill.

Mine eyes have seen the glory of the coming of the Lord:
He is trampling out the vintage where the grapes of wrath are stored;
He hath loosed the fateful lightning of his terrible swift sword:
    His truth is marching on.

I have seen him in the watch-fires of a hundred circling camps;
They have builded him an altar in the evening dews and damps;
I can read his righteous sentence by the dim and flaring lamps:
    His day is marching on.

He has sounded forth the trumpet that shall never call retreat;
He is sifting out the hearts of men before his judgment-seat:
O, be swift, my soul, to answer him! be jubilant, my feet!
    Our God is marching on.

In the beauty of the lilies Christ was born across the sea,
With a glory in his bosom that transfigures you and me;
As he died to make men holy, let us die to make men free,
    While God is marching on.

(Despite her super strong Union feeling, Julia was impressed enough and fair enough, that after Robert E. Lee's death she wrote an ode in his honor.)

Crossing the Bar
By Alfred Tennyson (1809-1892)

A beautiful, moving poem. A pilot
knows that when his ship has
crossed the bar, he is safely home,
and the trip is over. A favorite
request to be read at one's funeral; either of the two highlighted verses, or
the whole poem.

> **Sunset and evening star,**
> **And one clear call for me,**
> **And may there be no moaning of the bar,**
> **When I put out to sea.**

> But such a tide as moving seems asleep,
> Too full for sound and foam,
> When that which drew from out the boundless deep,
> Turns again home.

> **Twilight and evening bell,**
> **And after that the dark!**
> **And may there be no sadness of farewell,**
> **When I embark;**

> For tho' from out our bourne of time and place,
> The flood may bear me far,
> I hope to see my Pilot face to face,
> When I have crossed the bar.

A Lost Chord

by Adelaide Anne Procter (1825-1864)

My favorite organ rendition. Well done, it is
very moving.

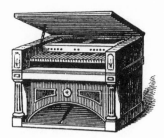

Seated one day at the Organ,
        I was weary and ill at ease,
And my fingers wandered idly
        Over the noisy keys.

I do not know what I was playing,
        Or what I was dreaming then;
But I struck one chord of music,
        Like the sound of a great Amen.

It flooded the crimson twilight,
        Like the close of an Angel's Psalm,
And it lay on my fevered spirit
        With a touch of infinite calm.

It quieted pain and sorrow,
        Like love overcoming strife;
It seemed the harmonious echo
        From our discordant life.

It linked all perplexed meanings,
        Into one perfect peace,
And trembled away into silence
        As if it were loth to cease.

I have sought, but I seek it vainly,
        That one lost chord divine,
Which came from the soul of the Organ,
        And entered into mine.

It may be that Death's bright angel
        Will speak in that chord again,—
It may be that only in Heaven
        I shall hear that grand Amen.

Each in His Own Tongue

by William Herbert Carruth

A middle road between religion and evolution,
beautifully put.

A fire-mist and a planet,
        A crystal and a cell,
A jelly-fish and a saurian,
        And caves where the cave-men dwell;
Then a sense of law and beauty
        And a face turned from the clod—
Some call it Evolution,
        And others call it God.

A haze on the far horizon,
        The infinite, tender sky,
The ripe rich tint of the cornfields,
        And the wild geese sailing high—
And all over upland and lowland
        The charm of the golden-rod—
Some of us call it Autumn
        And others call it God.

Like tides on a crescent sea-beach,
        When the moon is new and thin
Into our hearts high yearnings
        Come welling and surging in—
Come from the mystic ocean,
        Whose rim no foot has trod,—
Some of us call it Longing,
        And others call it God.

A picket frozen on duty,
        A mother starved for her brood,
Socrates drinking the hemlock,
        And Jesus on the rood;
And millions who, humble and nameless,
        The straight, hard pathway plod,—
Some call it Consecration,
        And others call it God.

Elegy Written in a Country Church-Yard

by Thomas Gray (1716-1771)

Unquestionably one of the greatest poems ever written. The title is important because Gray stresses that these are the graves of the poor people of a country village who loved their home and had no ambition to wander elsewhere. He urges us not to mock these country folk, since some might have been among the great of all time, if the chance had come their way. The highlighted sections are great to read over and over. Read it slowly! Get in the feeling. Sit in the church-yard while Gray tells you about these poor people buried here.

> The curfew tolls the knell of parting day,
>> The lowing herd winds slowly o'er the lea,
> The ploughman homeward plods his weary way,
>> And leaves the world to darkness and to me.
>
> Now fades the glimmering landscape on the sight,
>> And all the air a solemn stillness holds,
> Save where the beetle wheels his droning flight,
>> And drowsy tinklings lull the distant folds;
>
> Save that, from yonder ivy-mantled tower,
>> The moping owl does to the moon complain
> Of such as, wandering near her secret bower,
>> Molest her ancient, solitary reign.
>
> Beneath those rugged elms, that yew-tree's shade,
>> Where heaves the turf in many a mould'ring heap,
> Each in his narrow cell forever laid,
>> The rude forefathers of the hamlet sleep.
>
> The breezy call of incense-breathing morn,
>> The swallow twittering from the straw-built shed,
> The cock's shrill clarion, or the echoing horn,
>> No more shall rouse them from their lowly bed.

For them no more the blazing hearth shall burn,
    Or busy housewife ply her evening care;
No children run to lisp their sire's return,
    Or climb his knees the envied kiss to share.

Oft did the harvest to their sickle yield,
    Their furrow oft the stubborn glebe has broke;
How jocund did they drive their team afield!
    How bowed the woods beneath their sturdy stroke!

Let not ambition mock their useful toil,
    Their homely joys, and destiny obscure—
Nor grandeur hear with a disdainful smile
    The short and simple annals of the poor.

The boast of heraldry, the pomp of power,
    And all that beauty, all that wealth e'er gave,
Awaits alike the inevitable hour:
    The paths of glory lead but to the grave.

Nor you, ye proud, impute to these the fault,
    If memory o'er their tomb no trophies raise
Where through the long-drawn aisle and fretted vault
    The pealing anthem swells the note of praise.

Can storied urn or animated bust
    Back to its mansion call the fleeting breath?
Can Honor's voice provoke the silent dust
    Or Flattery soothe the dull cold ear of Death ?

Perhaps in this neglected spot is laid
    Some heart once pregnant with celestial fire;
Hands that the rod of empire might have swayed,
    Or wak'd to ecstasy the living lyre;

But Knowledge to their eyes her ample page,
    Rich with the spoils of time, did ne'er unroll;
Chill Penury repressed their noble rage,
    And froze the genial current of the soul.

Full many a gem of purest ray serene
　　The dark, unfathomed caves of ocean bear:
Full many a flower is born to blush unseen,
　　And waste its sweetness on the desert air.

Some village Hampden, that, with dauntless breast,
　　The little tyrant of his fields withstood,
Some mute, inglorious Milton, here may rest;
　　Some Cromwell guiltless of his country's blood.

The applause of list'ning senates to command,
　　The threats of pain and ruin to despise,
To scatter plenty o'er a smiling land,
　　And read their history in a nation's eyes,

Their lot forbade; nor circumscribed alone
　　Their growing virtues, but their crimes confined;
Forbade to wade thro' slaughter to a throne,
　　And shut the gates of mercy on mankind;

The struggling pangs of conscious truth to hide
　　To quench the blushes of ingenuous shame,
Or heap the shrine of Luxury and Pride
　　With incense kindled at the Muse's flame.

Far from the madding crowd's ignoble strife,
　　Their sober wishes never learned to stray;
Along the cool sequestered vale of life
　　They kept the noiseless tenor of their way.

Yet even these bones from insult to protect,
　　Some frail memorial still erected nigh,
With uncouth rhymes and shapeless sculpture decked,
　　Implores the passing tribute of a sigh.

Their names, their years, spelt by the unlettered Muse,
　　The place of fame and elegy supply—
And many a holy text around she strews
　　That teach the rustic moralist to die.

For who, to dumb forgetfulness a prey,
    This pleasing anxious being e'er resigned,
Left the warm precincts of the cheerful day,
    Nor cast one longing, lingering look behind?

On some fond breast the parting soul relies,
    Some pious drops the closing eye requires;
Ev'n from the tomb the voice of Nature cries,
    Ev'n in our ashes live their wonted fires.

For thee, who, mindful of the unhonor'd dead,
    Dost in these lines their artless tale relate;
If chance, by lonely contemplation led,
    Some kindred spirit shall inquire thy fate,—

Haply some hoary-headed swain may say:
    "Oft have we seen him, at the peep of dawn,
Brushing with hasty steps the dews away,
    To meet the sun upon the upland lawn.

"There at the foot of yonder nodding beech,
    That wreathes its old fantastic roots so high,
His listless length at noontide would he stretch,
    And pore upon the brook that babbles by.

"Hard by yon wood, now smiling as in scorn,
    Mutt'ring his wayward fancies, he would rove;—
Now drooping, woeful-wan, like one forlorn,
    Or craz'd with care, or cross'd in hopeless love.

"One morn I missed him on the custom'd hill,
    Along the heath, and near his favorite tree;
Another came,—nor yet beside the rill,
    Nor up the lawn, nor at the wood was he.

"The next, with dirges due, in sad array,
    Slowly through the church-way path we saw him borne;—
Approach and read (for thou canst read) the lay
    Grav'd on the stone beneath yon aged thorn."

THE EPITAPH

Here rests his head upon the lap of earth,
    A youth to fortune and to fame unknown;
Fair Science frown'd not on his humble birth,
    And Melancholy mark'd him for her own.

Large was his bounty, and his soul sincere;
    Heaven did a recompense as largely send:
He gave to misery all he had, a tear;
    He gained from heaven ('twas all he wished) a friend.

No farther seek his merits to disclose,
    Or draw his frailties from their dread abode,
(There they alike in trembling hope repose),
    The bosom of his Father and his God.

I Met the Master

by Unknown

Why does it take a crisis or disaster to bring about the meeting? Makes you stop and think, as we all did in those fox-holes.

I had walked life's way with an easy tread,
Had followed where comfort and pleasures led,
Until one day in a quiet place
I met the Master face to face.

With station and rank and wealth for my goal,
Much thought for my body, but none for my soul,
I had entered to win in life's mad race,
When I met the Master face to face.

I met Him, and knew Him and blushed to see
That His eyes full of sorrow, were fixed on me;
And I faltered and fell at His feet that day,
While my castles melted and vanished away.

Melted and vanished and in their place
Naught else did I see but the Master's face.
And I cried aloud, "Oh, make me meet
To follow the steps of Thy wounded feet."

My thought is now for the souls of men,
I have lost my life to find it again,
E'er since one day in a quiet place
I met the Master face to face.

I Saw Three Ships
by Unknown
A Christmas time standard.

> I saw three ships come sailing in,
>   On Christmas day, on Christmas day;
> I saw three ships come sailing in,
>   On Christmas day, in the morning.
>
> Pray, whither sailed those ships all three,
>   On Christmas day, on Christmas day?
> Pray, whither sailed those ships all three,
>   On Christmas day, in the morning?
>
> Oh, they sailed into Bethlehem,
>   On Christmas day, on Christmas day;
> Oh, they sailed into Bethlehem,
>   On Christmas day, in the morning.
>
> And all the bells on earth shall ring,
>   On Christmas day, on Christmas day;
> And all the bells on earth shall ring,
>   On Christmas day, in the morning.
>
> And all the angels in heaven shall sing,
>   On Christmas day, on Christmas day;
> And all the angels in heaven shall sing,
>   On Christmas day, in the morning.
>
> And all the souls on earth shall sing
>   On Christmas day, on Christmas day;
> And all the souls on earth shall sing,
>   On Christmas day, in the morning.

The Captain's Daughter

by James T. Fields (1816-1881)

The comfort and the power of faith—even if it is a
child's faith that sees them through.

We were crowded in the cabin,
    Not a soul would dare to sleep,—
It was midnight on the waters,
    And a storm was on the deep.

'Tis a fearful thing in winter
    To be shattered by the blast,
And to hear the rattling trumpet
    Thunder, "Cut away the mast!"

So we shuddered there in silence,—
    For the stoutest held his breath,
While the hungry sea was roaring
    And the breakers talked with Death.

As thus we sat in darkness,
    Each one busy with his prayers,
"We are lost!" the captain shouted
    As he staggered down the stairs.

But his little daughter whispered,
    As she took his icy hand,
"Isn't God, upon the ocean,
    Just the same as on the land?"

Then we kissed the little maiden,
    And we spoke in better cheer,
And we anchored safe in harbour
    When the morn was shining clear.

Pippa's Song

by Robert Browning (1812-1889)

A great "Good Morning"; off to a great start.

> The year's at the spring,
> > The day's at the morn;
> Morning's at seven;
> > The hillside's dew pearled;
>
> The lark's on the wing;
> > The snail's on the thorn;
> God's in His heaven—
> > All's right with the world.

The Ten Commandments

Delivered by God to Moses on Mount Sinai. Doesn't hurt to have them handy. Lest we forget!

1. I am the Lord thy God. Thou shalt have no other gods before me.
2. Thou shalt not make unto thee any graven image.
3. Thou shalt not take the name of the Lord thy God in vain.
4. Remember the Sabbath day, to keep it holy.
5. Honor thy father and thy mother.
6. Thou shalt not kill.
7. Thou shalt not commit adultery.
8. Thou shalt not steal.
9. Thou shalt not bear false witness against thy neighbor.
10. Thou shalt not covet.

This, Too, Shall Pass Away

by Lanta Wilson Smith

Nicely put—time soothes all. And remember, as
stated below, wealth and fame all end at the
grave, as far as we are all concerned.

When some great sorrow, like a mighty river,
    Flows through your life with peace-destroying power,
And dearest things are swept from sight forever,
    Say to your heart each trying hour:
        "This, too, shall pass away."

When ceaseless toil has hushed your song of gladness,
    And you have grown almost too tired to pray,
Let this truth banish from your heart its sadness,
    And ease the burdens of each trying day:
        "This, too, shall pass away."

When fortune smiles, and, full of mirth and pleasure,
    The days are flitting by without a care,
Lest you should rest with only earthly treasure,
    Let these few words their fullest import bear:
        "This, too, shall pass away."

When earnest labor brings you fame and glory,
    And all earth's noblest ones upon you smile,
Remember that life's longest, grandest story
    Fills but a moment in earth's little while:
        "This, too, shall pass away."

Through the Year

by Julian S. Cutler

A lovely year-round blessing. You can pick your season—mine's Spring.

God be with you in the Springtime
    When the violets unfold,
And the buttercups and cowslips
    Fill the fields with yellow gold;
In the time of apple blossoms,
    When the happy bluebirds sing,
Filling all the world with gladness—
    God be with you in the Spring!

God be with you in the Summer,
    When the sweet June roses blow,
When the bobolinks are laughing
    And the brooks with music flow;
When the fields are white with daisies
    And the days are glad and long—
God be with you in the Summer,
    Filling all your world with song.

God be with you in the Autumn,
    When the birds and flowers have fled,
And along the woodland pathways
    Leaves are falling, gold and red;
When the Summer lies behind you,
    In the evening of the year—
God be with you in the Autumn,
    Then to fill your heart with cheer.

God be with you in the Winter,
    When the snow lies deep and white,
When the sleeping fields are silent
    And the stars gleam cold and bright.
When the hand and heart are tired
    With life's long and weary quest—
God be with you in the Winter,
    Just to guide you into rest.

The Wonderer

by Robert Service (1874-1958)

The tough author, who braved the Yukon, cremated Sam McGee and watched the Shooting of Dan McGrew takes a moment to thank HIM and stand in "The Wonder and the awe of God," and the wondrous things He created, starting off with the hand, eyes, heart and brain.

I wish that I could understand
    The moving marvel of my Hand;
I watch my fingers turn and twist,
    The supple bending of my wrist,
The dainty touch of finger-tip,
    The steel intensity of grip;
A tool of exquisite design,
    With pride I think: "It's mine! It's mine!"

Then there's the wonder of my Eyes,
    Where hills and houses, seas and skies,
In waves of light converge and pass,
    And print themselves as on a glass.
Line, form and color live in me;
    I am the Beauty that I see;
Ah! I could write a book of size
    About the wonder of my Eyes.

What of the wonder of my Heart,
    That plays so faithfully its part?
I hear it running sound and sweet;
    It does not seem to miss a beat;
Between the cradle and the grave
    It never falters, stanch and brave.
Alas! I wish I had the art
    To tell the wonder of my Heart.

Then oh! but how can I explain
    The wondrous wonder of my Brain?
That marvellous machine that brings
    All consciousness of wanderings;
That lets me from myself leap out
    And watch my body walk about;
It's hopeless—all my words are vain
    To tell the wonder of my Brain.

But do not think, O patient friend,
>Who reads these stanzas to the end,
That I, myself, would glorify. . .
>You're just as wonderful as I,
And all Creation in our view
>Is quite as marvellous as you.

Come, let us on the sea-shore stand
>And wonder at a grain of sand;
And then into the meadow pass
>And marvel at a blade of grass;
Or cast our vision high and far
>And thrill with wonder at a star;
A host of stars-night's holy tent
>Huge-glittering with wonderment.

If wonder is in great and small,
>Then what of Him who made it all?
In eyes and brain and heart and limb
>Let's see the wondrous work of Him.
In house and hill and sward and sea,
>In bird and beast and flower and tree,
In everything from sun to sod,
>The wonder and the awe of God.

Ode On His Blindness
by John Milton (1608-1674)

How faith helped Milton accept the oncoming specter
of going blind. What a lift these simple lines have been
to thousands of blind people for over three centuries.

> When I consider how my light is spent
> Ere half my days, in this dark world and wide,
> And that one talent, which is death to hide,
> Lodged with me useless, though my soul more bent
> To serve therewith my Maker, and present
> My true account, lest He, returning, chide:
> "Doth God exact day labor, light denied?"
> I fondly ask; but Patience, to prevent
> That murmur, soon replies, "God doth not need
> Either man's work, or His own gifts; who best
> Bear His mild yoke, they serve Him best. His state
> Is kingly. Thousands at His bidding speed,
> And post o'er land and ocean without rest;
> **They also serve who only stand and wait."**

(Why do blind people always seem so pleasant and cheerful?)

Thanatopsis
by William Cullen Bryant (1794-1878)

(Thanatopsis means a view or contemplation of death.) Not a simple "dust
thou art and to dust returneth" theme, but rather a beautiful plea to
appreciate the wonders of nature and live a full life without fear of death.
If you are in a hurry, read the highlighted stanzas twice and skip the rest.
Those special lines are very special. This has to be one of the greatest
poems, but principally because of the great start and finish.

> **To him who in the love of Nature holds**
> **Communion with her visible forms, she speaks**
> **A various language; for his gayer hours**
> **She has a voice of gladness, and a smile**
> **And eloquence of beauty, and she glides**
> **Into his darker musings, with a mild**
> **And healing sympathy, that steals away**
> **Their sharpness, ere he is aware.** When thoughts
> Of the last bitter hour come like a blight
> Over thy spirit, and sad images

Of the stern agony, and shroud, and pall,
And breathless darkness, and the narrow house,
Make thee to shudder and grow sick at heart,—
Go forth, under the open sky, and list
To Nature's teachings, while from all around—
Earth and her waters, and the depths of air—
Comes a still voice:—

Yet a few days, and thee
The all-beholding sun shall see no more
In all his course; nor yet in the cold ground,
Where thy pale form was laid, with many tears,
Nor in the embrace of ocean, shall exist
Thy image. Earth, that nourished thee, shall claim
Thy growth, to be resolved to earth again,
And, lost each human trace, surrendering up
Thine individual being, shalt thou go
To mix forever with the elements,
To be a brother to the insensible rock
And to the sluggish clod, which the rude swain
Turns with his share, and treads upon. The oak
Shall send his roots abroad, and pierce thy mold.

Yet not to thine eternal resting-place
Shalt thou retire alone, nor couldst thou wish
Couch more magnificent. Thou shalt lie down
With patriarchs of the infant world—with kings,
The powerful of the earth—the wise, the good,
Fair forms, and hoary seers of ages past,
All in one mighty sepulcher. The hills
Rock-ribbed and ancient as the sun,—the vales
Stretching in pensive quietness between;
The venerable woods—rivers that move
In majesty, and the complaining brooks
That make the meadows green; and, poured round all,
Old Ocean's gray and melancholy waste,—
Are but the solemn decorations all
Of the great tomb of man. The golden sun,
The planets, all the infinite host of heaven,
Are shining on the sad abodes of death

Through the still lapse of ages. All that tread
The globe are but a handful to the tribes
That slumber in its bosom.—Take the wings
Of morning, pierce the Barcan wilderness,
Or lose thyself in the continuous woods
Where rolls the Oregon, and hears no sound,
Save his own dashings—yet the dead are there:
And millions in those solitudes, since first
The flight of years began, have laid them down
In their last sleep—the dead reign there alone.
So shalt thou rest, and what if thou withdraw
In silence from the living, and no friend
Take note of thy departure? All that breathe
Will share thy destiny. The gay will laugh
When thou are gone, the solemn brood of care
Plod on, and each one as before will chase
His favorite phantom; yet all these shall leave
Their mirth and their employments, and shall come
And make their bed with thee. As the long train
Of ages glides away, the sons of men—
The youth in life's fresh spring, and he who goes
In the full strength of years, matron and maid,
The speechless babe, and the gray-headed man—
Shall one by one be gathered to thy side,
By those, who in their turn shall follow them.

So live, that when thy summons comes to join
The innumerable caravan, which moves
To that mysterious realm, where each shall take
His chamber in the silent halls of death,
Thou go not, like the quarry-slave at night,
Scourged to his dungeon, but, sustained and soothed
By an unfaltering trust, approach thy grave
Like one who wraps the drapery of his couch
About him, and lies down to pleasant dreams.

Rocked in the Cradle of the Deep

by Emma Hart Willard (1787-1870)

A good song. A pleasant poem.

Rocked in the cradle of the deep
I lay me down in peace to sleep;
Secure I rest upon the wave,
For Thou, O Lord! hast power to save.
I know Thou wilt not slight my call,
For Thou dost mark the sparrow's fall;
And calm and peaceful shall I sleep,
Rocked in the cradle of the deep.

When in the dead of night I lie
And gaze upon the trackless sky,
The star-bespangled heavenly scroll,
The boundless waters as they roll,—
I feel Thy wonderous power to save
From perils of the stormy wave:
Rocked in the cradle of the deep,
I calmly rest and soundly sleep.

And such the trust that still were mine,
Though stormy winds swept o'er the brine,
Or though the tempest's fiery breath
Roused me from sleep to wreck and death.
In ocean cave, still safe with Thee
The germ of immortality!
And calm and peaceful shall I sleep,
Rocked in the cradle of the deep.

Requiem
by Robert Louis Stevenson (1850-1894)

Brief and beautiful farewell. Another very common gravestone carving.

Under the wide and starry sky
Dig the grave and let me lie.
Glad did I live and gladly die,
    And I laid me down with a will.

This be the verse you grave for me:
Here he lies where he longed to be;
Home is the sailor, home from sea,
    And the hunter home from the hill.

Onward, Christian Soldiers
by Sabine Baring-Gould

Possibly the most commonly sung church song. Certainly a Salvation Army favorite.

Onward, Christian soldiers!
    Marching as to war,
With the Cross of Jesus
    Going on before.
Christ the Royal Master
    Leads against the foe;
Forward into battle,
    See, His banners go!
    Onward, Christian soldiers!
        Marching as to war,
    With the Cross of Jesus
        Going on before.

At the sign of triumph
    Satan's host doth flee;
On, then, Christian soldiers,
    On to victory!
Hell's foundations quiver
    At the shout of praise;
Brothers, lift your voices,
    Loud your anthems raise!

Like a mighty army
  Moves the Church of God;
Brothers, we are treading
  Where the Saints have trod;
We are not divided
  All one body we,
One in hope and doctrine,
  One in charity.

Crowns and thrones may perish,
  Kingdoms rise and wane,
But the Church of Jesus
  Constant will remain;
Gates of hell can never
  'Gainst that Church prevail;
We have Christ's own promise,
  And that cannot fail.

Onward, then, ye people!
  Join our happy throng,
Blend with ours your voices
  In the triumph song;
Glory, laud, and honor
  Unto Christ the King,
This through countless ages
  Men and angels sing.
    Onward, Christian soldiers!
      Marching as to war,
    With the Cross of Jesus
      Going on before.

Nearer to Thee

by Sarah Flower Adams (1805-1845)

The story persists, with definite questions, that the band on the Titanic played this popular hymn as the ship was going down.

Nearer, my God, to Thee,
 Nearer to Thee!
E'en though it be a cross
 That raiseth me;
Still all my song shall be,
Nearer, my God, to Thee,
 Nearer to Thee!

Though like the wanderer,
 The sun gone down,
Darkness be over me,
 My rest a stone;
Yet in my dreams I'd be
Nearer, my God, to Thee,
 Nearer to Thee!

Light Shining out of Darkness

by William Cowper (1731-1800)

A touch of religion—made plain.

God moves in a mysterious way,
    His wonders to perform;
He plants His footsteps in the sea,
    And rides upon the storm.

Deep in unfathomable mines
    Of never-failing skill
He treasures up His bright designs,
    And works His sovereign will.

Ye fearful saints, fresh courage take;
    The clouds ye so much dread
Are big with mercy, and shall break
    In blessings on your head.

Judge not the Lord by feeble sense,
    But trust Him for His grace;
Behind a frowning Providence
    He hides a smiling face.

His purposes will ripen fast,
    Unfolding every hour;
The bud may have a bitter taste,
    But sweet will be the flower.

Blind unbelief is sure to err,
    And scan His work in vain;
God is His own interpreter,
    And He will make it plain.

INSPIRATION

A Psalm of Life

by Henry Wadsworth Longfellow (1807-1892)

An exceptional plea by Longfellow, that even though no one can live
forever, we can leave a worthwhile mark—Our footsteps on the sands of
time. I've highlighted four of the stanzas, but actually they are all
outstanding. A WINNER in all respects.

Tell me not, in mournful numbers,
    Life is but an empty dream!—
For the soul is dead that slumbers,
    And things are not what they seem.

Life is real! Life is earnest!
    And the grave is not its goal;
Dust thou art, to dust returnest,
    Was not spoken of the soul.

Not enjoyment, and not sorrow,
    Is our destined end or way;
But to act, that each tomorrow
    Find us farther than today.

Art is long, and Time is fleeting,
    And our hearts, though stout and brave,
Still, like muffled drums, are beating
    Funeral marches to the grave.

In the world's broad field of battle,
    In the bivouac of life,
Be not like dumb, driven cattle!
    Be a hero in the strife!

Trust no Future, howe'er pleasant!
    Let the dead Past bury its dead!
Act,—act in the living Present!
    Heart within, and God o'erhead!

Lives of great men all remind us
    We can make our lives sublime,
And, departing, leave behind us
    Footprints on the sands of time.

Footprints, that perhaps another,
    Sailing o'er life's solemn main,
A forlorn and shipwrecked brother,
    Seeing, shall take heart again.

Let us then be up and doing,
    With a heart for any fate;
Still achieving, still pursuing,
    Learn to labor and to wait.

Columbus

by Joaquin Miller (1841-1913) (the great lecturer
    and conservationist)

A moving story and inspiration for anyone faltering
or hesitating along life's way. We wonder how much
longer it would have taken to open the new world,
had Columbus said "Turn Back!"

Behind him lay the gray Azores,
Behind the Gates of Hercules*,
Before him not the ghost of shores,
Before him only shoreless seas.
The good mate said: "Now must we pray,
For lo! the very stars are gone.
Brave Adm'r'l, speak; what shall I say?"
"Why, say: 'Sail on! sail on! and on!'"

"My men grow mutinous day by day;
My men grow ghastly wan and weak."
The stout mate thought of home; a spray
Of salt wave washed his swarthy cheek.
"What shall I say, brave Adm'r'l, say,
If we sight naught but seas at dawn?"
"Why, you shall say, at break of day:
'Sail on! sail on! sail on! and on!'"

They sailed and sailed, as winds might blow,
Until at last the blanched mate said:
"Why, now not even God would know
Should I and all my men fall dead.
These very winds forget their way,
For God from these dread seas is gone.
Now speak, brave Adm'r'l; speak and say"—
He said: "Sail on! sail on! and on!"

They sailed. They sailed. Then spake the mate:
"This mad sea shows his teeth to-night;
He curls his lips, he lies in wait,
With lifted teeth, as if to bite:
Brave Adm'r'l, say but one good word;
What shall we do when hope is gone?"
The words leapt like a leaping sword:
"Sail on! sail on! sail on! and on!"

Then, pale and worn, he kept his deck,
And peered through darkness. Ah, that night
Of all dark nights! And then a speck—
A light! a light! a light! a light!
It grew, a starlit flag unfurled!
It grew to be Time's burst of dawn.
He gained a world; he gave that world
Its grandest lesson: "On! sail on!"

Gates of Hercules: the Straits of Gibraltar.

Happiness

by Priscilla Leonard

Priscilla says that happiness is accepting what
you have, and making the best of what you
have.

Happiness is like a crystal,
Fair and exquisite and clear,
Broken in a million pieces,
Shattered, scattered far and near.
Now and then along life's pathway,
Lo! some shining fragments fall;
But there are so many pieces
No one ever finds them all.

You may find a bit of beauty,
Or an honest share of wealth,
While another just beside you
Gathers honor, love, or health.
Vain to choose or grasp unduly,
Broken is the perfect ball;
And there are so many pieces
No one ever finds them all,

Yet the wise as on they journey
Treasure every fragment clear,
Fit them as they may together,
Imaging the shattered sphere,
Learning ever to be thankful,
Though their share of it is small;
For it has so many pieces
No one ever finds them all.

God Give us Men
by J.G. Holland (1819-1881)

A strong plea for a way to select men who will meet all the requirements of being a dedicated, honest, smart leader at all levels. Maybe it's no small wonder that so few step forward to fill such big shoes. Thought provoking.

> God give us men. The time demands
> Strong minds, great hearts, true faith and willing hands;
>   Men whom the lust of office does not kill;
> Men whom the spoils of office cannot buy;
>   Men who possess opinions and a will;
> Men who have honor; men who will not lie;
>   Men who can stand before a demagogue
> And damn his treacherous flatteries without winking;
>   Tall men, sun-crowned, who live above the fog
> In public duty and in private thinking!
> For while the rabble with their thumb-worn creeds,
> Their large professions and their little deeds
> Mingle in selfish strife; lo! Freedom weeps!
> Wrong rules the land, and waiting Justice sleeps!

(Untouchables!! Where are you?)

If I Can Stop One Heart from Breaking
by Emily Dickinson (1830-1886)

Simple acts—great rewards.

> If I can stop one heart from breaking,
> I shall not live in vain;
> If I can ease one life the aching,
> Or cool one pain,
> Or help one fainting robin
> Unto his nest again,
> I shall not live in vain.

It's Fine Today

by Douglas Malloch

Remember what a difference a day can make. Also, remember, on a clear day you can see forever.

Sure, this world is full of trouble—
    I ain't said it ain't.
Lord, I've had enough and double
    Reason for complaint;
Rain and storm have come to fret me,
    Skies are often gray;
Thorns and brambles have beset me
    On the road—but say,
        Ain't it fine today?

What's the use of always weepin',
    Making trouble last?
What's the use of always keepin'
    Thinkin' of the past?
Each must have his tribulation—
    Water with his wine;
Life, it ain't no celebration,
    Trouble?—I've had mine—
        But today is fine!

It's today that I am livin',
    Not a month ago.
Havin'; losin'; takin'; givin';
    As time wills it so.
Yesterday a cloud of sorrow
    Fell across the way;
It may rain again tomorrow,
    It may rain—but say,
        Ain't it fine today?

It Couldn't Be Done

by Edgar A. Guest

You've got to love and be inspired by this. By
the way, it has helped me in doing this book. I
like the swing and rhythm of Guest's poems.

Somebody said that it couldn't be done,
   But he with a chuckle replied
That "maybe it couldn't," but he would be one
   Who wouldn't say so till he'd tried.
So he buckled right in with the trace of a grin
   On his face. If he worried he hid it.
He started to sing as he tackled the thing
   That couldn't be done, and he did it.

Somebody scoffed: "Oh, you'll never do that;
   At least no one ever has done it;"
But he took off his coat and he took off his hat,
   And the first thing we knew he'd begun it.
With a lift of his chin and a bit of a grin,
   Without any doubting or quiddit,
He started to sing as he tackled the thing
   That couldn't be done, and he did it.

There are thousands to tell you it cannot be done,
   There are thousands to prophesy failure;
There are thousands to point out to you, one by one,
   The dangers that wait to assail you.
But just buckle in with a bit of a grin,
   Just take off your coat and go to it;
Just start to sing as you tackle the thing
   That "cannot be done," and you'll do it.

Thank you, Edgar.

Invictus
by William Ernest Henley (1849-1903)

Powerful! Great to not fear the present, the future, nor eternity. (Invictus is
Latin for Unconquered.)

Out of the night that covers me,
    Black as the Pit from pole to pole,
I thank whatever gods may be
    For my unconquerable soul.

In the fell clutch of circumstance
    I have not winced nor cried aloud.
Under the bludgeonings of chance
    My head is bloody, but unbowed.

Beyond this place of wrath and tears
    Looms but the horror of the shade,
And yet the menace of the years
    Finds, and shall find me, unafraid.

It matters not how strait the gate,
    How charged with punishments the scroll,
I am the master of my fate;
    I am the captain of my soul.

Keep a-Goin'
by Frank L. Stanton

If you've been down on your luck lately, try
this for size.

If you strike a thorn or rose,
    Keep a-goin'!
If it hails or if it snows,
    Keep a-goin'!
'Taint no use to sit an' whine
When the fish ain't on your line;
Bait your hook an' keep a-tryin'
    Keep a-goin'!

When the weather kills your crop,
        Keep a-goin'!
Though 'tis work to reach the top,
        Keep a-goin'!
S'pose you're out o' ev'ry dime,
Gittin' broke ain't any crime;
Tell the world you're feelin' prime—
        Keep a-goin'!

When it looks like all is up,
        Keep a-goin'!
Drain the sweetness from the cup,
        Keep a-goin'!
See the wild birds on the wing,
Hear the bells that sweetly ring,
When you feel like sighin', sing—
        Keep a-goin'!

Nobility

by Alice Cary

The author shows that the true meaning of nobility is not just appearing
regal but rather being kind, truthful, loving and honorable. And she
finishes by urging us to the old "Do unto others as you would have them
do unto you."

True worth is in being, not seeming,—
        In doing, each day that goes by,
Some little good-not in dreaming
        Of great things to do by and by.
For whatever men say in their blindness,
        And spite of the fancies of youth,
There's nothing so kingly as kindness,
        And nothing so royal as truth.

We get back our mete as we measure—
        We cannot do wrong and feel right,
Nor can we give pain and gain pleasure,
        For justice avenges each slight.

The air for the wing of the sparrow,
    The bush for the robin and wren,
But always the path that is narrow
    And straight, for the children of men.

'Tis not in the pages of story
    The heart of its ills to beguile,
Though he who makes courtship to glory
    Gives all that he hath for her smile.
For when from her heights he has won her,
    Alas! it is only to prove
That nothing's so sacred as honor,
    And nothing so loyal as love!

We cannot make bargains for blisses,
    Nor catch them like fishes in nets;
And sometimes the thing our life misses
    Helps more than the thing which it gets.
For good lieth not in pursuing,
    Nor gaining of great nor of small,
But just in the doing, and doing
    As we would be done by, is all.

Song

by Florence Smith

Unfortunately, I have to say, in my case, these people are getting fewer and fewer, and I love them, every one.

How pleasant it is that always
There's somebody older than you—
Someone to pet and caress you,
Someone to scold you, too!

Someone to call you a baby,
To laugh at you when you're wise;
Someone to care when you're sorry,
To kiss the tears from your eyes;

When life has begun to be weary,
And youth to melt like the dew,
To know, like the little children
Somebody's older than you.

The path cannot be so lonely,
For someone has trod it before;
The golden gates are the nearer,
That someone stands at the door.

I can think of nothing sadder
Than to feel, when days are few,
There's nobody left to lean on,
Nobody older than you!

The younger ones may be tender
To the feeble steps and slow;
But they can't talk the old times over—
Alas, how should they know!

'Tis a romance to them—a wonder
You were ever a child at play;
But the dear ones waiting in heaven
Know it is all as you say.

I know that the great All-Father
Loves us, and the little ones too;
Keep only childlike-hearted—
Heaven is older than you!

The Bridge Builder

by Will Allen Dromgoole

This will make you pause a minute and think and
remember the bridges that were built for you,
and who built them. Are you building your share?
Remember there are countless types of bridges to
be built. Anything that really helps forward
progress is a bridge to the future.

An old man, going a lone highway,
    Came at the evening, cold and gray,
To a chasm, vast and deep and wide,
    Through which was flowing a sullen tide.
The old man crossed in the twilight dim—
    That sullen stream had no fears for him;
But he turned, when he reached the other side,
    And built a bridge to span the tide.

"Old man," said a fellow pilgrim near,
    "You are wasting strength in building here.
Your journey will end with the ending day;
    You never again must pass this way.
You have crossed the chasm, deep and wide,
    Why build the bridge at the eventide?"

The builder lifted his old gray head.
    "Good friend, in the path I have come," he said,
"There followeth after me today
    A youth whose feet must pass this way.
This chasm that has been naught to me
    To that fair-haired youth may a pitfall be.
He, too, must cross in the twilight dim;
    Good friend, I am building the bridge for him."

The Day Is Done

by Henry Wadsworth Longfellow (1807-1892)

The theme of this book: the peace and
relaxation and contentment from poetry and
music. Not the complicated, contrived old
masters, but the free-flowing musical rhymes. I,
too, love poetry and music and therefore I like
to read this over and over, and enjoy it more
each time. I truly hope this feeling persists through this book. And I hope
the feeling is contagious.

> The day is done, and the darkness
> > Falls from the wings of Night,
> As a feather is wafted downward
> > From an eagle in his flight.
>
> I see the lights of the village
> > Gleam through the rain and the mist,
> And a feeling of sadness comes o'er me
> > That my soul cannot resist:
>
> A feeling of sadness and longing,
> > That is not akin to pain,
> And resembles sorrow only
> > As the mist resembles the rain.
>
> **Come, read to me some poem,**
> > **Some simple and heartfelt lay,**
> **That shall soothe this restless feeling,**
> > **And banish the thoughts of day.**
>
> **Not from the grand old masters,**
> > **Not from the bards sublime,**
> **Whose distant footsteps echo**
> > **Through the corridors of Time.**
>
> **For, like strains of martial music,**
> > **Their mighty thoughts suggest**
> **Life's endless toil and endeavor;**
> > **And tonight I long for rest.**

Read from some humbler poet,
　　Whose songs gushed from his heart,
As showers from the clouds of summer,
　　Or tears from the eyelids start;

Who, through long days of labor,
　　And nights devoid of ease,
Still heard in his soul the music
　　Of wonderful melodies.

Such songs have power to quiet
　　The restless pulse of care,
And come like the benediction
　　That follows after prayer.

Then read from the treasured volume
　　The poem of thy choice,
And lend to the rhyme of the poet
　　The beauty of thy voice.

And the night shall be filled with music
　　And the cares, that infest the day,
Shall fold their tents, like the Arabs,
　　And as silently steal away.

The Town of Don't-You-Worry

by I. J. Bartlett

Utopia on the river Smile. What? No smog,
traffic congestion, poverty, drugs nor
homelessness.

There's a town called Don't-You-Worry,
    On the banks of River Smile;
Where the Cheer-Up and Be-Happy
    Blossom sweetly all the while.
Where the Never-Grumble flower
    Blooms beside the fragrant Try,
And the Ne'er-Give-Up and Patience
    Point their faces to the sky.

In the valley of Contentment,
    In the province of I-Will,
You will find this lovely city,
    At the foot of No-Fret Hill.
There are thoroughfares delightful
    In this very charming town,
And on every hand are shade trees
    Named the Very-Seldom-Frown.

Rustic benches quite enticing
    You'll find scattered here and there;
And to each a vine is clinging
    Called the Frequent-Earnest-Prayer.
Everybody there is happy
    And is singing all the while,
In the town of Don't-You-Worry,
    On the banks of River Smile.

The Village Blacksmith

by Henry Wadsworth Longfellow (1807-1892)

If you hated this because you had to recite it, now love it for how great it is. Life, as it was hammered out on the blacksmith forge. Remember, the blacksmith of yesterday was as necessary to daily life as the auto repair man is today.

Under a spreading chestnut-tree
        The village smithy stands;
The smith, a mighty man is he.
        With large and sinewy hands,
And the muscles of his brawny arms
        Are strong as iron bands.

His hair is crisp, and black, and long;
        His face is like the tan;
His brow is wet with honest sweat,
        He earns whate'er he can,
And looks the whole world in the face,
        For he owes not any man.

Week in, week out, from morn till night,
        You can hear his bellows blow;
You can hear him swing his heavy sledge,
        With measured beat and slow,
Like a sexton ringing the village bell,
        When the evening sun is low.

And, children coming home from school
        Look in at the open door;
They love to see the flaming forge,
        And hear the bellows roar,
And catch the burning sparks that fly
        Like chaff from a threshing-floor.

He goes on Sunday to the church,
    And sits among his boys;
He hears the parson pray and preach,
    He hears his daughter's voice
Singing in the village choir,
    And it makes his heart rejoice.

It sounds to him like her mother's voice
    Singing in Paradise!
He needs must think of her once more,
    How in the grave she lies;
And with his hard, rough hand he wipes
    A tear out of his eyes.

Toiling,—rejoicing,—sorrowing,
    Onward through life he goes;
Each morning sees some task begin,
    Each evening sees it close;
Something attempted, something done,
    Has earned a night's repose.

Thanks, thanks to thee, my worthy friend,
    For the lesson thou hast taught!
Thus at the flaming forge of life
    Our fortunes must be wrought;
Thus on its sounding anvil shaped
    Each burning deed and thought.

Today

by Angela Morgan

Stop and think what our age has produced. In this
century alone, we have seen transportation advanced
from horse to train to auto to planes to spaceships.
What next, Jules Verne?

To be alive in such an age!
With every year a lightning page
Turned in the world's great wonder book
Whereon the leaning nations look.
When men speak strong for brotherhood,
For peace and universal good,
When miracles are everywhere,
And every inch of common air
Throbs a tremendous prophecy
Of greater marvels yet to be.
        O thrilling age,
        O willing age!
When steel and stone and rail and rod
Become the avenue of God—
A trump to shout His thunder through
To crown the work that man may do.

To be alive in such an age!
When man, impatient of his cage,
Thrills to the soul's immortal rage
For conquest—reaches goal on goal,
Travels the earth from pole to pole,
Garners the tempest and the tides
And on a Dream Triumphant rides.
When, hid within the lump of clay,
A light more terrible than day
Proclaims the presence of that Force
Which hurls the planets on their course.
        O age with wings
        O age that flings
A challenge to the very sky,
Where endless realms of conquest lie!
When, earth on tiptoe, strives to hear
The message of a sister sphere,

Yearning to reach the cosmic wires
That flash Infinity's desires.

To be alive in such an age!
That blunders forth its discontent
With futile creed and sacrament,
Yet craves to utter God's intent,
Seeing beneath the world's unrest
Creation's huge, untiring quest,
And through Tradition's broken crust
The flame of Truth's triumphant thrust;
Below the seething thought of man
The push of a stupendous Plan.
  O age of strife!
  O age of life!
When Progress rides her chariots high,
And on the borders of the sky
The signals of the century
Proclaims the things that are to be—
The rise of woman to her place,
The coming of a nobler race.

To be alive in such an age—
  To live in it,
  To give to it!
Rise, soul, from thy despairing knees.
What if thy lips have drunk the lees?
Fling forth thy sorrows to the wind
And link thy hope with humankind—
The passion of a larger claim
Will put thy puny grief to shame.
Breathe the world thought, do the world deed,
Think hugely of thy brother's need.
And what thy woe, and what thy weal?
Look to the work the times reveal!
Give thanks with all thy flaming heart—
Crave but to have in it a part.
Give thanks and clasp thy heritage—
To be alive in such an age!

Yes, Angela, it is truly great to be alive in such an age.

Where Are You Going, Greatheart?

by John Oxenham

Another great tribute to Teddy Roosevelt. Citing the very progressive and varied talents of that great outdoorsman and Rough Rider, our 26th President from 1901-1909.

Where are you going, Greatheart?
With your eager face and your fiery grace?
Where are you going, Greatheart?

"To fight a fight with all my might,
For Truth and Justice, God and Right,
To grace all Life with His fair Light."
Then God go with you, Greatheart!

Where are you going, Greatheart?
"To beard the Devil in his den,
To smite him with the strength of ten;
To set at large the souls of men."
Then God go with you, Greatheart!

* * * * *

Where are you going, Greatheart?
"To cleanse the earth of noisome things;
To draw from life its poison stings;
To give free play to Freedom's wings."
Then God go with you, Greatheart!

Where are you going, Greatheart?
"To lift Today above the Past;
To make Tomorrow sure and fast;
To nail God's colors to the mast."
Then God go with you, Greatheart!

Where are you going, Greatheart?
"To break down old dividing lines;
To carry out my Lord's designs;
To build again His broken shrines."
Then God go with you, Greatheart!

Where are you going, Greatheart?
"To set all burdened peoples free;
To win for all God's liberty;
To establish His sweet sovereignty."
God goeth with you, Greatheart!

Where There's a Will There's a Way

by Eliza Cook

This sounds convincing. I've heard it since child-
hood so it must be true. Anyhow, it surely makes
it sound simple and easy. Definitely worth a try.

We have faith in old proverbs full surely,
    For Wisdom has traced what they tell,
And Truth may be drawn up as purely
    From them, as it may from "a well."
Let us question the thinkers and doers,
    And hear what they honestly say;
And you'll find they believe, like bold wooers,
    In "Where there's a will there's a way."

The hills have been high for man's mounting,
    The woods have been dense for his axe,
The stars have been thick for his counting,
    The sands have been wide for his tracks.
The sea has been deep for his diving,
    The poles have been broad for his sway,
But bravely he's proved in his striving,
    That "Where there's a will there's a way."

Have ye vices that ask a destroyer?
    Or passions that need your control?
Let Reason become your employer,
    And your body be ruled by your soul.
Fight on, though ye bleed in the trial,
    Resist with all strength that ye may;
Ye may conquer Sin's host by denial;
    For "Where there's a will there's a way."

Have ye Poverty's pinching to cope with?
　　　Does Suffering weigh down your might?
Only call up a spirit to hope with,
　　　And dawn may come out of the night.
Oh! much may be done by defying
　　　The ghosts of Despair and Dismay;
And much may be gained by relying
　　　On "Where there's a will there's a way."

Should ye see afar off that worth winning,
　　　Set out on the journey with trust;
And ne'er heed if your path at beginning
　　　Should be among brambles and dust.
Though it is but by footsteps ye do it.
　　　And hardships may hinder and stay,
Walk with faith, and be sure you'll get through it;
　　　For "Where there's a will there's a way."

Worth While

by Ella Wheeler Wilcox (1855-1919)

The first stanza really presents a worthwhile aim for all of us. Virtue a la mode is virtue with a smile.

It is easy enough to be pleasant,
　　　When life flows by like a song,
But the man worth while is one who will smile,
　　　When everything goes dead wrong.
For the test of the heart is trouble,
　　　And it always comes with the years,
And the smile that is worth the praises of earth
　　　Is the smile that shines through tears.

It is easy enough to be prudent,
　　　When nothing tempts you to stray,
When without or within no voice of sin
　　　Is luring your soul away;
But it's only a negative virtue
　　　Until it is tried by fire,
And the life that is worth the honor on earth
　　　Is the one that resists desire.

By the cynic, the safe, the fallen,
　　Who had no strength for the strife,
The world's highway is cumbered to-day;
　　They make up the sum of life.
But the virtue that conquers passion,
　　And the sorrow that hides in a smile,
It is these that are worth the homage on earth
　　For we find them but once in a while.

You Mustn't Quit

by Unknown

The last line is a great summary.

When things go wrong, as they sometimes will,
When the road you're trudging seems all uphill,
When the funds are low and the debts are high
And you want to smile, but you have to sigh,
Rest! if you must—but never quit.

Life is queer, with its twists and turns,
As every one of us sometimes learns,
And many a failure turns about
When he might have won if he'd stuck it out;
Stick to your task, though the pace seems slow—
You may succeed with one more blow.

Success is failure turned inside out—
The silver tint of the clouds of doubt—
And you never can tell how close you are,
It may be near when it seems afar;
So stick to the fight when you're hardest hit—
It's when things seem worst that YOU MUSTN'T QUIT.

The Ordinary Man

by Robert Service (1874-1958)

A real man, a true man, a common man, yes,
just an ordinary man. After all, down deep,
isn't that most of us?

If you and I should chance to meet,
I guess you wouldn't care;
I'm sure you'd pass me in the street
As if I wasn't there;
You'd never look me in the face,
My modest mug to scan,
Because I'm just a commonplace
      And Ordinary Man.

But then, it may be, you are too
A guy of every day,
Who does the job he's told to do
And takes the wife his pay;
Who makes a home and kids his care,
And works with pick or pen....
Why, Pal, I guess we're just a pair
      Of Ordinary Men.

We plug away and make no fuss,
Our feats are never crowned;
And yet it's common coves like us
Who make the world go round.
And as we steer a steady course
By God's predestined plan,
Hats off to that almighty Force:
      THE ORDINARY MAN.

What I Live For

by George Linneaus Banks

High hopes—but then, who knows?

    I live for those who love me,
        Whose hearts are kind and true;
    For the Heaven that smiles above me,
        And awaits my spirit too;
    For all human ties that bind me,
    For the task by God assigned me,
    For the bright hopes yet to find me,
        And the good that I can do.

    I live to learn their story
        Who suffered for my sake;
    To emulate their glory,
        And follow in their wake;
    Bards, patriots, martyrs, sages,
    The heroic of all ages,
    Whose deeds crowd History's pages,
        And Time's great volume make.

    I live to hold communion
        With all that is divine,
    To feel there is a union
        'Twixt Nature's heart and mine;
    To profit by affliction,
    Reap truth from fields of diction,
    Grow wiser from conviction,
        And fulfill God's grand design.

    I live to hail that season
        By gifted ones foretold,
    When men shall live by reason,
        And not alone by gold;
    When man to man united,
    And every wrong thing righted,
    The whole world shall be lighted
        As Eden was of old.

I live for those who love me,
>   For those who know me true,
For the Heaven that smiles above me,
>   And awaits my spirit too;
For the cause that lacks assistance,
For the wrong that needs resistance,
For the future in the distance,
>   And the good that I can do.

The Manly Man

by Unknown

Always looked up to, the manly man.

The world has room for the manly man, with
>   the spirit of manly cheer;
The world delights in the man who smiles
>   when his eyes keep back the tear;
It loves the man who, when things are wrong,
>   can take his place and stand
With his face to the fight and his eyes to the light, and toil with a
>   willing hand.

The manly man is the country's need, the moment's need, forsooth,
With a heart that beats to the pulsing troop of the lilied leagues of
>   truth;
The world is his and it waits for him, and it leaps to hear the ring
Of the blow he strikes and the wheels he turns and hammers he
>   dares to swing;
It likes the forward look on his face, the poise of his noble head,
And the onward lunge of his tireless will and the sweep of his
>   dauntless tread!

Hurrah for the manly man who comes with sunlight on his face,
And the strength to do and the will to dare and the courage to find
>   his place!
The world delights in the manly man, and the weak and evil flee
When the manly man goes forth to hold his own on land or sea!

The Common Road

by Silas H. Perkins

Not a bad agenda for anyone on life's highway.

I want to travel the common road
With the great crowd surging by,
Where there's many a laugh and many a load,
And many a smile and sigh.
I want to be on the common way
With its endless tramping feet,
In the summer bright and winter gray,
In the noonday sun and heat.
In the cool of evening with shadows nigh,
At dawn, when the sun breaks clear,
I want the great crowd passing by,
To ken what they see and hear.
I want to be one of the common herd,
Not live in a sheltered way,
Want to be thrilled, want to be stirred
By the great crowd day by day;
To glimpse the restful valleys deep,
To toil up the rugged hill,
To see the brooks which shyly creep,
To have the torrents thrill.
I want to laugh with the common man
Wherever he chance to be,
I want to aid him when I can
Whenever there's need of me.
I want to lend a helping hand
Over the rough and steep
To a child too young to understand—
To comfort those who weep.
I want to live and work and plan
With the great crowd surging by,
To mingle with the common man,
No better or worse than I.

The Chambered Nautilus

by Oliver Wendell Holmes (1809-1894)

About the spiraled shell that enlarges its home each year
with pearly additions. This inspired Holmes to the
thought of the last seven lines which are terrific and
stimulating. A lesson from Nature to keep building
bigger and better things from the past. He urges us to build our aims in
life higher and higher each year, just as the nautilus builds its shell.

This is the ship of pearl which, poets *feign,*
    Sails the unshadowed main,
    The venturous bark that flings
On the sweet summer wind its purpled wings
In gulfs enchanted, where the Siren sings,
    And coral reefs lie bare,
Where the cold sea-maids rise to sun their streaming hair.

Its webs of living gauze no more unfurl;
    Wrecked is the ship of pearl!
    And every chambered cell,
Where its dim dreaming life was wont to dwell,
As the frail tenant shaped his growing shell,
    Before thee lies revealed,—
Its irised ceiling rent, its sunless crypt unsealed

Year after year beheld the silent toil
    That spread his lustrous coil;
    Still, as the spiral grew,
He left the past year's dwelling for the new,
Stole with soft step its shining archway through,
    Built up its idle door,
Stretched in his last-found home, and knew the old no more.

Thanks for the heavenly message brought by thee,
    Child of the wandering sea,
    Cast from her lap, forlorn!
From thy dead lips a clearer note is born
Than ever Triton blew from wreath'ed horn!
    While on mine ear it rings,
Through the deep caves of thought I hear a voice that sings:—

Build thee more stately mansions, O my soul,
    As the swift seasons roll!
    Leave thy low-vaulted past!
Let each new temple, nobler than the last,
Shut thee from heaven with a dome more vast,
    Till thou at length art free,
Leaving thine outgrown shell by life's unresting sea!

One, Two, Three

by Henry Cuyler Bunner (1855-1896)

A delightful made-up game, with two unlikely
contestants and two winners. A heart warmer.

It was an old, old, old, old lady,
    And a boy that was half-past three;
And the way that they played together
    Was beautiful to see.

She couldn't go running and jumping,
    And the boy, no more could he;
For he was a thin little fellow,
    With a thin little twisted knee.

They sat in the yellow sunlight,
    Out under the Maple tree;
And the game that they played I'll tell you,
    Just as it was told to me.

It was Hide-and-Go-Seek they were playing,
    Though you'd never have known it to be—
With an old, old, old, old lady,
    And a boy with a twisted knee.

The boy would bend his face down
    On his one little sound right knee,
And he'd guess where she was hiding,
    In guesses One, Two, Three!

"You are in the china-closet!"
	He would cry, and laugh with glee—
It wasn't the china closet,
	But he still had Two and Three.

"You are up in papa's big bedroom,
	In the chest with the queer old key!"
And she said: "You are warm and warmer;
	But you're not quite right," said she.

" It can't be the little cupboard
	Where mamma's things used to be—
So it must be the clothes-press, Gran'ma!"
	And he found her with his Three.

Then she covered her face with her fingers,
	That were wrinkled and white and wee,
And she guessed where the boy was hiding,
	With a One and a Two and a Three.

And they never had stirred from their places,
	Right under the maple tree—
This old, old, old, old lady
	And the boy with the lame little knee—
This dear, dear, dear old lady,
	And the boy who was half-past three.

The Miller of the Dee

by Charles Mackay (1814-1889)

There are some jobs better than being King.
Don't believe it? Ask the King.

There dwelt a miller, hale and bold,
　　Beside the River Dee;
He wrought and sang from morn till night,
　　No lark more blithe than he;
And this the burden of his song
　　Forever used to be,
"I envy no man, no, not I,
　　And no one envies me!"

"Thou'rt wrong, my friend!" said old King Hal,
　　"As wrong as wrong can be;
For could my heart be light as thine,
　　I'd gladly change with thee.
And tell me now what makes thee sing
　　With voice so loud and free,
While I am sad, though I'm the King,
　　Beside the River Dee?"

The miller smiled and doffed his cap:
　　"I earn my bread," quoth he;
"I love my wife, I love my friend,
　　I love my children three.
I owe no one I cannot pay,
　　I thank the River Dee,
That turns the mill that grinds the corn
　　To feed my babes and me!"

"Good friend," said Hal, and sighed the while,
　　"Farewell! and happy be;
But say no more, if thou'dst be true,
　　That no one envies thee.
Thy mealy cap is worth my crown;
　　Thy mill my kingdom's fee!
Such men as thou are England's boast,
　　Oh, miller of the Dee!"

Inspiration
by Robert Service (1874-1958)

How to write a poem. See how easy it is? A straightforward way to describe the music of poetry and nature—that's why I like him.

How often have I started out
    With no thought in my noddle,
And wandered here and there about,
    Where fancy bade me toddle;
Till feeling faunlike in my glee
    I've voiced some gay distiches,
Returning joyfully to tea,
    A poem in my britches.

A-squatting on a thymy slope
    With vast of sky about me,
I've scribbled on an envelope
    The rhymes the hills would shout me;
The couplets that the trees would call,
    The lays the breezes proffered ...
Oh no, I didn't think at all—
    I took what Nature offered.

For that's the way you ought to write
    Without a trace of trouble;
Be super-charged with high delight
    And let the words out-bubble;
Be voice of vale and wood and stream
    Without design or proem:
Then rouse from out a golden dream
    To find you've made a poem.

So I'll go forth with mind a blank,
    And sea and sky will spell me;
And lolling on a thymy bank
    I'll take down what they tell me;
As Mother Nature speaks to me
    Her words I'll gaily docket,
So I'll come singing home to tea
    A poem in my pocket.

Great-Heart

by Rudyard Kipling (1865-1936)

Kipling, Mr. Englishman himself, was obviously
extremely impressed by the down-to-earth, friendly,
warm-hearted great American, Teddy Roosevelt, in
whose memory he wrote this outstanding passage.

Concerning brave Captains
    Our age hath made known
For all men to honor,
    One standeth alone,
Of whom, o'er both oceans
    Both Peoples may say:
"Our realm is diminished,
    With Great-Heart away."

In purpose unsparing,
    In action no less,
The labors he praised
    He would seek and profess
Through travail and battle,
    At hazard and pain...
And our world is none the braver
    Since Great-Heart was ta'en.

Plain speech with plain folk,
    And plain words for false things,
Plain faith in plain dealing
    'Twixt neighbors or kings
He used and he followed,
    However it sped...
Oh, our world is one more honest
    Now Great-Heart is dead!

The heat of his spirit
        Struck warm through all lands;
For he loved such as showed
        'Emselves men of their hands;
In love, as in hate,
        Paying home to the last...
But our world is none the kinder
        Now Great-Heart has passed!

Hard-schooled by long power,
        Yet most humble of mind
Where aught that he was
        Might advantage mankind.
Leal servant, loved master,
        Rare comrade, sure guide...
Oh, our world is none the safer
        Now Great-Heart hath died!

Let those who would handle
        Make sure they can wield
His far-reaching sword
        And his close-guarding shield;
For those who must journey
        Henceforward alone
Have need of stout convoy
        Now Great-Heart is gone.

Under the Portrait of Milton

by John Dryden (1631-1700)

The highest tribute Dryden could offer. Milton was a famous English poet of the 17th century.

    Three Poets, in three distant ages born,
    Greece, Italy, and England did adorn.
    The first in loftiness of thought surpassed;
    The next in majesty; in both the last.
    The force of Nature could no further go:
    To make a third she joined the former two.

(The Greek was Homer and the Italian was Virgil.)

FRIENDSHIP

A Friend or Two

by Wilbur D. Nesbit

A toast to one of life's greatest treasures.

> There's all of pleasure and all of peace
> In a friend or two;
> And all your troubles may find release
> Within a friend or two,
> It's in the grip of the sleeping hand
> On native soil or in alien land,
> But the world is made—do you understand—
> Of a friend or two.
>
> A song to sing and a crust to share
> With a friend or two;
> A smile to give and a grief to bear
> With a friend or two;
> A road to walk and a goal to win,
> An inglenook to find comfort in,
> The gladdest hours that we know begin
> With a friend or two.
>
> A little laughter, perhaps some tears
> With a friend or two;
> The days, the weeks, and the months and years
> With a friend or two;
> A vale to cross and a hill to climb,
> A mock at age and a jeer at time—
> The prose of life takes the lilt of rhyme
> With a friend or two.

The brother-soul and the brother-heart
    Of a friend or two
Make us drift on from the crowd apart,
    With a friend or two;
For come days happy or come days sad
We count no hours but the ones made glad
By the hale good times we have ever had
    With a friend or two.

Then brim the goblet and quaff the toast
    To a friend or two,
For glad the man who can always boast
    Of a friend or two;
But fairest sight is a friendly face,
The blithest tread is a friendly pace,
And heaven will be a better place
    For a friend or two.

Good King Wenceslas

by John Neal (1793-1876)

A Christmas regular and too good a poem to
leave out. Makes you feel good, too. Great foot-
steps to follow in, as the King's page found out.

Good King Wenceslas looked out,
    On the Feast of Stephen,
When the snow lay round about,
    Deep, and crisp, and even:
Brightly shone the moon that night,
    Though the frost was cruel,
When a poor man came in sight,
    Gathering winter fuel.

"Hither, page, and stand by me,
    If thou know'st it, telling,
Yonder peasant, who is he?
    Where and what his dwelling?"
"Sire, he lives a good league hence,
    Underneath the mountain;
Right against the forest fence,
    By Saint Agnes' fountain."

"Bring me flesh, and bring me wine,
    Bring me pine logs hither;
Thou and I will see him dine,
    When we bear them thither."
Page and monarch forth they went,
    Forth they went together;
Through the rude wind's wild lament,
    And the bitter weather.

"Sire, the night is darker now,
    And the wind blows stronger;
Fails my heart, I know not how,
    I can go no longer."
"Mark my footsteps, good my page!
    Tread thou in them boldly;
Thou shalt find the winter's rage
    Freeze thy blood less coldly."

In his master's steps he trod,
    Where the snow lay dinted;
Heat was in the very sod
    Which the saint had printed.
Therefore, Christian men, be sure,
    Wealth or rank possessing,
Ye who now will bless the poor,
    Shall yourselves find blessing.

A Friend's Greeting

by Edgar A. Guest

Great at Christmas, but also great any day.
Typical Guest. A little sugary.

I'd like to be the sort of friend that you have been to me;
I'd like to be the help that you've been always glad to be;
I'd like to mean as much to you each minute of the day
As you have meant, old friend of mine, to me along the way.

I'd like to do the big things and the splendid things for you,
To brush the gray from out your skies and leave them only blue;
I'd like to say the kindly things that I so oft have heard,
And feel that I could rouse your soul the way that mine you've
    stirred.

I'd like to give back the joy that you have given me,
Yet that were wishing you a need I hope will never be;
I'd like to make you feel as rich as I, who travel on
Undaunted in the darkest hours with you to lean upon.

I'm wishing at this Christmas time that I could but repay
A portion of the gladness that you've strewn along my way;
And could I have one wish this year, this only would it be:
I'd like to be the sort of friend that you have been to me.

Ingratitude

by William Shakespeare (1564-1616)

Will is sure that an icy winter wind does not bite as
sharply as being forgotten by a friend.

Blow, blow, thou winter wind,
Thou are not so unkind
        As man's ingratitude;
Thy tooth is not so keen
Because thou art not seen,
        Although thy breath be rude.

Freeze, freeze, thou bitter sky,
Thou dost not bite so nigh
    As benefits forgot;
Though thou the waters warp,
Thy sting is not so sharp
    As friend remembered not.

A Mile with Me

by Henry Van Dyke

A friendly walk through sunshine, and rain, to
the rainbow.

O, who will walk a mile with me
    Along life's merry way?
A comrade blithe and full of glee,
Who dares to laugh out loud and free,
And let his frolic fancy play,
Like a happy child, through the flowers gay
That fill the field and fringe the way
    Where he walks a mile with me.

And who will walk a mile with me
    Along life's weary way?
A friend whose heart has eyes to see
The stars shine out o'er the darkening lea,
And the quiet rest at the end o' the day,—
A friend who knows, and dares to say,
The brave, sweet words that cheer the way
    Where he walks a mile with me.

With such a comrade, such a friend,
I fain would walk till journey's end,
Through summer sunshine, winter rain,
And then?—Farewell, we shall meet again!

Auld Lang Syne

by Robert Burns (1759-1796)

Brush up on your Scottish brogue and smile through Bobbie Burns's lines that became the International song at New Year's, and the theme song of the Great Guy Lombardo band. It literally means "old long since"; hence, times long past, or the good old times.

Should auld acquaintance be forgot,
    And never brought to min'?
Should auld acquaintance be forgot,
    And days o' lang syne?

For auld lang syne, my dear,
    For auld lang syne,
We'll tak a cup o' kindness yet
    For auld lang syne.

We twa hae rin about the braes,
    And pu'd the gowans fine;
But we've wandered monie a weary fit
    Sin' auld lang syne.

We twa hae paidl't I' the burn,
    Frae mornin' sun til dine;
But seas between us braid hae roared
    Sin' auld lang syne.

And here's a hand, my trusty fiere,
    And gie's a hand o' thine;
And we'll tak a right guid willie-waught
    For auld lang syne.

And surely ye'll be your pint-stowp,
    And surely I'll be mine,
And we'll take a cup o' kindness yet
    For auld lang syne!

twa: two	*rin: run*
braes: hills	*willie-waught: big drink*
gowan: flower;	*stowp: stoup*
burn: stream	*fiere: companion*

Fellowship

by Unknown

What a satisfying feeling—a friendly hand upon
your shoulder.

When a feller hasn't got a cent
And is feelin' kind of blue,
And the clouds hang thick and dark
And won't let the sunshine thro',
It's a great thing, oh my brethren,
For a feller just to lay
His hand upon your shoulder in a friendly sort o' way.

It makes a man feel queerish,
It makes the tear-drops start.
And you kind o' feel a flutter
In the region of your heart.
You can't look up and meet his eye,
You don't know what to say
When a hand is on your shoulder in a friendly sort o' way.

Oh this world's a curious compound
With its honey and its gall;
Its cares and bitter crosses,
But a good world after all.
And a good God must have made it,
Leastwise that is what I say,
When a hand is on your shoulder in a friendly sort o' way.

Loyalty

by Berton Braley

The kind of friend we all have, and like to have, but don't brag about.

> He may be six kinds of a liar,
>> He may be ten kinds of a fool,
> He may be a wicked highflyer
>> Beyond any reason or rule;
> There may be a shadow above him
>> Of ruin and woes to impend,
> And I may not respect, but I love him,
>> Because—well, because he's my friend.
>
> I know he has faults by the billion,
>> But his faults are a portion of him;
> I know that his record's vermilion,
>> And he's far from the sweet Seraphim;
> But he's always been square with yours truly,
>> Ready to give or to lend,
> And if he is wild and unruly,
>> I like him—because he's my friend.
>
> I criticize him but I do it
>> In just a frank, comradely key,
> And back-biting gossips will rue it
>> If ever *they* knock him to me!
> I never make diagrams of him,
>> No maps of his soul have I penned;
> I don't analyze—I just love him,
>> Because—well, because he's my friend.

Our Own

by Margaret E. Sangster (1838-1912)

We see this happen much too often. A quote from
an oldie, *The Wreck of Old '97*—"Never breathe
harsh words to your true love or husband. He
may leave you and never return." Don't let it
happen to you.

> If I had known in the morning
>> How wearily all the day
> The words unkind would trouble my mind
>> That I said when you went away,
> I had been more careful, darling,
>> Nor given you needless pain;
> But we vex our own with look and tone
>> We may never take back again.
>
> For though in the quiet evening
>> You may give me the kiss of peace,
> Yet it well might be that never for me
>> The pain of the heart should cease!
> How many go forth at morning
>> Who never come home at night!
> And hearts have broken for harsh words spoken
>> That sorrow can ne'er set right.
>
> We have careful thought for the stranger,
>> And smiles for the sometime guest;
> But oft for "our own" the bitter time,
>> Though we love our own the best.
> Ah! lips with the curve impatient,
>> Ah! brow with the shade of scorn,
> 'Twere a cruel fate, were the night too late
>> To undo the work of the morn!

New Friends and Old Friends
by Joseph Parry

Gold is valuable, but silver isn't cheap, and both are very attractive and great to have around.

> Make new friends, but keep the old;
> Those are silver, these are gold.
> New-made friendships, like new wine,
> Age will mellow and refine.
> Friendships that have stood the test—
> Time and change—are surely best;
> Brow may wrinkle, hair grow gray,
> Friendship never knows decay.
> For 'mid old friends, tried and true,
> Once more we our youth renew.
> But old friends, alas! may die,
> New friends must their place supply.
> Cherish friendship in your breast—
> New is good, but old is best;
> Make new friends, but keep the old;
> Those are silver, these are gold.

The House by the Side of the Road
by Sam Walter Foss (1858-1911)

Sounds as if he has made it a Home by the side of the road with a friendly guy in it. Come on, let's drop in—I can't wait to meet him.

"He was a friend to man, and he lived In a house by the side of the road."—Homer

> There are hermit souls that live withdrawn
>   In the place of their self-content;
> There are souls like stars, that dwell apart,
>   In a fellowless firmament;
> There are pioneer souls that blaze their paths
>   Where highways never ran—
> But let me live by the side of the road
>   And be a friend to man.

Let me live in a house by the side of the road,
    Where the race of men go by—
The men who are good and the men who are bad,
    As good and as bad as I.
I would not sit in the scorner's seat,
    Or hurl the cynic's ban—
Let me live in a house by the side of the road
    And be a friend to man.

I see from my house by the side of the road,
    By the side of the highway of life,
The men who, press with the ardor of hope,
    The men who are faint with the strife.
But I turn not away from their smiles nor their tears,
    Both parts of an infinite plan—
Let me live in a house by the side of the road
    And be a friend to man.

I know there are brook-gladdened meadows ahead
    And mountains of wearisome height;
That the road passes on through the long afternoon
    And stretches away to the night.
But still I rejoice when the travelers rejoice,
    And weep with the strangers that moan,
Nor live in my house by the side of the road
    Like a man who dwells alone.

Let me live in my house by the side of the road
    It's here the race of men go by.
They are good, they are bad, they are weak, they are strong,
    Wise, foolish—so am I;
Then why should I sit in the scorner's seat,
    Or hurl the cynic's ban?
Let me live in my house by the side of the road
    And be a friend to man.

To a Friend

by Grace Stricker Dawson

What a blessing to have friends like this.
However, we should turn the tables, too.

You entered my life in a casual way,
    And saw at a glance what I needed;
There were others who passed me or met me each day,
    But never a one of them heeded.

Perhaps you were thinking of other folks more,
    Or chance simply seemed to decree it;
I know there were many such chances before,
    But the others—well, they didn't see it.

You said just the thing that I wished you would say,
    And you made me believe that you meant it;
I held up my head in the old gallant way,
    And resolved you should never repent it.

There are times when encouragement means such a lot,
    And a word is enough to convey it;
There were others who could have, as easy as not—
    But, just the same, they didn't say it

There may have been someone who could have done more
    To help me along, though I doubt it;
What I needed was cheering, and always before
    They had let me plod onward without it.

You helped to refashion the dream of my heart,
    And made me turn eagerly to it;
There were others who might have (I question that part)—
    But, after all, they didn't do it!

Touching Shoulders

by Unknown

Obviously a wonderful lot rubbed off
with each touch.

There's a comforting thought at the close of the day,
When I'm weary and lonely and sad,
That sort of grips hold of my crusty old heart
And bids it be merry and glad.
It gets in my soul and it drives out the blues,
And finally thrills through and through.
It is just a sweet memory that chants the refrain:
"I'm glad I touch shoulders with you!"

Did you know you were brave, did you know you were strong?
Did you know there was one leaning hard?
Did you know that I waited and listened and prayed,
And was cheered by your simplest word?
Did you know that I longed for that smile on you face,
For the sound of your voice ringing true?
Did you know I grew stronger and better because
I had merely touched shoulders with you?

I am glad that I live, that I battle and strive
For the place that I know I must fill;
I am thankful for sorrows, I'll meet with a grin
What fortune may send, good or ill.
I may not have wealth, I may not be great,
But I know I shall always be true,
For I have in my life that courage you gave
When once I rubbed shoulders with you.

❦ CHALLENGE ❧

Always Finish

by Unknown

Reciting this should be compulsory by age 6, and rechecked at 16, and always remembered.

> If a task is once begun
>> Never leave it til it's done.
> Be the labor great or small,
>> Do it well or not at all.

Carry On!

by Robert Service (1874-1958)

This should encourage and cheer up a lot of people. Carry on! Carry on!

> It's easy to fight when everything's right,
> And you're mad with the thrill and the glory;
> It's easy to cheer when victory's near,
> And wallow in fields that are gory.
> It's a different song when everything's wrong
> When you're feeling infernally mortal;
> When it's ten against one, and hope there is none,
> Buck up, little soldier, and chortle:

>> Carry on! Carry on!
>> There isn't much punch in your blow.
> You're glaring and staring and hitting out blind;
> You're muddy and bloody, but never you mind.
>> Carry on! Carry on!
>> You haven't the ghost of a show.
> It's looking like death, but while you've a breath,
>> Carry on, my son! Carry on!

And so in the strife of the battle of life
It's easy to fight when you're winning;
It's easy to slave, and starve and be brave,
When the dawn of success is beginning.
But the man who can meet despair and defeat
With a cheer, there's the man of God's choosing;
The man who can fight to Heaven's own height
Is the man who can fight when he's losing.

Carry on! Carry on!
Things never were looming so black.
But show that you haven't a cowardly streak,
And though you're unlucky you never are weak.
Carry on! Carry on!
Breach up for another attack.
It's looking like hell, but—you never can tell:
Carry on, old man! Carry on!

There are some who drift out in the deserts of doubt,
And some who in brutishness wallow;
There are others, I know, who in piety go
Because of a Heaven to follow.
But to labor with zest, and to give of your best,
For the sweetness and joy of the giving;
To help folks along with a hand and a song;
Why, there's the real sunshine of living.

Carry on! Carry on!
Fight the good fight and true;
Believe in your mission, greet life with a cheer;
There's big work to do, and that's why you are here.
Carry on! Carry on!
Let the world be the better for you;
And at last when you die, let this be your cry:
Carry on, my soul! Carry on!

Give Us Men!

by Josiah Gilbert Holland (1819-1881)

Should we apply this when choosing our representatives, especially Presidents, Senators, Representatives, Governors and Judges? Could we find enough qualified applicants? Especially when we think of the men in the Continental Congress by comparison, undoubtedly the greatest collection of statesmen ever assembled. Fortunately, we have always found them when the tempest of war appears.

Give us Men!
Men—from every rank,
Fresh and free and frank;
Men of thought and reading,
Men of light and leading,
Men of loyal breeding,
The nation's welfare speeding;
Men of faith and not of fiction,
Men of lofty aim in action;
    Give us Men—I say again,
        Give us Men!

Give us Men!
Strong and stalwart ones;
Men whom highest hope inspires,
Men whom purest honor fires,
Men who trample self beneath them,
Men who make their country wreathe them
    As her noble sops,
      Worthy of their sires;
Men who never shame their mothers,
Men who never fail their brothers,
True, however false are others:
    Give us Men—I say again,
        Give us Men!

Give us Men!
Men who, when the tempest gathers,
Grasp the standard of their fathers
    In the thickest fight;

Men who strike for home and altar,
(Let the coward cringe and falter),
　　God defend the right!
True as truth the lorn and lonely,
Tender, as the brave are only;
Men who tread where saints have trod,
Men for Country, Home—and God:
　　Give us Men! I say again—again—
　　Give us Men!

Never Say Fail!

by Unknown

Keep pushing—'tis wiser
　　Than sitting aside,
And dreaming and sighing,
　　And waiting the tide,
In life's earnest battle
　　They only prevail
Who daily march onward
　　And never say fail!

With an eye ever open,
　　A tongue that's not dumb,
And a heart that will never
　　To sorrow succumb—
You'll battle and conquer,
　　Though thousands assail:
How strong and how mighty
　　Who never say fail!

The spirit of angels
　　Is active, I know,
As higher and higher
　　In glory they go;
Methinks on bright pinions
　　From Heaven they sail,
To cheer and encourage
　　Who never say fail!

Ahead, then, keep pushing,
　　　And elbow your way,
Unheeding the envious,
　　　And asses that bray;
All obstacles vanish,
　　　All enemies quail,
In the might of their wisdom
　　　Who never sail fail!

In life's early morning,
　　　In manhood's firm pride,
Let this be your motto
　　　Your footsteps to guide;
In storm and in sunshine,
　　　Whatever assail,
We'll onward and conquer,
　　　And never say fail!

I Shall Not Pass This Way Again

by Eva Rose York

We have but one life to live, so enjoy the beauty and
the music along the way, and stop and smell the
roses. And on the way, give a hand or a kind word
to those in trouble, so that they, too, can smell the
roses, and hear the music.

　　　I shall not pass this way again
　　　　　Although it bordered be with flowers,
　　　　　Although I rest in fragrant bowers,
　　　　　And hear the singing
　　　　　Of song-birds winging
　　　To highest heaven their gladsome flight;
　　　Though moons are full and stars are bright,
　　　And winds and waves are softly sighing,
　　　While leafy trees make low replying;
　　　Though voices clear in joyous strain
　　　Repeat a jubilant refrain;
　　　Though rising suns, their radiance throw
　　　On summer's, green and winter's snow,
　　　In such rare splendor that my heart

Would ache from scenes like these to part;
    Though beauties heighten,
    And life-lights brighten,
And joys proceed from every pain,
I shall not pass this way again.

Then let me pluck the flowers that blow,
And let me listen as I go
        To music rare
        That fills the air;
        And let hereafter
        Songs and laughter
Fill every pause along the way;
And to my spirit let me say:
"O soul, be happy; soon 'tis trod,
The path made thus for thee by God.
Be happy, thou, and bless his name.
By whom such marvellous beauty came."
And let no chance by me be lost
To kindness show at any cost.
I shall not pass this way again;
Then let me now relieve some pain,
Remove some barrier from the road,
Or brighten some one's heavy load;
A helping hand to this one lend,
Then turn some other to befriend.

        O God, forgive
        That now I live
As if I might, sometime, return
To bless the weary ones that yearn
For help and comfort every day,—
For there be such along the way.
God, forgive that I have seen
The beauty only, have not been
Awake to sorrow such as this;
That I have drunk the cup of bliss
Remembering not that those there be
Who drink the dregs of misery.
I love the beauty of the scene,

Would roam again o'er fields so green;
But since I may not, let me spend
My strength for others to the end,—
For those who tread on rock and stone,
And bear their burdens all alone,
Who loiter not in leafy bowers,
Nor hear the birds nor pluck the flowers.
A larger kindness give to me,
A deeper love and sympathy;
    Then, O, one day
    May someone say—
Remembering a lessened pain—
"Would she could pass this way again."

I Shall Not Pass This Way Again

by Unknown

Seems "Unknown" felt the same way that Eva
York felt in the previous poem, and didn't want
his plans to be "Unknown."

Through this toilsome world, alas!
    Once and only once I pass;
If a kindness I may show,
    If a good deed I may do
To a suffering fellow man,
    Let me do it while I can.
No delay, for it is plain
    I shall not pass this way again.

IF

by Rudyard Kipling (1865-1936)

A great challenge to throw at every teenager—and while you are at it, every age including me at 84. A great poem to be posted in every home. How many "Ifs" can you handle? Maybe more next year? And daughters should just substitute "you'll be a real woman, my daughter!" for the last line.

> If you can keep your head when all about you
>   Are losing theirs and blaming it on you;
> If you can trust yourself when all men doubt you,
>   But make allowance for their doubting too:
> If you can wait and not be tired by waiting,
>   Or, being lied about, don't deal in lies,
> Or being hated, don't give way to hating,
>   And yet don't look too good, nor talk too wise;
>
> If you can dream—and not make dreams your master,
>   If you can think—and not make thoughts your aim,
> If you can meet with Triumph and Disaster
>   And treat those two impostors just the same:
> If you can bear to hear the truth you've spoken
>   Twisted by knaves to make a trap for fools,
> Or watch the things you gave your life to, broken,
>   And stoop and build 'em up with worn-out tools;
>
> If you can make one heap of all your winnings
>   And risk it on one turn of pitch-and-toss,
> And lose, and start again at your beginnings,
>   And never breathe a word about your loss:
> If you can force your heart and nerve and sinew
>   To serve your turn long after they are gone,
> And so hold on when there is nothing in you
>   Except the Will which says to them: "Hold on!"
>
> If you can talk with crowds and keep your virtue,
>   Or walk with Kings—nor lose the common touch,
> If neither foes nor loving friends can hurt you,
>   If all men count with you, but none too much:
> If you can fill the unforgiving minute
>   With sixty seconds' worth of distance run,
> Yours is the Earth and everything that's in it,
>   And—which is more—you'll be a Man, my son!

Lord, Make a Regular Man Out of Me

by Edgar A. Guest

About as fine a New Year's Resolution as one could dream up. This guy should pass the *If* quiz in style.

This I would like to be—braver and bolder,
Just a bit wiser because I am older,
Just a bit kinder to those I may meet,
Just a bit manlier taking defeat;
This for the New Year my wish and my plea—
Lord, make a regular man out of me.

This I would like to be—just a bit finer,
More of a smiler and less of a whiner,
Just a bit quicker to stretch out my hand
Helping another who's struggling to stand,
This is my prayer for the New Year to be,
Lord, make a regular man out of me.

This I would like to be—just a bit fairer,
Just a bit better, and just a bit squarer,
Not quite so ready to censure and blame,
Quicker to help every man in the game,
Not quite so eager men's failings to see,
Lord, make a regular man out of me.

This I would like to be—just a bit truer,
Less of the wisher and more of the doer,
Broader and bigger, more willing to give,
Living and helping my neighbor to live!
This for the New Year my prayer and my plea—
Lord, make a regular man out of me.

It Can Be Done

By Unknown

To find out how, read *It Couldn't Be Done*. That
sounds backwards, doesn't it?

> The man who misses all the fun
> Is he who says, "It can't be done."
> In solemn pride he stands aloof
> And greets each venture with reproof.
> Had he the power he'd efface
> The history of the human race;
> We'd have no radio or motor cars,
> No streets lit by electric stars;
> No telegraph nor telephone,
> We'd linger in the age of stone.
> The world would sleep if things were run
> By men who say, "It can't be done."

Myself

by Edgar A. Guest

A satisfying look in the mirror. What a great feeling to
be content with what you see.

> I have to live with myself, and so
> I want to be fit for myself to know,
> I want to be able, as days go by,
> Always to look myself straight in the eye;
> I don't want to stand, with the setting sun,
> And hate myself for things I have done.
>
> I don't want to keep on a closet shelf
> A lot of secrets about myself,
> And fool myself, as I come and go,
> Into thinking that nobody else will know
> The kind of a man I really am;
> I don't want to dress up myself in sham.

I want to go out with my head erect,
I want to deserve all men's respect;
But here in the struggle for fame and pelf
I want to be able to like myself.
I don't want to look at myself and know
That I'm bluster and bluff and empty show.

I can never hide myself from me;
I see what others may never see;
I know what others may never know,
I never can fool myself, and so,
Whatever happens, I want to be
Self-respecting and conscience free.

Soliloquy from "Hamlet"
by William Shakespeare (1564-1616)

Oops, not a poem, but isn't the rhythm poetic,
especially the first 13 lines. He certainly makes the
"to be" look much better after all, than the "not to
be." Shakespeare at his finest.

To be, or not to be; that is the question;
Whether 'tis nobler in the mind to suffer
The slings and arrows of outrageous fortune,
Or to take arms against a sea of troubles,
And by opposing end them. To die: to sleep:
No more; and by a sleep to say we end
The heart-ache and the thousand natural shocks
That flesh is heir to; 'tis a consummation
Devoutly to be wished. To die; to sleep;
To sleep: perchance to dream: aye, there's the rub;
For, in that sleep of death, what dreams may come,
When we have shuffled off this mortal coil,
Must give us pause: there's the respect
That makes calamity of so long life;
For who would bear the whips and scorns of time,
The oppressor's wrong, the proud man's contumely,
The pangs of despis'd love, the law's delay, [1]
The insolence of office, and the spurns

That patient merit of the unworthy takes,
When he himself might quietus make
With a bare bodkin²? Who would fardels³ bear,
To grunt and sweat under a weary life,
But that the dread of something after death—
The undiscovered country from whose bourn
No traveler returns—puzzles the will
And makes us rather bear those ills we have
Than fly to others that we know not of?
Thus conscience does make cowards of us all,
And thus the native hue of resolution
Is sicklied o'er with the pale cast of thought,
And enterprises of great pith and moment
With this regard their currents turn away,
And lose the name of action.

¹ *Law's delay: Things haven't changed. Even Shakespeare bemoaned the terrible
slowness of legal actions.*

² *Bodkin: a small pointed instrument*

³ *Fardel: a bundle or burden*

The Coming American

By Sam Walter Foss (1858-1911)

Horace Greely had said "Go West young man!"
Hard for a young man to turn down this plea.
Foss has changed that to "Come West, real men."
Obviously a lot of men (and women) listened to
both of them.

Bring me men to match my mountains,
Bring me men to match my plains,
Men with empires in their purpose
And new eras in their brains.
Bring me men to match my prairies,
Men to match my inland seas,
Men whose thoughts shall pave a highway
Up to ampler destinies,
Pioneers to cleanse thought's marshlands,
        And to cleanse old error's fen;
Bring me men to match my mountains—
        Bring me men!

Bring me men to match my forests,
Strong to fight the storm and beast,
Branching toward the skyey future,
Rooted on the futile past.
Bring me men to match my valleys,
　　　Tolerant of rain and snow,
Men within whose fruitful purpose
　　　Time's consummate blooms shall grow,
Men to tame the tigerish instincts
　　　Of the lair and cave and den,
Cleanse the dragon slime of nature—
　　　Bring me men!

Bring me men to match my rivers,
　　　Continent cleansers, flowing free,
Drawn by eternal madness,
　　　To be mingled with the sea—
Men of oceanic impulse,
　　　Men whose moral currents sweep
Toward the wide, infolding ocean
　　　Of an undiscovered deep—
Men who feel the strong pulsation
　　　Of the central sea, and then
Time their currents by its earth throbs—
　　　Bring me Men!

The Quitter

by Unknown

Mighty good advice. So "Restart your motors,
Gentlemen" and keep them well-oiled and
running smoothly, and give it another try.

It ain't the failures he may meet
     That keeps a man from winnin',
It's the discouragement complete
     That blocks a new beginnin';
You want to quit your habits bad,
     And, when the shadows flitten'
Make life seem worthless an' sad,
     You want to quit your quittin'!

You want to quit a-layin' down
     An' sayin' hope is over,
Because the fields are bare an' brown
     Where once we lived in clover.
When jolted from the water cart
     It's painful to be hittin'
The earth; but make another start.
     Cheer up, an' quit your quittin'!

Although the game seems rather stiff
     Don't be a doleful doubter;
There's always one more innin' if
     You're not a down-and-outer.
But fortune's pretty sure to flee
     From folks content with sittin'
Around an' sayin' life's N.G.
     You've got to quit your quittin'.

The Things That Haven't Been Done Before

by Edgar Guest

Stop and think what this type of person has accomplished in the 20th century. Contrast this to *The Calf Path*.

> The things that haven't been done before,
>   Those are the things to try;
> Columbus dreamed of an unknown shore
>   At the rim of the far-flung sky,
> And his heart was bold and his faith was strong
>   As he ventured in dangers new,
> And he paid no heed to the jeering throng
>   Or the fears of the doubting crew.
>
> The many will follow the beaten track
>   With guideposts on the way.
> They live and have lived for ages back
>   With a chart for every day.
> Someone has told them it's safe to go
>   On the road he has traveled o'er,
> And all that they ever strive to know
>   Are the things that were known before.
>
> A few strike out, without map or chart,
>   Where never a man has been,
> From the beaten paths they draw apart
>   To see what no man has seen.
> There are deeds they hunger alone to do;
>   Though battered and bruised and sore,
> They blaze the path for the many, who
>   Do nothing not done before.
>
> The things that haven't been done before
>   Are the tasks worthwhile today;
> Are you one of the flock that follows, or
>   Are you one that shall lead the way?
> Are you one of the timid souls that quail
>   At the jeers of a doubting crew,
> Or dare you, whether you win or fail,
>   Strike out for a goal that's new?

Try, Try Again
by William Edward Hickson

'Tis a fact. It will work.

'Tis a lesson you should heed,
    Try, try again;
If at first you don't succeed,
    Try, try again;
Then your courage should appear,
For, if you will persevere,
You will conquer, never fear;
    Try, try again.

Once or twice, though you should fail,
    Try again;
If you would at last prevail,
    Try again;
If we strive, 'tis no disgrace
Though we do not win the race;
What should we do in that case?
    Try again.

If you find your task is hard,
    Try again;
Time will bring you your reward,
    Try again;
All that other folks can do,
Why, with patience, may not you?
Only keep this rule in view,
    Try again.

The Men That Don't Fit In

by Robert Service (1874-1958)

Service, no doubt, saw hundreds of these men during
his days in the Yukon. Homeless, restless, penniless—
and always missing their chances. If they just stuck to
it, they could have fulfilled their dreams. The greenest
grass is most often your own—well-watered.

There's a race of men that don't fit in,
　　A race that can't stay still;
So they break the hearts of kith and kin,
　　And they roam the world at will.
They range the field and they rove the flood,
　　And they climb the mountain's crest;
Theirs is the curse of the gypsy blood,
　　And they don't know how to rest.

If they just went straight they might go far;
　　They are strong and brave and true;
But they're always tired of the things that are,
　　And they want the strange and new.
They say: "Could I find my proper groove,
　　What a deep mark I would make!"
So they chop and change, and each fresh move
　　Is only a fresh mistake.

And each forgets, as he strips and runs
　　With a brilliant, fitful pace,
It's the steady, quiet, plodding ones
　　Who win in the lifelong race.
And each forgets that his youth has fled,
　　Forgets that his prime is past,
Till he stands one day, with a hope that's dead,
　　In the glare of the truth at last.

He has failed, he has failed; he has missed his chance;
　　He has just done things by half.
Life's been a jolly good joke on him,
　　And now is the time to laugh.
Ha, ha! He is one of the Legion Lost;
　　He was never meant to win;
He's a rolling stone, and it's bred in the bone;
　　He's a man who won't fit in.

Work: A Song of Triumph

by Angela Morgan

The song of a real doer and go-getter. May her tribe increase. Her enthusiasm sure makes a man feel better. She knew what made America great and emotionally and forcefully stated it.

Work!
Thank God for the might of it,
The ardor, the urge, the delight of it—
Work that springs from the heart's desire,
Setting the brain and the soul on fire—
Oh, what is so good as the heat of it,
And what is so glad as the beat of it,
And what is so kind as the stern command,
Challenging brain and heart and hand?

Work!
Thank God for the pride of it,
For the beautiful, conquering tide of it.
Sweeping the life in its furious flood,
Thrilling the arteries, cleansing the blood,
Mastering stupor and dull despair,
Moving the dreamer to do and dare.
Oh, what is so good as the urge of it,
And what is so glad as the surge of it,
And what is so strong as the summons deep,
Rousing the torpid soul from sleep?

Work!
Thank God for the pace of it,
For the terrible, keen, swift race of it;
Fiery steeds in full control,
Nostrils a-quiver to meet the goal.
Work, the Power that drives behind,
Guiding the purposes, taming the mind,
Holding the runaway wishes back,
Reining the will to one steady track,
Speeding the energies faster, faster,
Triumphing over disaster.

Oh, what is so good as the pain of it,
And what is so great as the gain of it?
And what is so kind as the cruel goad,
Forcing us on through the rugged road?

Work!
Thank God for the swing of it,
For the clamoring, hammering ring of it,
Passion of labor daily hurled
On the mighty anvils of the world.
Oh, what is so fierce as the flame of it?
And what is so huge as the aim of it?
Thundering on through dearth and doubt,
Calling the plan of the Maker out.
Work, the Titan; Work, the friend,
Shaping the earth to a glorious end,
Draining the swamps and blasting the hills,
Doing whatever the Spirit wills—
Rending a continent apart,
To answer the dreams of the Master heart.
Thank God for a world where none may shirk—
Thank God for the splendor of work!

The Law of the Yukon

by Robert Service (1874-1958)

This is a very powerful, stirring story by one who has surely been there and knows the real truth of the hardships of late 19th century Alaska. It's told by the Yukon Territory as first person, bemoaning the numerous riff-raff that have come to profit from the sudden riches, and pleading for the strong who will build the cities, dig the mines, and create a great land in this harsh domain. However, in contrast to *The Spell of the Yukon*, it stresses the rough, tough side of the area rather than the super pleasant side. She, the Yukon, welcomes you, but warns you.

This is the law of the Yukon, and ever she makes it plain:
"Send not your foolish and feeble; send me your strong and your sane—
Strong for the red rage of battle; sane, for I harry them sore;
Send me men girt for the combat, men who are grit to the core;
Swift as the panther in triumph, fierce as the bear in defeat,
Sired of a bulldog parent, steeled in the furnace heat.
Send me the best of your breeding, lend me your chosen ones;
Them will I take to my bosom, them will I call my sons;
Them will I gild with my treasure, them will I glut with my meat;
But the others—the misfits, the failures—I trample under my feet.
Dissolute, damned and despairful, crippled and palsied and slain,
Ye would send me the spawn of your gutters—Go! take back your
    spawn again.

"Wild and wide are my borders, stern as death is my sway;
From my ruthless throne I have ruled alone for a million years and a
    day;
Hugging my mighty treasure, waiting for man to come,
Till he swept like a turbid torrent, and after him swept—the scum.
The pallid pimp of the dead-line, the enervate of the pen,
One by one I weeded them out, for all that I sought was—Men.
One by one I dismayed them, frighting them sore with my glooms;
One by one I betrayed them unto my manifold dooms.
Drowned them like rats in my rivers, starved them like curs on my plains,
Rotted the flesh that was left them, poisoned the blood in their veins;
Burst with my winter upon them, searing forever their sight,
Lashed them with fungus-white faces, whimpering wild in the night;

"Staggering blind through the storm-whirl, stumbling mad through
    the snow,
Frozen stiff in the ice-pack, brittle and bent like a bow;
Featureless, formless, forsaken, scented by wolves in their flight,
Left for the wind to make music through ribs that are glittering
white;
Gnawing the black crust of failure, searching the pit of despair,
Crooking the toe in the trigger, trying to patter a prayer;
Going outside with an escort, raving with lips all afoam,
Writing a cheque for a million, driveling feebly of home;
Lost like a louse in the burning...or else in the tented town
Seeking a drunkard's solace, sinking and sinking down;
Steeped in the slime at the bottom, dead to a decent world,
Lost 'mid the human flotsam, far on the frontier hurled;
In the camp at the bend of the river, with its dozen saloons aglare,
Its gambling dens ariot, its gramophones all ablare;
Crimped with the crimes of a city, sin-ridden and bridled with lies,
In the hush of my mountained vastness, in the flush of my midnight skies,
Plague-spots, yet tools of my purpose, so natheless I suffer them thrive,
Crushing my Weak in their clutches, that only my Strong may survive.

"But the others, the men of my mettle, the men who would 'stablish
    my fame
Unto its ultimate issue, winning me honor, not shame;
Searching my uttermost valleys, fighting each step as they go,
Shooting the wrath of my rapids, scaling my ramparts of snow;
Ripping the guts of my mountains, looting the beds of my creeks,
Them will I take to my bosom, and speak as a mother speaks.
I am the land that listens, I am the land that broods;
Steeped in eternal beauty, crystalline waters and woods.
Long have I waited lonely, shunned as a thing accurst,
Monstrous, moody, pathetic, the last of the lands and the first;
Visioning camp-fires at twilight, and with a longing forlorn,
Feeling my womb o'er—pregnant with the seed of cities unborn.

Wild and wide are my borders, stern as death is my sway,
And I wait for the men who will win me—and I will not be won in a day;
And I will not be won by weaklings, subtle, suave and mild,
But by men with the hearts of vikings, and the simple faith of a
     child;
Desperate, strong and resistless, unthrottled by fear or defeat,
Them will I gild with my treasure, them will I glut with my meat.

"Lofty I stand from each sister land, patient and wearily wise,
With the weight of a world of sadness in my quite, passionless eyes;
Dreaming alone of a people, dreaming alone of a day,
When men shall not rape my riches, and curse me and go away;
Making a bawd of my bounty, fouling the hand that gave—
Till I rise in my wrath and I sweep on their path and I stamp them
     into a grave.
Dreaming of men who will bless me, of women esteeming me good.
Of children born in my borders of radiant motherhood.
Of cities leaping to stature, of fame like a flag unfurled,
As I pour the tide of my riches in the eager lap of the world."

This is the Law of the Yukon, that only the Strong shall thrive;
That surely the Weak shall perish, and only the Fit survive.
Dissolute, damned and despairful, crippled and palsied and slain,
This is the Will of the Yukon—Lo, how she makes it plain!

The Two Glasses

by Ella Wheeler Wilcox (1855-1919)

A clever debate between John Barleycorn and
Cool Waters. You be the judge. There were no
rebuttals.

There sat two glasses filled to the brim,
On a rich man's table, rim to rim;
One was ruddy and red as blood,
And one as clear as the crystal flood.

Said the glass of wine to the paler brother:
"Let us tell the tales of the past to each other;
I can tell of banquet and revel and mirth,
And the proudest and grandest souls on earth
Fell under my touch as though struck by blight,
Where I was king, for I ruled in might;
From the heads of kings I have torn the crown,
From the heights of fame I have hurled men down:
I have blasted many an honored name;
I have taken virtue and given shame;
I have tempted the youth with a sip, a taste,
That has made his future a barren waste.
Greater, far greater than king am I,
Or than any army beneath the sky.
I have made the arm of the driver fail,
And sent the train from the iron rail;
I have made good ships go down at sea,
And the shrieks of the lost were sweet to me,
For they said, 'Behold how great you be!
Fame, strength, wealth, genius before you fall,
For your might and power are over all.'
Ho! ho! pale brother," laughed the wine,
"Can you boast of deeds as great as mine?"

Said the water glass: "I cannot boast
Of a king dethroned or a murdered host;
But I can tell of a heart once sad,
By my crystal drops made light and glad;
Of thirsts I've quenched, of brows I've laved,
Of hands I have cooled, and souls I have saved;
I have leaped through the valley, dashed down the mountain,
Flowed in the river and played in the fountain,
Slept in the sunshine and dropped from the sky,
And everywhere gladdened the landscape and eye.
I have eased the hot forehead of fever and pain;
I have made the parched meadows grow fertile with grain;
I can tell of the powerful wheel of the mill,
That ground out the flour and turned at my will,
I can tell of manhood debased by you,
That I have lifted and crowned anew.
I cheer, I help, I strengthen and aid;
I gladden the heart of man and maid;
I set the chained wine-captive free;
And all are better for knowing me."

These are the tales they told each other,
The glass of wine and the paler brother,
As they sat together filled to the brim,
On the rich man's table, rim to rim.

Humor

The Duel

by Eugene Field (1850-1895)

A delightful bit. Don't let the title fool you.
Very clever.

    The gingham dog and the calico cat
    Side by side on the table sat;
    'Twas half-past twelve, and (what do you think!)
    Nor one nor t' other had slept a wink!
The old Dutch clock and the Chinese plate
Appeared to know as sure as fate
    There was going to be a terrible spat.

    (I wasn't there; I simply state
    What was told to me by the Chinese plate!)

    The gingham dog went "bow-wow-wow!"
    And the calico cat replied "mee-ow!"
    The air was littered, an hour or so,
    With bits of gingham and calico,
While the old Dutch clock in the chimney-place
Up with its hands before its face,
    For it always dreaded a family row!

    (Never mind: I'm only telling you
    What the old Dutch clock declares is true!)

    The Chinese plate looked very blue,
    And wailed, "Oh, dear! what shall we do!"
    But the gingham dog and the calico cat
    Wallowed this way and tumbled that,
Employing every tooth and claw
In the awfullest way you ever saw
    And, oh! how the gingham and calico flew!

    (Don't fancy I exaggerate-
    I got my news from the Chinese plate!)

Next morning where the two had sat
They found no trace of dog or cat;
And some folks think unto this day
That burglars stole that pair away!
But the truth about the cat and pup
Is this: they ate each other up!
Now what do you really think—of that!

*(The old Dutch clock it told me so,
And that is how I came to know.)*

The Chaperon
by Henry Cuyler Bunner (1855-1896)

A person who has become so rare that I almost
put in a definition. A little whimsy.

I take my chaperon to the play—
    She thinks she's taking me.
And the gilded youth who owns the box,
    A proud young man is he;
But how would his young heart be hurt
    If he could only know
    That not for his sweet sake I go
    Nor yet to see the trifling show;
But to see my chaperon flirt.

Her eyes beneath her snowy hair
    They sparkle young as mine;
There's scarce a wrinkle in her hand
    So delicate and fine.
And when my chaperon is seen,
    They come from everywhere—
    The dear old boys with silvery hair,
    With old-time grace and old-time air,
To greet their old-time queen.

They bow as my young Midas here
    Will never learn to bow
(The dancing masters do not teach
    That gracious reverence now);
With voices quavering just a bit,
    They play their old parts through,
    They talk of folk who used to woo,
    Of hearts that broke in 'fifty-two—
Now none the worse for it.

And as those aged crickets chirp,
    I watch my chaperon's face,
And see the dear old features take
    A new and tender grace;
And in her happy eyes I see
    Her youth awakening bright;
    With all its hope, desire, delight—
    Ah, me! I wish that I were quite
As young—as young as she!

The Blind Men and the Elephant
by John Godfrey Saxe (1816-1887)

A Hindu fable. Interesting observations of people with limited information. Do you think there are blind men or just elephant-feelers in our great halls of Congress?

It was six men of Indostan
    To learning much inclined,
Who went to see the Elephant
    (Though all of them were blind),
That each by observation
    Might satisfy his mind.

The *First* approached the Elephant,
    And happening to fall
Against his broad and sturdy side,
    At once began to bawl;
"God bless me! but the Elephant
    Is very like a wall!"

The *Second*, feeling of the tusk,
　　Cried, "Ho! what have we here
So very round and smooth and sharp?
　　To me 'tis mightly clear
This wonder of an Elephant
　　Is very like a spear!"

The *Third* approached the animal,
　　And happening to take
The squirming trunk within his hands,
　　Thus boldly up and spake:
"I see," quoth he, "the Elephant
　　Is very like a snake!"

The *Fourth* reached out an eager hand,
　　And felt about the knee.
"What most this wondrous beast is like
　　Is mighty plain," quoth he;
"'Tis clear enough the Elephant
　　Is very like a tree!"

The *Fifth* who chanced to touch the ear,
　　Said: "E'en the blindest man
Can tell what this resembles most;
　　Deny the fact who can,
This marvel of an elephant
　　Is very like a fan!"

The *Sixth* no sooner had begun
　　About the beast to grope,
Than, seizing on the swinging tail
　　That fell within his scope,
"I see," quoth he, "the Elephant
　　Is very like a rope!"

And so these men of Indostan
　　Disputed loud and long,
Each in his own opinion
　　Exceeding stiff and strong,
Though each was partly in the right
　　And all were in the wrong!

Moral

So oft in theologic wars,
    The disputants, I ween,
Rail on in utter ignorance
    Of what each other mean,
And prate about an Elephant
    Not one of them has seen!

He Worried About It

by Sam Walter Foss (1858-1911)

How many of your friends fit this Joe's pattern?
He sounds like Mark Twain, who said "I have
had a lot of worries in my life, most of which never happened."

The sun's heat will give out in ten million years more—
    And he worried about it.
It will sure give out then, if it doesn't before—
    And he worried about it.
It will surely give out, so the scientists said
In all scientific books he had read,
And the whole boundless universe then will be dead—
    And he worried about it.

And some day the earth will fall into the sun—
    And he worried about it.
Just as sure and as straight as if shot from a gun—
    And he worried about it.
"When strong gravitation unbuckles her straps,
Just picture," he said, "what a fearful collapse!
It will come in a few million ages, perhaps"—
    And he worried about it.

And the earth will become much too small for the race—
    And he worried about it.
When we'll pay thirty dollars an inch for pure space—
    And he worried about it.
The earth will be crowded so much, without doubt,
That there won't be room for one's tongue to stick out,
Not room for one's thoughts to wander about—
    And he worried about it.

And the Gulf Stream will curve, and New England grow torrider—
    And he worried about it.
Than was ever the climate of southernmost Florida—
    And he worried about it.
Our ice crop will be knocked into small smithereens,
And crocodiles block up our mowing-machines,
And we'll lose our fine crops of potatoes and beans—
    And he worried about it.

And in less than ten thousand years, there's no doubt—
    And he worried about it.
Our supply of lumber and coal will give out—
    And he worried about it.
Just then the ice age will return cold and raw,
Frozen men will stand stiff with arms outstretched in awe,
As if vainly beseeching a general thaw—
    And he worried about it.

His wife took in washing—half a dollar a day—
    He didn't worry about it—
His daughter sewed shirts, the rude grocer to pay—
    He didn't worry about it—
While his wife beat her tireless rub-a-dub-dub
On the washboard drum of her old wooden tub,
He sat by the stove, and he just let her rub—
    He didn't worry about it.

The Female of the Species
by Rudyard Kipling (1865-1936)

If you have, or had, any doubts about which is the
more deadly of the species, Kipling will convince you
conclusively. Furthermore, he wrote this before the days
of Eva Peron and Hillary Clinton.

When the Himalayan peasant meets the he-bear in his pride,
He shouts to scare the monster, who will often turn aside;
But the she-bear thus accosted rends the peasant tooth and nail,
For the female of the species is more deadly than the male.

When Nag the basking cobra hears the careless foot of man,
He will sometimes wriggle sideways and avoid it as he can;
But his mate makes no such motion where she camps beside the trail,
For the female of the species is more deadly than the male.

When the early Jesuit fathers preached to Hurons and Choctaws,
They prayed to be delivered from the vengeance of the squaws.
'Twas the women, not the warriors, turned those stark enthusiasts pale,
For the female of the species is more deadly than the male.

Man's timid heart is bursting with the things he must not say,
For the Woman that God gave him isn't his to give away;
But when the hunter meets with husband, each confirms the other's
    tale—
The female of the species is more deadly than the male.

Man, a bear in most relations—worm and savage otherwise,—
Man propounds negotiations, Man accepts the compromise.
Very rarely will he squarely push the logic of a fact
To its ultimate conclusion in unmitigated act.

Fear, or foolishness, impels him, ere he lay the wicked low,
To concede some form of trial even to his fiercest foe.
Mirth obscene diverts his anger! Doubt and Pity oft perplex
Him in dealing with an issue—to the scandal of The Sex!

But the Woman that God gave him, every fibre of her frame
Proves her launched for one sole issue, armed and engined for the same;
And to serve that single issue, lest the generations fail,
For the female of the species must be deadlier than the male.

She who faces Death by torture for each life beneath her breast
May not deal in doubt or pity—must not swerve for fact or jest.
These be purely male diversions—not in these her honour dwells.
She the Other Law we live by, is that Law and nothing else.

She can bring no more to living than the powers that make her great
And the Mother of the Infant and the Mistress of the Mate!
And when Babe and Man are lacking and she strides unclaimed to claim
Her right as femme (and baron), her equipment is the same.

She is wedded to convictions—in default of grosser ties;
Her contentions are her children, Heaven help him who denies!—
He will meet no suave discussion, but the instant, white-hot, wild,
Wakened female of the species warring as for spouse and child.

Unprovoked and awful changes—even so the she-bear fights,
Speech that drips, corrodes, and poisons—even so the cobra bites,
Scientific vivisection of one nerve till it is raw,
And the victim writhes in anguish—like the Jesuit with the squaw!

So it comes that Man the coward, when he gathers to confer
With her fellow-braves in council, dare not leave a place for her
Where, at war with Life Conscience, he uplifts his erring hands
To some God of Abstract Justice—which no woman understands.

And Man knows it! Knows, moreover, that the Woman that God gave him
Must command but may not govern—shall enthrall but not enslave him.
And She knows, because She warns him, and Her instincts never fail,
That the Female of Her Species is more deadly than the Male.

My Familiar

by John Godfrey Saxe (1816-1887)

Thank goodness there are not too many
"Familiars" around. However, you will greatly
enjoy his characterizations, and recognize a few
"Familiars" of your own.

Again I hear that creaking step!—
    He's rapping at the door!—
Too well I know the boding sound
    That ushers in a bore.
I do not tremble when I meet
    The stoutest of my foes,
But Heaven defend me from the friend
    Who comes—but never goes!

He drops into my easy chair,
    And asks about the news,
He peers into my manuscript,
    And gives his candid views;
He tells me where he likes the line,
    And where he's forced to grieve;
He takes the strangest liberties,—
    But never takes his leave!

He reads my daily paper through
    Before I've seen a word;
He scans the lyric (that I wrote),
    And thinks it quite absurd;
He calmly smokes my last cigar,
    And cooly asks for more;
He opens everything he sees—
    Except the entry door!!

He talks about his fragile health,
    And tells me of the pains
He suffers from a score of ills
    Of which he ne'er complains;
And how he struggled once with Death
    To keep the fiend at bay;
On themes like those away he goes—
    But never goes away!

He tells me of the carping words
    Some shallow critic wrote;
And every precious paragraph
    Familiarity can quote;
He thinks the writer did me wrong;
    He'd like to run him through!
He says a thousand pleasant things—
    But never says, "Adieu!"

Whene'er he comes—that dreadful man—
    Disguise it as I may,
I know that, like an autumn rain,
    He'll last throughout the day.
In vain I speak of urgent tasks;
    In vain I scowl and pout;
A frown is no extinguisher—
    It does not put him out!

I mean to take the knocker off,
    Put crape upon the door,
Or hint to John that I am gone
    To stay a month or more.
I do not tremble when I meet
    The stoutest of my foes,
But Heaven defend me from the friend
    Who never, never goes!

Captain Jinks

by Unknown

A little high-jinks out of the past; we used to love
to sing it as kids.

I'm Captain Jinks of the Horse Marines,
I feed my horse on corn and beans,
And sport young ladies in their teens,
        Though a captain in the army.
I teach young ladies how to dance,
How to dance, how to dance,
I teach young ladies how to dance,
        For I'm the pet of the army.

Chorus:
Captain Jinks of the Horse Marines,
I feed my horse on corn and beans,
And often live beyond my means,
        Though a captain in the army.

I joined my corps when twenty-one,
Of course I thought it capital fun;
When the enemy came, of course I run,
        For I'm not cut out for the army.
When I left home, mama she cried,
Mama she cried, mama she cried,
When I left home, mama she cried:
        "He's not cut out for the army."

The first time I went out to drill,
The bugle sounding made me ill;
Of the battle field I'd had my fill,
        For I'm not cut out for the army.
The officers they all did shout,
They all did shout, they all did shout,
The officers they all did shout:
        "Why, kick him out of the army."

Casey At the Bat

by Ernest Lawrence Thayer

Baseball is the All-American sport and this
is the All-American poem. No American kid
should grow up without reading it, and
maybe even reciting it. From the best sources I could find, the related
events refer to a game in or near Stockton, California.

The outlook wasn't brilliant for the Mudville nine that day;
The score stood two to four, with but an inning left to play.
So, when Cooney died at second, and Burrows did the same,
A pallor wreathed the features of the patrons of the game.

A straggling few got up to go, leaving there the rest,
With that hope which springs eternal within the human breast.
For they thought: "If only Casey could get a whack at that,"
They'd put even money now, with Casey at the bat.

But Flynn preceded Casey, as did also Jimmy Blake,
And the former was a pudd'n, and the latter was a fake.
So on that stricken multitude a deathlike silence sat;
For there seemed but little chance of Casey's getting to the bat.

But Flynn let drive a "single," to the wonderment of all.
And the much-despised Blakey "tore the cover off the ball."
And when the dust had lifted, and they saw what had occurred,
There was Blakey safe at second, and Flynn a-huggin' third.

Then from the gladdened multitude went up a joyous yell—
It rumbled in the mountaintops, it rattled in the dell;
It struck upon the hillside and rebounded on the flat;
For Casey, mighty Casey, was advancing to the bat.

There was ease in Casey's manner as he stepped into his place,
There was pride in Casey's bearing and a smile on Casey's face;
And when responding to the cheers he lightly doffed his hat,
No stranger in the crowd could doubt 'twas Casey at the bat.

Ten thousand eyes were on him as he rubbed his hands with dirt,
Five thousand tongues applauded when he wiped them on his shirt;
Then when the writhing pitcher ground the ball into his hip,
Defiance glanced in Casey's eye, a sneer curled Casey's lip.

And now the leather-covered sphere came hurtling through the air,
And Casey stood a-watching it in haughty grandeur there.
Close by the sturdy batsman the ball unheeded sped;
"That ain't my style," said Casey. "Strike one," the umpire said.

From the benches, black with people, there went up a muffled roar,
Like the beating of the storm waves on the stern and distant shore.
"Kill him! kill the umpire!" shouted someone on the stand;
And it's likely they'd have killed him had not Casey raised his hand.

With a smile of Christian charity great Casey's visage shone;
He stilled the rising tumult, he bade the game go on.
He signaled to the pitcher, and once more the spheroid flew;
But Casey still ignored it, and the umpire said, "Strike two."

"Fraud!" cried the maddened thousands, and the echo answered "Fraud!"
But one scornful look from Casey and the audience was awed;
They saw his face grow stern and cold, they saw his muscles strain,
And they knew that Casey wouldn't let the ball go by again.

The sneer is gone from Casey's lips, his teeth are clenched in hate,
He pounds with cruel vengeance his bat upon the plate;
And now the pitcher holds the ball, and now he lets it go,
And now the air is shattered by the force of Casey's blow.

Oh, somewhere in this favored land the sun is shining bright,
The band is playing somewhere, and somewhere hearts are light;
And somewhere men are laughing, and somewhere children shout,
But there is no joy in Mudville: Mighty Casey has struck out.

Casey's Revenge

by Ames Wilson

Being a Reply to the Famous Baseball Classic, *Casey At the Bat*. Can't touch the original, but still good.

There were saddened hearts in Mudville for a
  week or even more;
There were muttered oaths and curses—every
  fan in town was sore.
"Just think," said one, "how soft it looked with Casey at the bat!
And then to think he'd go and spring a bush-league trick like that."

All his fame was forgotten; he was now a hopeless "shine,"
They called him "Strike-out Casey" from the mayor down the line,
And as he came to bat each day his bosom heaved a sigh,
While a look of hopeless fury shone in mighty Casey's eye.

The lane is long, someone has said, that never turns again,
And Fate, thought fickle, often gives another chance to men.
And Casey smiled—his rugged face no longer wore a frown;
The pitcher who had started all the trouble came to town.

All Mudville had assembled; ten thousand fans had come
To see the twirler who had put big Casey on the bum;
And when he stepped into the box the multitude went wild.
He doffed his cap in proud disdain—but Casey only smiled.

"Play ball!" the umpire's voice rang out, and then the game began;
But in that throng of thousands there was not a single fan
Who thought that Mudville had a chance; and with the setting sun
Their hopes sank low—the rival team was leading "four to one."

The last half of the ninth came round, with no change in the score;
But when the first man up hit safe the crowd began to roar.
The din increased, the echo of ten thousand shouts was heard
When the pitcher hit the second and gave "four balls" to the third.

Three men on base—nobody out—three runs to tie the game!
A triple meant the highest niche in Mudville's hall of fame;
But here the rally ended and the gloom was deep as night
When the fourth one "fouled to catcher" and the fifth "flew out to right."

A dismal groan in chorus came—a scowl was on each face—
When Casey walked up, bat in hand, and slowly took his place;
His bloodshot eyes in fury gleamed; his teeth were clinched in hate;
He gave his cap a vicious hook and pounded on the plate.

But fame is fleeting as the wind, and glory fades away;
There were no wild and woolly cheers, no glad acclaim this day.
They hissed and groaned and hooted as they clamored, "Strike him out!"
But Casey gave no outward sign that he had heard this shout.

The pitcher smiled and cut one loose, across the plate it spread;
Another hiss, another groan. "Strike one!" the umpire said.
Zip! Like a shot, the second curve broke just below his knee—
"Strike two!" the umpire roared aloud; but Casey made no plea.

No roasting for the umpire now—his was an easy lot;
But here the pitcher whirled again—was that a rifle shot?
A whack! a crack! and out through space the leather pellet flew,
A blot against the distant sky, a speck against the blue.

Above the fence in center field, in rapid whirling flight,
The sphere sailed on; the blot grew dim and then was lost to sight.
Ten thousand hats were thrown in air, ten thousand threw a fit;
But no one ever found the ball that mighty Casey hit!

Oh, somewhere in this favored land dark clouds may hide the sun,
And somewhere bands no longer play and children have no fun;
And somewhere over blighted lives there hangs a heavy pall;
But Mudville hearts are happy now—for Casey hit the ball!

I Had But Fifty Cents

by Unknown

Get ready for a laugh; and the price is right.

       I took my girl to a fancy ball;
       It was a social hop;
       We waited till the folks got out,
       And the music it did stop.
       Then to a restaurant we went,
       The best one on the street;
       She said she wasn't hungry,
       But this is what she eat:
       A dozen raw, a plate of slaw,
       A chicken and a roast,
       Some applesass, and sparagrass,
       And soft-shell crabs on toast.
       A big box stew, and crackers too;
       Her appetite was immense!
       When she called for pie,
       I thought I'd die,
       For I had but fifty cents.

       She said she wasn't hungry
       And didn't care to eat,
       But I've got money in my clothes
       To bet she can't be beat;
       She took it in so cozy,
       She had an awful tank;
       She said she wasn't thirsty,
       But this is what she drank:
       A whisky skin, a glass of gin,
       Which made me shake with fear,
       A ginger pop, with rum on top,
       A schooner then of beer,
       A glass of ale, a gin cocktail;
       She should have had more sense;
       When she called for more,
       I fell on the floor,
       For I had but fifty cents.
       Of course I wasn't hungry,

And didn't care to eat,
Expecting every moment
To be kicked into the street;
She said she'd fetch her family round,
And some night we'd have fun;
When I gave the man the fifty cents,
This is what he done:
He tore my clothes,
He smashed my nose,
He hit me on the jaw,
He gave me a prize
Of a pair of black eyes
And with me swept the floor.
He took me where my pants hung loose,
And threw me over the fence;
Take my advice, don't try it twice
If you've got but fifty cents!

Methuselah

by Unknown

A clever slap at today's diet craze. But
I bet he didn't smoke.

Methuselah ate what he found on his plate,
And never, as people do now,
Did he note the amount of the calory count;
He ate it because it was chow.
He wasn't disturbed as at dinner he sat,
Devouring a roast or a pie,
To think it was lacking in granular fat
Or a couple of vitamins shy.
He cheerfully chewed each species of food,
Unmindful of troubles or fears
Lest his health might be hurt
By some fancy dessert;
And he lived over nine hundred years.

I Never Even Suggested It

by Ogden Nash

Sound familiar? OK, fellow chickens. This has the classic Ogden <u>Gnash,</u> or bite.

I know lots of men who are in love and lots
    of men who are married and lots of men who are both,
And to fall out with their loved ones is what all of them are most
    loth.
They are conciliatory at every opportunity,
Because all they want is serenity and a certain amount of impunity,
Yes, many the swain who has finally admitted that the earth is flat
Simply to sidestep a spat.

Many the masculine, Positively, or, Absolutely, which has been
    diluted to an If
Simply to avert a tiff,
Many the two-fisted executive whose domestic conversation is
    limited to a tactfully interpolated Yes,
And then he is amazed to find that he is being raked backwards over
    a bed of coals nevertheless.
These misguided fellows are under the impression that it takes two
    to make a quarrel, that you can sidestep a crisis by nonaggression
    and nonresistance,
Instead of removing yourself to a discreet distance.

Passivity can be a provoking *modus operandi*;
Consider the Empire and Gandhi.
Silence is golden, but sometimes invisibility is golder,
Because loved ones may not be able to make bricks without straw
    but often they don't need any straw to manufacture a bone to
    pick or blood in their eye or a chip for their soft white shoulder.
It is my duty, gentlemen, to inform you that women are dictators all,
    and I recommend to you this moral:
In real life it takes only one to make a quarrel.

Johnny's Hist'ry Lesson

by Nixon Waterman

Unfortunately there are millions of Johnnys in the U.S.A.
today, and some don't even remember 1492.

I think of all the things at school
    A boy has got to do,
That studyin' hist'ry, as a rule,
    Is worst of all, don't you?
Of dates there are an awful sight,
An' though I study day an' night,
There's only one I've got just right—
    That's fourteen ninety-two.

Columbus crossed the Delaware
    In fourteen ninety-two;
We whipped the British, fair an' square,
    In fourteen ninety-two.
At Concord an' at Lexington
We kept the redcoats on the run
While the band played "Johnny Get Your Gun,"
    In fourteen ninety-two.

Pat Henry, with his dyin' breath—
    In fourteen ninety-two—
Said "Gimme liberty or death!"
    In fourteen ninety-two.
An' Barbara Fritchie, so 'tis said,
Cried, "Shoot if you must this old gray head,
But I'd rather 'twould be your own instead!"
    In fourteen ninety-two.

The Pilgrims came to Plymouth Rock
    In fourteen ninety-two,
An' the Indians standin' on the dock
    Asked "What are you goin' to do?"
An' they said, "We seek your harbor drear
That our children's children's children dear
May boast that their forefathers landed here
    In fourteen ninety-two.

Miss Pocahontas saved the life,
    In fourteen ninety-two,
Of John Smith, an' became his wife
    In fourteen ninety-two.
An' the Smith tribe started then an' there,
An' now there are John Smiths everywhere,
But they didn't have any Smiths to spare
    In fourteen ninety-two.

Kentucky was settled by Daniel Boone
    In fourteen ninety-two,
An' I think the cow jumped over the moon
    In fourteen ninety-two.
Ben Franklin flew his kite so high
He drew the lightnin' from the sky,
An' Washington couldn't tell a lie,
    In fourteen ninety-two.

(Did you pick up the unexpected error about Pocahontas and John Smith? She saved Smith's life, but married John Rolfe. Back to school, Mr. Waterman.)

The Optimist

by Unknown

A little tall tale.

The optimist fell ten stories.
    At each window bar
He shouted to his friends:
    "All is well so far."

O'Grady's Goat

by Will S. Hays

Too funny to leave out. This animal got a lot of
peoples' goat.

O'Grady lived in Shanty row;
    The neighbors often said
They wished that he would move away
    Or that his goat was dead.
He kept the neighborhood in fear,
    And the children always vexed;
They couldn't tell just when or where
    The goat would pop up next.

Ould widow Casey stood wan day
    The dirty clothes to rub
Upon the washboard, when she dived
    Head foremost o'er the tub;
She lit upon her back and yelled,
    As she was lying flat:
"Go git your goon an' shoot thot baste,
    O'Grady's goat doon that."

Pat Doolan's woife hung out the wash
    Upon the line to dry;
She wint to take it in at night,
    But stopped to have a cry.
The sleeves av two red flannel shirts,
    That once were worn by Pat,
Were chewed off almost to the neck—
    O'Grady's goat doon that.

They had a party at McCune's,
    An' they were having foon,
When suddinly ther was a crash
    An' ivirybody roon.
The iseter soup fell on the floor,
    An' nearly drowned the cat;
The stove was knocked to smithereens—
    O'Grady's goat doon that.

Moike D'yle was courtin' Biddy Shea,
 Both standin' at the gate,
An' they wor jist about to kiss
 Aich oother sly and shwate.
They coom togither like two rams,
 An' mashed their noses flat.
They niver shpake whin they goes by,
 O'Grady's goat doon that.

Folks in O'Grady's neighborhood
 All live in fear or fright;
They think it's certain death to go
 Around there after night.
An' in their shlape they sees a ghost
 Upon the air afloat,
An' wake thimselves by shoutin' out:
 "Luck out for Grady's goat."

One winter morning whin the shnow
 Was deep upon the ground,
Men, women, children—in a crowd—
 Were sad an' shtandin' 'round
The form of wan, cold, stiff an' dead,
 An' shtickin' down his throat
Was Mag McGinty's bushtlefast,
 That inded Grady's goat.

Some Little Bug
by Roy Atwell

Easy to go on a strict diet (boiled water) after reading this
delightful bit of humor.

In these days of indigestion
It is oftentimes a question
    As to what to eat and what to leave alone;
For each microbe and bacillus
Has a different way to kill us,
    And in time they always claim us for their own.
There are germs of every kind
In any food that you can find
    In the market or upon the bill of fare.
Drinking water's just as risky
As the so-called deadly whiskey,
    And it's often a mistake to breathe the air.

Some little bug is going to find you some day,
Some little bug will creep behind you some day,
    Then he'll send for his bug friends
    And all your earthly trouble ends;
Some little bug is going to find you some day.
The inviting green cucumber
Gets most everybody's number,
    While the green corn has a system of its own;
Though a radish seems nutritious
Its behaviour is quite vicious,
    And a doctor will be coming to your home.
Eating lobster cooked or plain
Is only flirting with ptomaine,
    While an oyster sometimes has a lot to say,
But the clams we eat in chowder
Make the angels chant the louder,
    For they know that we'll be with them right away.

Take a slice of nice fried onion
And you're fit for Dr. Munyon,
    Apple dumplings kill you quicker than a train.
Chew a cheesy midnight "rabbit"

And a grave you'll soon inhabit—
    Ah, to eat at all is such a foolish game.
Eating huckleberry pie
Is a pleasing way to die.
    While sauerkraut brings on softening of the brain.
When you eat banana fritters
Every undertaker titters,
    And the casket makers nearly go insane.

Some little bug is going to find you some day,
Some little bug will creep behind you some day,
    With a nervous little quiver
    He'll give cirrhosis of the liver;
Some little bug is going to find you some day.
When cold storage vaults I visit
I can only say what is it
    Makes poor mortals fill their systems with such stuff?
Now, for breakfast, prunes are dandy
If a stomach pump is handy
    And your doctor can be found quite soon enough.
Eat a plate of fine pigs' knuckles
And the headstone cutter chuckles,
    While the grave digger makes a note upon his cuff.
Eat that lovely red bologna
And you'll wear a wooden kimona,
    As your relatives start scrappin' 'bout your stuff.

Some little bug is going to find you some day,
Some little bug will creep behind you some day,
    Eating juicy sliced pineapple
    Makes the sexton dust the chapel;
Some little bug is going to find you some day.

All those crazy foods they mix
Will float us 'cross the River Styx,
    Or they'll start us climbing up the milky way.
And the meals we eat in courses
Mean a hearse and two black horses
    So before a meal some people always pray.
Luscious grapes breed 'pendicitis,
And the juice leads to gastritis,

So there's only death to greet us either way;
And fried liver's nice, but, mind you,
Friends will soon ride slow behind you
    And the papers then will have nice things to say.

Some little bug is going to find you some day,
Some little bug will creep behind you some day
    Eat some sauce, they call it chili,
    On your breast they'll place a lily;
Some little bug is going to find you some day.

The Patter of the Shingle

by Unknown

Maybe a few more shingles would help reduce the
present juvenile problems. Just kidding, A.C.L.U.

When the angry passion gathering in my mother's face I see,
And she leads me to the bedroom gently lays me on her knee,
Then I know that I will catch it, and my flesh in fancy itches
As I listen for the patter of the shingle on my breeches.

Every tingle of the shingle has an echo and a sting
And a thousand burning fancies into active being spring,
And a thousand bees and hornets 'neath my coattail seem to swarm,
As I listen to the patter of the shingle, oh, so warm.

In a splutter comes my father—who I supposed had gone—
To survey the situation and tell her to lay it on,
To see her bending o'er me as I listen to the strain
Played by her and by the shingle in a wild and weird refrain.

In a sudden intermission, which appears my only chance,
I say, "Strike gently, Mother, or you'll split my Sunday pants!"
She stops a moment, draws her breath, and the shingle holds aloft,
And says "I had not thought of that, my son, just take them off."

Holy Moses and the angels! cast your pitying glances down,
And thou, O family doctor, put a good soft poultice on.
And may I with fools and dunces everlastingly commingle,
If I ever say another word when my mother wields the shingle!

The Walrus and the Carpenter
by Lewis Carroll (1832-1898)

A most entertaining parody on the machinations of this very odd pair and their "friends," the oysters. The highlighted verse is often quoted. This is taken from Carroll's second book about Alice's adventures, *Through the Looking Glass.*

The sun was shining on the sea
        Shining with all his might:
He did his very best to make
        The billows smooth and bright—
And this was odd, because it was
        The middle of the night.

The moon was shining sulkily,
        Because she thought the sun
Had got no business to be there
        After the day was done—
"It's very rude of him," she said,
        "To come and spoil the fun!"

The sea was wet as wet could be,
        The sands were dry as dry.
You could not see a cloud, because
        No cloud was in the sky:
No birds were flying overhead—
        There were no birds to fly.

The Walrus and the Carpenter
    Were walking close at hand:
They wept like anything to see
    Such quantities of sand.
"If this were only cleared away,"
    They said, "it would be grand!"

"If seven maids with seven mops
    Swept it for half a year,
Do you suppose," the Walrus said,
    "That they could get it clear?"
"I doubt it," said the Carpenter,
    And shed a bitter tear.

"O Oysters, come and walk with us!"
    The Walrus did beseech.
"A pleasant talk, a pleasant walk,
    Along the briny beach:
We cannot do with more than four,
    To give a hand to each."

The eldest Oyster looked at him,
    But never a word he said:
The eldest Oyster winked his eye,
    And shook his heavy head—
Meaning to say he did not choose
    To leave the oyster-bed.

But four young Oysters hurried up,
    All eager for the treat:
Their coats were brushed, their faces washed,
    Their shoes were clean and neat—
And this was odd, because, you know,
    They hadn't any feet.

Four other Oysters followed them,
    And yet another four;
And thick and fast they came at last,
    And more, and more, and more—
All hopping through the frothy waves,
    And scrambling to the shore.

The Walrus and the Carpenter
　　Walked on a mile or so,
And then they rested on a rock
　　Conveniently low:
And all the little Oysters stood
　　And waited in a row.

"The time has come," the Walrus said,
　　"To talk of many things:
Of shoes and ships and sealing-wax,
　　Of cabbages and kings;
And why the sea is boiling hot—
　　And whether pigs have wings."

"But wait a bit," the Oysters cried,
　　"Before we have our chat;
For some of us are out of breath,
　　And all of us are fat!"
"No hurry!" said the Carpenter.
　　They thanked him much for that.

"A loaf of bread," the Walrus said,
　　"Is what we chiefly need:
Pepper and vinegar besides
　　Are very good indeed—
Now, if you're ready, Oysters dear,
　　We can begin to feed."

"But not on us!" the Oysters cried,
　　Turning a little blue.
"After such kindness, that would be
　　A dismal thing to do!"
"The night is fine," the Walrus said.
　　"Do you admire the view?"

"It was so kind of you to come!
     And you are very nice!"
The Carpenter said nothing but
     "Cut us another slice.
I wish you were not quite so deaf—
     I've had to ask you twice!"

"It seems a shame," the Walrus said,
     "To play them such a trick,
After we've brought them out so far,
     And made them trot so quick!"
The Carpenter said nothing but
     "The butter's spread too thick!"

"I weep for you," the Walrus said:
     "I deeply sympathize."
With sobs and tears he sorted out
     Those of the largest size,
Holding his pocket-handkerchief
     Before his streaming eyes.

"O Oysters," said the Carpenter,
     "You've had a pleasant run!
Shall we be trotting home again?"
     But answer came there none—
And this was scarcely odd, because
     They'd eaten every one.

King John and the Abbot of Canterbury

by Unknown

A very entertaining story with a very ingenious finale.

An ancient story I'll tell you anon
        Of a notable prince, that was called King John;
And he ruled England with main and with might,
        For he did great wrong and maintained little right.

And I'll tell you a story, a story so merry,
        Concerning the Abbot of Canterbury;
How for his housekeeping and high renown,
        They rode post for him to fair London town.

An hundred men, the King did hear say,
        The Abbot kept in his house every day;
And fifty gold chains, without any doubt,
        In velvet coats waited the Abbot about.

"How now, Father Abbot, I hear it of thee,
        Thou keepest a far better house than me;
And for thy housekeeping and high renown,
        I fear thou work'st treason against my crown."

"My liege," quo' the Abbot, "I would it were knowne,
        I never spend nothing but what is my owne;
And I trust your Grace will not put me in fear,
        For spending of my owne true-gotten gear."

"Yes, yes, Father Abbot, thy fault is highe,
        And now for the same thou needst must die;
For except thou canst answer me questions three,
        Thy head shall be smitten from thy bodie.

"And first," quo' the King, "when I'm in this stead,
  With my crowns of gold so faire on my head,
Among all my liege-men, so noble of birthe,
  Thous must tell to one penny what I am worthe.

"Secondlye, tell me, without any doubt,
  How soon I may ride the whole world about,
And at the third question thou must not shrink,
  But tell me here truly what I do think."

"Oh, these are hard questions for my shallow wit,
  Nor can I answer your Grace as yet;
But if you will give me but three weeks space,
  I'll do my endeavor to answer your Grace."

"Now three weeks' space to thee will I give,
  And that is the longest time thou hast to live;
For if thou dost not answer my questions three,
  Thy land and thy livings are forfeit to me."

Away rode the Abbot all sad at that word,
  And he rode to Cambridge and Oxenford;
But never a doctor there was so wise,
  That could with his learning an answer devise.

Then home rode the Abbot of comfort so cold,
  And he met his Shepherd a-going to fold:
"How now, my Lord Abbot, you are welcome home;
  What news do you bring us from good King John?"

"Sad news, sad news, Shepherd, I must give,
  That I have but three days more to live;
I must answer the King his questions three,
  Or my head will be smitten from my bodie.

"The first is to tell him, there in that stead,
  With his crown of gold so fair on his head,
Among all his liege-men so noble of birth
  To within one penny of what he is worth.

"The seconde, to tell him, without any doubt,
How soone he may ride this whole world about:
And at the third question I must not shrink,
But tell him truly what he does think."

"Now cheer up, Sire Abbot, did you never hear yet,
That a fool he may learne a wise man wit?
Lend me a horse, and serving-men, and your apparel,
And I'll ride to London to answer your quarrel.

"Nay, frown not, if it hath bin told unto me,
I am like your Lordship, as ever may be:
And if you will but lend me your gown,
There is none shall know us in fair London town."

"Now horses and serving-men thou shalt have,
With sumptuous array most gallant and brave;
With crozier, and mitre, and rochet, and cope,
Fit to appear 'fore our Father the Pope."

"Now welcome, Sire Abbot," the King he did say,
"'Tis well thou'rt come back to keep thy day;
For and if thou canst answer my questions three,
Thy living and thy life both saved shall be.

"And first, when thou seest me, here in this stead,
With my crown of golde so fair on my head,
Among all my liege-men so noble of birth,
Tell me to one penny what I am worth."

"For thirty pence our Saviour was sold
Among the false Jews, as I have been told:
And twenty-nine is the worth of thee,
For I think, thou art one penny worse than he."

The King he laughed, and swore by St. Bittel,
"I do not think I had been worth so little!
Now, secondly, tell me, without any doubt,
How soon I may ride this whole world about."

"You must rise with the sun, and ride with the same,
    Until the next morning he riseth again;
And then your Grace need not make any doubt
    But in twenty-four hours you'll ride it about."

The King he laughed, and swore by St. Jone,
    "I did not think it could be done so soon.
Now from the third question thou must not shrink,
    But tell me here truly what I do think."

"Yes, that I shall do and make your Grace merry;
    You think I'm the Abbot of Canterbury;
But I'm his poor shepherd, as plain you may see,
    That am come to beg pardon for him and for me."

The King he laughed, and swore by the mass,
    "I'll make thee Lord Abbot this day in his place!"
"Nay, nay, my Liege, be not in such speed,
    For alack, I can neither write nor read."

"Four nobles a week, then, I will give thee,
    For this merry jest thou hast shown unto me;
And tell the old Abbot, when thou gettest home,
    Thou hast brought him a pardon from good King John."

The Goat

by Unknown

This has been around for years. Here are two
versions. I learned the second as a child. I like
my version by far.

There was a man, now please take note,
There was a man, who had a goat.
He lov'd that goat, indeed he did,
He lov'd that goat, just like a kid.

One day that goat felt frisk and fine,
Ate three red shirts from off the line.
The man he grabbed him by the back,
And tied him to a railroad track.

But when the train hove into sight,
That goat grew pale and green with fright.
He heaved a sigh, as if in pain,
Coughed up those shirts and flagged the train.

❖ ❖ ❖ ❖ ❖

There was a man, his name was Bert,
His wife bought him a bright red shirt.
Bert had a goat, his name was Kid.
Now I'll tell you, what that goat did.

He ate that shirt, right off the line,
But good old Bert, caught him in time,
He swore he would, that shirt get back,
So he tied that goat, to the railroad track.

Now Mrs. Bert began to cry,
That goat he was too cute to die.
Kid coughed and kicked, with might and main,
Coughed up that shirt, and flagged the train.

The Deacon's Masterpiece
or "The One-Hoss Shay"
by *Oliver Wendell Holmes (1809-1894)*

If you can read this without laughing, you either
deserve a medal for control or else have no sense
of humor whatsoever. Another of what I call the "Great Ones."

Have you heard of the wonderful one-hoss shay,
That was built in such a logical way
It ran a hundred years to a day,
And then, of a sudden, it—ah, but stay,
I'll tell you what happened without delay,
Scaring the parson into fits,
Frightening people out of their wits,
Have you heard of that, I say?

Seventeen hundred and fifty-five.
Georgius Secundus[1] was then alive,—
Snuffy old drone from the German hive.
That was the year[2] when Lisbon-town
Saw the earth open and gulp her down,
And Braddock's army[3] was done so brown,
Left without a scalp to its crown.
It was on the terrible Earthquake-day
That the Deacon finished the one-hoss shay.

Now in building of chaises, I tell you what,
There is always somewhere a weakest spot,—
In hub, tire, felloe[4], in spring or thill,[5]
In panel, or crossbar, or floor, or sill,
In screw, bolt, thoroughbrace[6],—lurking still,
Find it somewhere you must and will,—
Above or below, or within or without,—
And that's the reason, beyond a doubt,
A chaise breaks down, but doesn't wear out.

But the Deacon swore (as Deacons do,
With an "I dew vum," or an "I tell yeou")
He would build one shay to beat the taown
'N' the keounty 'n' all the kentry raoun';
It should be so built that it couldn' break daown
"Fur," said the Deacon, "'t's mighty plain
Thut the weakes' places mus' stan' the strain;
'N' the way t' fix it, uz I maintain, is only jest
T' make that place uz strong uz the rest."

So the Deacon inquired of the village folk
Where he could find the strongest oak,
That couldn't be split nor bent nor broke,—
That was for spokes and floor and sills;
He sent for lancewood to make the thills;
The crossbars were ash, from the straightest trees;
The panels of white-wood, that cuts like cheese,
But lasts like iron for things like these;
The hubs of logs from the "Settler's ellum,"—
Last of its timber,—they couldn't sell 'em,
Never an axe had seen their chips,
And the wedges flew from between their lips,
Their blunt ends frizzled like celery-tips;
Step and prop-iron, bolt and screw,
Spring, tire, axle, and linchpin too,
Steel of the finest, bright and blue;
Thoroughbrace bison-skin, thick and wide;
Boot, top, dasher, from tough old hide
Found in the pit when the tanner died.
That was the way he "put her through."—
"There!" said the Deacon, "naow she'll dew!"

Do! I tell you, I rather guess
She was a wonder, and nothing less!
Colts grew horses, beards turned gray,
Deacon and deaconess dropped away,
Children and grandchildren—where were they?
But there stood the stout old one-hoss shay
As fresh as on Lisbon-earthquake-day!

EIGHTEEN HUNDRED;—it came and found
The Deacon's masterpiece strong and sound.
Eighteen hundred increased by ten;—
"Hahnsum kerridge" they called it then.
Eighteen hundred and twenty came;—
Running as usual; much, the same.
Thirty and forty at last arrive,
And then come fifty, and FIFTY-FIVE.

Little of all we value here
Wakes on the morn of its hundredth year
Without both feeling and looking queer.
In fact, there's nothing that keeps its youth,
So far as I know, but a tree and truth.
(This is a moral that runs at large;
Take it. You're welcome. No extra Charge.)
FIRST OF NOVEMBER,—the Earthquake-day.—
There are traces of age in the one-hoss shay,
A general flavor of mild decay,
But nothing local as one may say.
There couldn't be,—for the Deacon's art
Had made it so like in every part
That there wasn't a chance for one to start.
For the wheels were just as strong as the thills,
And the floor was just as strong as the sills,
And the panels just as strong as the floor.
And the whippletree[7] neither less nor more,
And the back-crossbar as strong as the fore,
And spring, and axle and hub encore.
And yet, as a whole, it is past a doubt
In another hour it will be worn out!

First of November, Fifty-five!
This morning the parson takes a drive.
Now, small boys, get out of the way!
Here comes the wonderful one-hoss shay,
Drawn by a rat-tailed, ewe-necked bay.
"Huddup" said the parson. Off went they.
The parson was working his Sunday's text,—
Had got to fifthly, and stopped perplexed

At what the—Moses—was coming next.
All at once the horse stood still,
Close by the meet'n'-house on the hill.
First a shiver, and then a thrill,
Then something decidedly like a spill,—
And the parson was sitting up on a rock,
At half-past nine by the meet'n'-house clock,
Just the hour of the Earthquake shock!
What do you think the parson found,
When he got up and stared around?
The poor old chaise in a heap or mound,
As if it had been to the mill and ground!
You see, of course, if you're not a dunce,
How it went to pieces all at once,—
All at once, and nothing first,—
Just as bubbles do when they burst.

End of the wonderful one-hoss shay,
Logic is logic. That's all I say.

---

[1] *King George II of England 1683-1760. He preceded George III who was King during the Revolutionary War.*

[2] *A terrible earthquake destroyed Lisbon, Portugal on November 1, 1755.*

[3] *General Braddock, who was leading the British against the French and Indians, was badly beaten but was saved from total disaster by his aide George Washington. He subsequently died from the wounds received in this battle.*

[4] *Felloe - The Rim of the Wheel.*

[5] *Thill - one of the shafts to attach to the horse*

[6] *Thoroughbrace - strong brace between front and back springs.*

[7] *Whippletree - the crossbar behind the horse.*

The Cremation of Sam McGee
by Robert Service (1874-1958)

Gruesome but funny. A real combination you won't soon forget. With the great rhythmic beat of the poetry that is so classic of Service. This must be the best example of "double rhyming" in all of poetry. That is rhyming within each line and at the ends of the line for the entire poem. Robert Service was born in England but moved to Western Canada when he was around 20. He spent many years in the Yukon, which enabled him to so accurately picture that area in this poem, and in other poems in this book, notably *The Spell of the Yukon*, *The Law of the Yukon*, and *The Shooting of Dan McGrew*.

> There are strange things done in the midnight sun
> By the men who moil for gold;
> The Arctic trails have their secret tales
> That would make your blood run cold;
> The Northern Lights have seen queer sights,
> But the queerest they ever did see
> Was that night on the marge of Lake Lebarge
> I cremated Sam McGee.

Now Sam McGee was from Tennessee, where the cotton blooms and blows.
Why he left his home in the South to roam 'round the Pole, God only knows.
He was always cold, but the land of gold seemed to hold him like a spell;
Though he'd often say in his homely way that "he'd sooner live in hell."

On a Christmas Day we were mushing our way over the Dawson trail.
Talk of your cold! through the parka's fold it stabbed like a driven nail.
If our eyes we'd close, then the lashes froze till sometimes we couldn't see;
It wasn't much fun, but the only one to whimper was Sam McGee.

And that very night, as we lay packed tight in our robes beneath the
    snow,
And the dogs were fed, and the stars o'erhead were dancing heel
    and toe,
He turned to me, and "Cap," says he, "I'll cash in this trip, I guess;
And if I do, I'm asking that you won't refuse my last request."

Well, he seemed so low that I couldn't say no; then he says with a
    sort of moan:
"It's the curs'ed cold, and it's got right hold till I'm chilled clean
    through to the bone.
Yet 'tain't being dead—it's my awful dread of the icy grave that pains;
So I want you to swear that, foul or fair, you'll cremate my last
    remains."

A pal's last need is a thing to heed, so I swore I would not fail;
And we started on at the streak of dawn; but God! he looked ghastly
    pale.
He crouched on the sleigh, and he raved all day of his home in
    Tennessee;
And before nightfall a corpse was all that was left of Sam McGee.

There wasn't a breath in that land of death, and I hurried, horror-
    driven,
With a corpse half hid that I couldn't get rid, because of a promise
    given;
It was lashed to the sleigh, and it seemed to say: "You may tax your
    brawn and brains,
But you promised true, and it's up to you to cremate those last
    remains."

Now a promise made is a debt unpaid, and the trail has its own
    stern code.
In the days to come, though my lips were dumb, in my heart how I
    cursed that load.
In the long, long night, by the lone firelight, while the huskies,
    round in a ring,
Howled out their woes to the homeless snows—O God! how I
    loathed the thing.

And every day that quiet clay seemed to heavy and heavier grow;
And on I went, though the dogs were spent and the grub was getting
    low;
The trail was bad, and I felt half mad, but I swore I would not give in;
And I'd often sing to the hateful thing, and it hearkened with a grin.

Till I came to the marge of Lake Lebarge, and a derelict there lay;
It was jammed in the ice, but I saw in a trice it was called the "Alice
    May."
And I looked at it, and I thought a bit, and I looked at my frozen
    chum;
Then "Here, " said I, with a sudden cry, "is my cre-ma-tor-eum."

Some planks I tore from the cabin floor, and I lit the boiler fire;
Some coal I found that was lying around, and I heaped the fuel
    higher;
The flames just soared, and the furnace roared—such a blaze you
    seldom see;
And I burrowed a hole in the glowing coal, and I stuffed in Sam
    McGee.

Then I made a hike, for I didn't like to hear him sizzle so;
And the heavens scowled, and the huskies howled, and the wind
    began to blow.
It was icy cold, but the hot sweat rolled down my cheeks, and I don't
    know why;
And the greasy smoke in an inky cloak went streaking down the sky.

I do not know how long in the snow I wrestled with grisly fear;
But the stars came out and they danced about ere again I ventured
    near;
I was sick with dread, but I bravely said: "I'll just take a peep inside.
I guess he's cooked, and it's time I looked"; . . . then the door I
    opened wide.

And there sat Sam, looking cool and calm, in the heart of the
    furnace roar;
And he wore a smile you could see a mile, and he said: "Please close
    that door.
It's fine in here, but I greatly fear you'll let in the cold and storm—
Since I left Plumtree, down in Tennessee, it's the first time I've been
    warm."

There are strange things done in the midnight sun
    By the men who moil for gold;
The Arctic trails have their secret tales
    That would make your blood run cold;
The Northern Lights have seen queer sights,
    But the queerest they ever did see
Was that night on the marge of Lake Lebarge
    I cremated Sam McGee.

Time's Revenge
by *Walter Learned (1847-1915)*

As the saying goes, "It's all in the eyes of the
beholder."

When I was ten and she was fifteen—
    Ah, me! How fair I thought her.
She treated with disdainful mien
    The homage that I brought her,
And, in a patronizing way,
Would of my shy advances say:
    "It's really quite absurd, you see;
    He's very much too young for me."

I'm twenty now, she twenty-five—
    Well, well! How old she's growing.
I fancy that my suit might thrive
    If pressed again; but, owing
To great discrepancy in age,
Her marked attentions don't engage
    My young affections, for, you see,
    She's really quite too old for me.

Repentance

by Robert Service (1874-1958)

Just like us all—"manana, is good enough for me."
However, the advice is not the best; too many
people wait too long to repent, and miss the last
bus.

"If you repent," the Parson said,
   "Your sins will be forgiven.
Aye, even on your dying bed
   You're not too late for Heaven."

That's just my cup of tea, I thought,
   Though for my sins I sorrow;
Since salvation is easy bought
   I will repent... to-morrow.

To-morrow and to-morrow went,
   But though my youth was flying,
I was reluctant to repent,
   Having no fear of dying.

'Tis plain, I mused, the more I sin,
   (To Satan's jubilation)
When I repent the more I'll win
   Celestial approbation.

So still I sin, and though I fail
   To get snow-whitely shriven,
My timing's good—I hope to hail
   The last bus up to Heaven.

Maternity
by Robert Service (1874-1958)

A <u>plane</u> lesson in solid geometry (or maybe, '<u>trickanometry</u>'.)

> There once was a Square, such a square little Square,
>   And he loved a trim Triangle;
> But she was a flirt and around her skirt
>   Vainly she made him dangle.
> Oh he wanted to wed and he had no dread
>   Of domestic woes and wrangles;
> For he thought that his fate was to procreate
>   Cute little Squares and Triangles.
>
> Now it happened one day on that geometric way
>   There swaggered a big bold Cube,
> With a haughty stare and he made that Square
>   Have the air of a perfect boob;
> To his solid spell the Triangle fell,
>   And she thrilled with love's sweet sickness,
> For she took delight in his breadth and height
>   But how she adored his thickness!
>
> So that poor little Square just died of despair,
>   For his love he could not strangle;
> While the bold Cube led to the bridal bed
>   That cute and acute Triangle.
> The Square's sad lot she has long forgot,
>   And his passionate pretensions . . .
> For she dotes on her kids—Oh such cute Pyramids
>   In a world of three dimensions.

The Birth of St. Patrick

by Samuel Lover (1797-1868)

They could sure use a Father Mulcahy over there
now. Just try mentioning compromise.

On the eighth day of March it was, some people say,
That Saint Pathrick at midnight he first saw the day;
While others declare 'twas the ninth he was born,
And 'twas all a mistake between midnight and morn;
For mistakes will occur in a hurry and shock,
And some blamed the babby—and some blamed the clock—
Till with all their cross-questions sure no one could know
If the child was too fast, or the clock was too slow.

Now the first faction-fight in owld Ireland, they say,
Was all on account of Saint Pathrick's birthday:
Some fought for the eighth—for the ninth more would die,
And who wouldn't see right, sure they blackened his eye!
At last, both the factions so positive grew,
That each kept a birthday, so Pat then had two,
Till Father Mulcahy, who showed them their sins,
Said, "No one could have two birthdays, but a twins."

Says he, "Boys, don't be fightin' for eight or for nine,
Don't be always dividin'—but sometimes combine;
Combine eight with nine, and seventeen is the mark,
So let that be his birthday." — "Amen," says the clerk.
"If he wasn't a twins, sure our hist'ry will show
That, at least, he's worth any two saints that we know!"
Then they all got blind dhrunk—which complated their bliss,
And we keep up the practice from that day to this.

The V-A-S-E

by James Jeffrey Roche (1847-1908)

And the winner, my deahr! (I wonder how they would have done with an Urn.)

From the madding crowd they stand apart,
The maidens four and the Work of Art;

And none might tell from sight alone
In which had Culture ripest grown,—

The Gotham Million fair to see,
The Philadelphia Pedigree,

The Boston Mind of azure hue,
Or the soulful Soul from Kalamazoo,—

For all loved Art in a seemly way,
With an earnest soul and a capital A.

Long they worshipped; but no one broke
The sacred stillness, until up spoke

The Western one from the nameless place,
Who blushing said: "What a lovely vace!"

Over three faces a sad smile flew,
And they edged away from Kalamazoo.

But Gotham's haughty soul was stirred
To crush the stranger with one small word.

Deftly hiding reproof in praise,
She cries: "'Tis, indeed, a lovely vaze!"

But brief her unworthy triumph when
The lofty one from the home of Penn,

With the consciousness of two grandpapas,
Exclaims: "It is quite a lovely vahs!"

And glances round with an anxious thrill,
Awaiting the word of Beacon Hill.

But the Boston maid smiles courteouslee,
And gently murmurs: "Oh pardon me!

"I did not catch your remark, because
I was so entranced with that charming vaws!"

(She must not have been a Cabot! She wouldn't have been talking to these inferiors.)

The Purple Cow

by Gelett Burgess (1866-
A Classic. I'll take my chances on quoting it here.

I never saw a Purple Cow;
       I never hope to see one;
But I can tell you, anyhow,
       I'd rather see than be one.

—(five years later)—

Ah, yes, I wrote the "Purple Cow"—
       I'm sorry, now, I wrote it!
But I can tell you, anyhow,
       I'll kill you if you quote it!

—(thousands of chuckles later)—

(Gelett, We enjoy your "Purple Cow"
       And although you say don't quote it,
I'm going to tell you anyhow
       I'm awfully glad you wrote it.
                        –The Editor)

The Twins

by Henry Sambrooke Leigh (1837-1883)

A clever little poem—double trouble, with a
twist.

In form and feature, face and limb,
    I grew so like my brother,
That folks got taking me for him,
    And each for one another.
It puzzled all our kith and kin,
    It reached a fearful pitch;
For one of us was born a twin,
    Yet not a soul knew which.

One day, to make the matter worse,
    Before our names were fixed,
As we were being washed by a nurse,
    We got completely mixed;
And thus, you see, by fate's decree,
    Or rather nurse's whim,
My brother John got christened me,
    And I got christened him.

The fatal likeness even dogged
    My footsteps when at school,
And I was always getting flogged,
    For John turned out a fool.
I put this question, fruitlessly,
    To every one I knew,
"What *would* you do, if you were me,
    To prove that you were *you?*"

Our close resemblance turned the tide
    Of my domestic life,
For somehow, my intended bride
    Became my brother's wife.
In fact, year after year the same
    Absurd mistakes went on,
And when I died, the neighbors came
    And buried brother John.

The Little Elf

by John Kendrick Bangs (1862-1922)

Can't beat this repartee; that's really thinking on your feet.

> I met a little Elf-man, once,
>> Down where the lilies blow.
> I asked him why he was so small,
>> And why he didn't grow.
>
> He slightly frowned, and with his eye
>> He looked me through and through,
> "I'm quite as big for me," said he,
>> "As you are big for you."

On the Aristocracy of Harvard

by John Collins Bassidy

A Harvard truism.

> And this is good old Boston,
>> The home of the bean and the cod,
> Where the Lowells talk to the Cabots
>> And the Cabots talk only to God.

On the Democracy of Yale

by Frederick Scheetz Jones

An Eli retort.

> Here's to the town of New Haven,
>> The home of the Truth and the Light,
> Where God talks to Jones in the very same tones
>> That He uses with Hadley and Dwight!

Lay of Ancient Rome

by Thomas Ybarra

If you didn't study any Latin, I'm sorry. If you did,
you'll love this bit of erratum.

Oh, the Roman was a rogue,
    He erat was, you bettum;
He ran his automobolis
    And smoked his cigarettum;
He wore a diamond studibus
    And elegant cravattum,
A maxima cum laude shirt,
    And such a stylish hattum!

He loved the luscious hic-hæc-hoc,
    And bet on games and equi;
At times he won; at others, though,
    He got it in the nequi;
He winked (quo usque tandem?)
    At puellas on the Forum,
And sometimes even made
    Those goo-goo oculorum!

He frequently was seen
    At combats gladiatorial,
And ate enough to feed
    Ten boarders at Memorial;
He often went on sprees
    And said, on starting homus,
"Hic labor—opus est,
    Oh, where's my hic—hic—domus?"

Although he lived in Rome—
    Of all the arts the middle—
He was (excuse the phrase)
    A horrid individ'l;
Ah! what a different thing
    Was the homo (dative, hominy)
Of far away B.C.
    From us of Anno Domini.

Fore

by Samuel N. Etheredge

Duck! Here comes another goof ball.

He may have seemed entirely sane
    With no signs of softening of the brain,
But then he sank his first long putt;
    Voila! Presto! A hopeless golf nut.

A hunter always took time to spread the word,
    How much fun it was to shoot a bird.
But now you ought to hear his noise,
    When his bird on eighteen beats all the boys.

And the fisherman with his hook and line
    That was tangled almost half the time.
Now he never hits a drive without thinking twice,
    Will it hold the line, will it hook, or slice.

We know doctors never make an incision
    Without first making a firm decision.
But now their only decision seems to be
    Should I hit a full four-iron, or an easy three.

That young lawyer always wants to go back to
    His favorite claim, that crazy ipso facto.
But no matter what new law he propounds
    The fact is just this; his ball's out of bounds.

Tennis players are sure golf's just another racket,
    They've hit so many balls with a racquet.
But their hands turn to butter when they grasp a putter
    And Oh Boy! you should hear what they mutter.

The ladies, God bless 'em, have found it fun too
    When the kids are in school, there's a game to run to.
But with some of the he-men, they don't make a hit,
    When they step up and outdrive them by quite a little bit.

So, here's to the great leveler of the whole human race
    It's only a game, but it's firmed up its place,
As hacker and pro, the great and the small,
    Try to solve the enigma of that little golf ball.

~~Contract~~ Contact Bridge

by Unknown

This one has to bring a smile to bridge players of all abilities. I hope you love Bridge as much as I do. What a wonderful invention.

"It was the night before Christmas,
    Two guests in our house
Had started to play bridge
    With me and my spouse."

"Please tell me," she shouted,
    "Why didn't you double?
Twas plain from the start
    That we had them in trouble."

"Tis futile, my dear,"
    Said I, taking no stand,
"To discuss it with you—
    Let us play the next hand."

"Remember next time,"
    Said she making a frown,
"To double a contract
    That is sure to go down."

So I picked up my cards
    In a downtrodden state,
Then I opened one spade
    And awaited my fate.

The guy sitting South
    Was like many I've known,
He played and he bid
    In a world all his own.

East dealer
North-South vulnerable.

NORTH
S: 9 8 7 6
H: 6 5 4 3 2
D: 8 7 6 5
C:—

WEST
S:—
H: Q J 10 9
D: K Q J 10 9
C: K Q J 10

EAST
S: A K Q J 10
H: A K 8 7
D:—
C: A 9 8 7

SOUTH
S: 5 4 3 2
H:—
D: A 4 3 2
C: 6 5 4 3 2

"Two diamonds," he countered
    With scarcely a care,
The ace in his hand
    Gave him courage to spare.

My wife, she smiled faintly,
    And tossing her head,
Leaned over the table;
    "I double," she said.

And North for some reason
    I cannot determine,
Bid two hearts as though
    He were preaching a sermon.

I grinned as I doubled,
    Enjoying the fun,
And turned round to South
    To see where he would run.

But South, undistressed,
  Not at loss for a word,
Came forth with two spades—
  Did I hear what I heard?

The other two passed
  And in sheer disbelief,
I said, "Double, my friend,
  That'll bring you to grief."

South passed with a nod,
  His composure serene;
My wife with a flourish
  Led out the heart queen.

I sat there and chuckled
  Inside o'er their fix—
But South very calmly
  Ran off eight straight tricks.

He ruffed the first heart
  In his hand right away,
And then trumped a club
  On the very next play.

He crossruffed the hand
  At a breathtaking pace
Till I was left holding
  Five spades to the ace.

In anguish my wife cried,
  "Your mind's growing old,
Don't you see six no-trump
  In this hand is ice cold?"

By doubling this time
  I'd committed a sin.
It just goes to prove
  That you never can win.

(Why did she get so upset? The difference was a mere 1860 points! Also, had she, on a hunch, led the King of Diamonds, East-West could have taken all 13 tricks for an eight trick set, doubled. For a 2300, plus 150 honors, set!)

The Shooting of Dan McGrew
by Robert Service (1874-1958)

Back in Yukon territory again. Typical Robert Service.
Not for the tender-hearted, but great for the strong.
Gal Lou was true to her lover, down to the last poke
of gold he had.

A bunch of the boys were whooping it up in
the Malamute saloon;
The kid that handles the music-box was hitting a jag-time tune;
Back of the bar, in a solo game, sat Dangerous Dan McGrew,
And watching his luck was his light-o'-love, the lady that's known as
Lou.

When out of the night, which was fifty below, and into the din and
the glare,
There stumbled a miner fresh from the creeks, dog-dirty, and loaded
for bear.
He looked like a man with a foot in the grave and scarcely the
strength of a louse,
Yet he tilted a poke of dust on the bar, and he called for drinks for
the house.
There was none could place the stranger's face, though we searched
ourselves for a clue;
But we drank his health, and the last to drink was Dangerous Dan
McGrew.

There's men that somehow just grip your eyes, and hold them hard
like a spell;
And such was he, and he looked to me like a man who had lived in
hell;
With a face most hair, and the dreary stare of a dog whose day is done,
As he watered the green stuff in his glass, and the drops fell one by
one.
Then I got to figgering who he was, and wondering what he'd do,
And I turned my head—and there watching him was the lady that's
known as Lou.

His eyes went rubbering round the room, and he seemed in a kind
    of daze,
Till at last that old piano fell in the way of his wandering gaze.
The rag-time kid was having a drink; there was no one else on the
    stool,
So the stranger stumbles across the room, and flops down there like
    a fool.
In a buckskin shirt that was glazed with dirt he sat, and I saw him
    sway;
Then he clutched the keys with his talon hands—my God! but that
    man could play.

Were you ever out in the Great Alone, when the moon was awful
    clear,
And the icy mountains hemmed you in with a silence you most
    could hear;
With only the howl of a timber wolf, and you camped there in the
    cold,
A half-dead thing in a stark, dead world, clean mad for the muck
    called gold;
While high overhead, green, yellow and red, the North Lights swept
    in bars?—
Then you've a hunch what the music meant . . . hunger and night
    and the stars.

And hunger not of the belly kind, that's banished with bacon and
    beans,
But the gnawing hunger of lonely men for a home and all that it
    means;
For a fireside far from the cares that are, four walls and a roof above;
But oh! so cramful of cosy joy, and crowned with a woman's love—
A woman dearer than all the world, and true as Heaven is true—
(God! how ghastly she looks through her rouge,—the lady that's
    known as Lou.)

Then on a sudden the music changed, so soft that you scarce could
    hear;
But you felt that your life had been looted clean of all that it once
    held dear;
That someone had stolen the woman you loved; that her love was a
    devil's lie;
That your guts were gone, and the best for you was to crawl away
    and die.
'Twas the crowning cry of a heart's despair, and it thrilled you
    through and through—
"I guess I'll make it—a spread misere," said Dangerous Dan McGrew.

The music almost died away . . . then it burst like a pent-up flood;
And it seemed to say, "Repay, repay," and my eyes were blind with
    blood.
The thought came back of an ancient wrong, and it stung like a
    frozen lash,
And the lust awoke to kill, to kill . . . then the music stopped with a
    crash,
And the stranger turned, and his eyes they burned in a most
    peculiar way.
In a buckskin shirt that was glazed with dirt he sat, and I saw him
    sway;
Then his lips went in, in a kind of grin, and he spoke, and his voice
    was calm,
And "Boys," says he, "you don't know me, and none of you care a
    damn;
But I want to state, and my words are straight, and I'll bet my poke
    they're true,
That one of you is a hound of hell and that one is Dan McGrew."

Then I ducked my head, and the lights went out, and two guns
    blazed in the dark,
And a woman screamed, and the lights went up, and two men lay
    stiff and stark.
Pitched on his head, and pumped full of lead, was Dangerous Dan
    McGrew,
While the man from the creeks lay clutched to the breast of the lady
    that's known as Lou.
These are the simple facts of the case, and I guess I ought to know.
They say that the stranger was crazed with "hooch," and I'm not
    denying it's so.
I'm not so wise as the lawyer guys, but strictly between us two—
**The woman that kissed him and—pinched his poke—was the lady
    that's known as Lou.**

WALLY'S BITS OF
❦ WIT AND WISDOM ❧

Who is Wally? Wally Riddell is a golfing friend of mine at our Country Club. Born in Berkeley, California in 1915 and a product of the University of California, Wally showed an early talent for his writing and advice-oriented ditties. After service in the Navy in World War II, he helped found an advertising agency in San Francisco. "It Hasta be Shasta" was one of his brain children. He is now retired, but still writing. Wally has served as editor and contributing writer for our club paper for many years with a column *From Bad to Verse*. I have enjoyed his witticisms for 40 years. Wally's other well-known talent is being a genius at finding golf balls. Two notable records are 289 in one day and 350,000 total over the years. They end up with friends, club juniors or local charities. Thanks for sharing your clever "Bits" with us, Wally.

Wally on Business

Best way to double your money?
(Don't knock it)
Just fold it over once
And put it in your pocket!

❖

Inflation has changed our language
It has added a couple of "Naughts"—
Today, the old saying goes:
"$1.00 for your thoughts!"

❖

They say "Giving up work
Can be hazardous to your health."
I say it can even be
Hazardous to your wealth!

❖

Our two biggest problems
In business, my friend,
Are making ends meet, and
Making meetings end!

❖

The wealth of rich men
(Should you aspire it)
Should be measured by
The means they acquire it.

❖

Office absentee excuses
Are becoming astuter—
Like: "I caught a virus
From the computer."

❖

"A fool and her money
Are soon courted."
That's an old, familiar saying
Quite properly distorted.

❖

If your broker says: "I want an
Answer right away,"
Nothing is sometimes the
Right thing to say.

Money can sometimes
Be a disaster...
An excellent servant
But a terrible master!

❖

Your chance of winning
The lottery jackpot
Is the same whether
You play or not!

Wally on Sports

From a psychiatrist comes news
You should take to heart:
If you play golf, stop;
If you don't play, don't start.

❖

They're burying golfers at sea,
And we know you'll be glad;
They've found that deep down
Golfers really aren't so bad!

Besides backward caps
This has to go:
The after-touchdown
Minstrel show!

❖

Don't ask your kids:
If they won.
Your question should be:
"Was it fun?"

Wally on Daily Life

They served me a one-legged
Crab for dinner—
I know they love to fight,
But bring me the winner!

❖

A white lie, perhaps,
Can be your salvation:
"A little inaccuracy sometimes
Saves tons of explanation!"

❖

Attention all you drivers
Who want to stay alive—
About 7pm Saturday is
The deadliest time to drive.

❖

Kids aren't happy with
Nothing to ignore,
And that's what parents
Were created for.

❖

Our six-year-old
Couldn't be cuter
But better than that,
He understands a computer.

❖

It's not the things I failed to do
That make me wipe this eye,
It's things I should and could have done
And simply failed to try.

❖

Dieters at the break of day
Have these hopeful words to say:
"Mirror, mirror on the dresser,
Do I look a little lesser?"

❖

The hardest job kids face today
(Among many),
Is learning good manners
Without seeing any!

❖

The trouble started the night
I came home and said, "Honey,
Why is so much month left
At the end of the money?"

❖

Home is where you can say
What you want to say,
Because nobody will listen
To you anyway!

❖

This bit of awareness
The passing years bring:
"I'm not young enough
To know everything!"

❖

My wife finds TV educating:
When I take a look,
She goes in the other room
And reads a book!

❖

Why are true friends so rare
I ask with mournful sigh
I ought to ask instead
What kind of friend am I?

❖

Memory is what tells you,
"Hey...
Your wife's birthday was
Yesterday!"

❖

The modern American
(Including me and thou)
Prays for patience
And wants it right now!

❖

Here is a truth
That you can't disparage:
Love is a brief insanity
Curable by marriage.

❖

Bachelors know more about women
Than married men do.
If they didn't they'd be
Married men, too!

❖

The world's most dangerous device
Is the auto, it's reckoned;
But who would guess the stair step
Comes in second?

❖

When you read this
Prepare yourself for trouble
In just thirty years
The earth's population will double!

❖

Mankind owes its existence
(One who knows explains)
To the six inches of topsoil
And the fact that it rains.

The kids phone home, and
I've come to expect
When youth calls to age
It's always collect.

❖

Some minds are like concrete
(And many I've met)—
They're thoroughly mixed
And permanently set!

❖

If you two are a teenager's
Father and Mother,
You're probably wondering
About each other!

❖

The best thing about spring,
Let's toast—
It comes around when we
Need it most!

Wally on Government

No wonder the US budget
Is in such a pickle:
It costs us 50 cents
Just to coin a nickel.

❖

This fact makes all
The oil companies drool:
Aircraft carriers get six inches
From a gallon of fuel!

❖

This truth is spreading
Across the land:
"The supply of government
Exceeds the demand."

❖

A revolt is brewing
Across the nation
"No taxation
Without simplification!"

❖

If you're a typical taxpayer
This will spoil your mood:
You spend three times more on taxes
Than you spend on food.

❖

To get rich quick,
Just find an easy pigeon,
Then invent a patent medicine
Or a new religion.

❖

Limiting politician's terms
Is the perfect idea, at last;
Now they can go home and live
Under the laws they've passed!

❖

Totally confused
With your tax form deductions?
You ain't seen nothin'
'Til you read the IRS instructions!

❖

The mint prints a dollar
For a two-and-a-half-cents.
So they print 'em by the millions
Because the profit's so immense.

❖

Congress mails 12,000 letters
For every one they get.
No wonder our Treasury's
Three trillion bucks in debt!

❖

Blessed are the young,
You bet,
For they shall inherit
The National Debt!

❖

"Buy American" is a slogan
In need of some reviewing
Since that's exactly what
Foreign companies are doing.

❖

Here's why the taxpayer
Can never relax
1,000 government bodies
Have the power to tax!

❖

Incongruous
(I've learned at last)
Is not the place
Where laws are passed.

❖

Wally's Advice

"Think like a man of action
Act like a man of thought"—
Another bit of good advice
That costs you exactly naught.

❖

Gift shopping for
Your wife? Be wise!
Never try to guess
Her dress size.
Just buy any dress
That's marked "Petite"...
And—be sure to
Keep the receipt!

❖

A woman should never
Chase a man, they say—
Unless, of course,
He's trying to get away.

❖

Traveling? Here's advice
From one who knows
Take twice the cash
And half the clothes.

❖

Honesty pays dividends,
You'll find,
Both in dollars and
In peace of mind.

❖

Wherever you may come
    from,
Wherever you roam
When you look like your
    passport photo
It's time to go home!

❖

To hear words which are both
Curt and cursory
Just forget to remember your
Wedding anniversary!

❖

Good old Ben Franklin
It was he who said:
"Three can keep a secret
If two of them are dead."

❖

Wally on Education

With a college degree
You've several ways to impress
If you can't dazzle them with
    your brilliance,
Baffle them with your B.S.!

❖

4649 x 239=
The answer's a surprise;
Try it on your calculator,
You'll see a road of railroad ties!

❖

No wonder they say
Many Americans are schnooks:
A study shows we're spending more
On chewing gum than on books!

❖

We have no more right
To consume happiness without
    inducing it,
Than we have to consume wealth
Without personally producing it.

❖

Pollsters say:
Three in a hundred
College students answer
That Mikhail Gorbachev
Is a ballet dancer.

❖

This came to me
As quite a surprise:
All windmills turn
Counter-clockwise.

❖

What you're now reading
May be a surprise:
70% of all you learn
Comes through your eyes.

❖

"There's nothing more
    terrifying
Than ignorance in action:"
For instance, my trying to
Divide with a fraction.

❖

.

❧ LOVE AND ROMANCE ❧

When I Was One-and-Twenty
by Alfred Edward Housman

What a glorious, care-free, and exciting time.

When I was one-and-twenty
        I heard a wise man say,
"Give crowns and pounds and guineas
        But not your heart away;
Give pearls away and rubies
        But keep your fancy free."
But I was one-and-twenty,
        No use to talk to me.

When I was one-and-twenty
        I heard him say again,
"The heart out of the bosom
        Was never given in vain,
'Tis paid with sighs a-plenty
        And sold for endless rue."
And I am two-and-twenty,
        And oh, 'tis true, 'tis true.

Should You Go First

by A. K. Rowswell

A look into the uncertain future, by longtime
friends or lovers.

Should you go first and I remain
        To walk the road alone,
I'll live in memory's garden, dear,
        With happy days we've known.
In Spring I'll wait for roses red,
        When fades the lilac blue,
In early Fall, when brown leaves call
        I'll catch a glimpse of you.

Should you go first and I remain
        For battles to be fought,
Each thing you've touched along the way
        Will be a hallowed spot.
I'll hear your voice, I'll see your smile,
        Though blindly I may grope,
The memory of your helping hand
        Will buoy me on with hope.

Should you go first and I remain
        To finish with the scroll,
No length'ning shadows shall creep in
        To make this life seem droll.
We've known so much of happiness,
        We've had our cup of joy,
And memory is one gift of God
        That death cannot destroy.

Should you go first and I remain,
        One thing I'd have you do:
Walk slowly down that long, lone path,
        For soon I'll follow you.
I'll want to know each step you take
        That I may walk the same,
For some day down that lonely road
        You'll hear me call your name.

When Lovely Woman
by Phoebe Cary (1824-1871)

What a sneaky way!

> When lovely woman wants a favor,
>> And finds, too late, that man won't bend,
> What earthly circumstances can save her
>> From disappointment in the end?
>
> The only way to bring him over,
>> The last experiment to try,
> Whether a husband or a lover,
>> If he have feeling is—to cry.

Annabel Lee
by Edgar Allan Poe (1809-1849)

To me, the most beautiful poem ever written. Poe's tribute to his 13-year-old cousin and bride, Virginia Glenn, his beautiful Annabel Lee, dead at the age of 24.

> It was many and many a year ago,
>> In a kingdom by the sea,
> That a maiden there lived whom you may know
>> By the name of Annabel Lee;—
> And this maiden she lived with no other thought
>> Than to love and be loved by me.
>
> I was a child and she was a child,
>> In this kingdom by the sea,
> But we loved with a love that was more than love—
>> I and my Annabel Lee—
> With a love that the winged seraphs in Heaven
>> Coveted her and me.

And this was the reason that, long ago,
    In this kingdom by the sea,
A wind blew out of a cloud, chilling
    My beautiful Annabel Lee;
So that her high-born kinsmen came
    And bore her away from me,
To shut her up in a sepulcher
    In this kingdom by the sea.

The angels, not half so happy in Heaven,
    Went envying her and me:—
Yes!—that was the reason (as all men know,
    In this kingdom by the sea)
That the wind came out of the cloud, by night,
    Chilling and killing my Annabel Lee.

But our love it was stronger by far than the love
    Of those who were older than we—
    Of many far wiser than we—
And neither the angels in Heaven above,
    Nor the demons down under the sea,
Can ever dissever my soul from the soul
    Of the beautiful Annabel Lee:—

For the moon never beams without bringing me dreams
    Of the beautiful Annabel Lee;
And the stars never rise but I feel the bright eyes
    Of the beautiful Annabel Lee;
And so, all the night-tide, I lie down by the side
Of my darling,—my darling,—my life and my bride,
    In her sepulcher there by the sea—
    In her tomb by the sounding sea.

To Helen

by Edgar Allan Poe (1809-1849)

Poe, in a lighter mood.

Helen, thy beauty is to me
    Like those Nicæan barks of yore,
That gently, o'er a perfumed sea,
    The weary, wayworn wanderer bore
    To his own native shore.

On desperate seas long wont to roam,
    Thy hyacinth hair, thy classic face,
Thy Naiad airs have brought me home
    To the glory that was Greece
    And the grandeur that was Rome.

Lo! In yon brilliant window-niche
    How statue-like I see thee stand,
The agate lamp within thy hand!
    Ah, Psyche, from the regions which
    Are Holy Land!

To Celia

From "The Forest"
by Ben Jonson (1573-1637)

Four centuries old, but still great.

Drink to me only with thine eyes,
    And I will pledge with mine;
Or leave a kiss but in the cup,
    And I'll not look for wine.

The thirst that from the soul doth rise
    Doth ask a drink divine,
But might I of Job's nectar sup
    I would not change for thine.

A Red, Red Rose

by Robert Burns (1759-1796)

Burns obviously didn't spend all his time plowing up a mouse's home as he described in *To a Mouse.*

> O, my luve's like a red, red rose
> > That's newly sprung in June;
> O, my luve's like the melodie
> > That's sweetly played in tune.
>
> As fair thou art, my bonnie lass
> > So deep in luve am I;
> And I will luve thee still my dear,
> > Till a' the seas gang dry.
>
> Till a' the seas gang dry, my dear
> > And the rocks melt wi' the sun;
> I will luve thee still, my dear,
> > While the sands o' life shall run.
>
> And fare-thee-weel, my only luve!
> > And fare-thee-weel a while!
> And I will come again, my luve,
> > Though it were ten thousand mile.

The Night Has a Thousand Eyes

by Francis William Bourdillon

A brief comparison of the setting of the sun with the death of love.

> The night has a thousand eyes,
> > And the day but one;
> Yet the light of the bright world dies
> > With the dying sun.
>
> The mind has a thousand eyes,
> > And the heart but one;
> Yet the light of a whole life dies
> > When love is done.

The White Flag

by John Hay (1838-1905)

A rose is a rose—usually. Gertrude Stein
was wrong here. This could up the sale of
red and white roses.

I sent my love two roses,—one
    As white as driven snow,
And one a blushing royal red,
    A flaming Jacqueminot.

I meant to touch and test my fate;
    That night I should divine,
The moment I should see my love,
    If her true heart were mine.

For if she holds me dear, I said,
    She'll wear my blushing rose;
If not, she'll wear my cold Lamarque,
    As white as winter's snows.

My heart sank when I met her: sure
    I had been overbold,
For on her breast my pale rose lay
    In virgin whiteness cold.

Yet with low words she greeted me,
    With smiles divinely tender;
Upon her cheek the red rose dawned,—
    The white rose meant surrender.

Tell Her So

by Unknown

Hey, all you lucky husbands, I couldn't find you better advice than this. And it doesn't hurt to repeat and repeat, and not just on Valentine's Day and birthdays.

> Amid the cares of married life,
> In spite of toil and business strife,
> If you value your sweet wife,
>   Tell her so!
>
> Prove to her you don't forget
> The bond to which your seal is set;
> She's of life's sweet the sweetest yet—
>   Tell her so!
>
> When days are dark and deeply blue,
> She has her troubles, same as you;
> Show her that your love is true—
>   Tell her so!
>
> In former days you praised her style,
> And spent much care to win her smile;
> 'Tis just as well now worth your while—
>   Tell her so!
>
> There was a time when you thought it bliss
> To get a favor of one kiss;
> A dozen now won't come amiss—
>   Tell her so!
>
> Your love for her is no mistake—
> You feel it dreaming or awake—
> Don't conceal it; for her sake
>   Tell her so!
>
> You'll never know what you have missed,
> If you make love a game of whist;
> Lips mean more—than to be kissed!
>   Tell her so!

Don't act as if she'd passed her prime,
As though to please her was a crime—
If e'er you loved her, now's the time;
    Tell her so!

She'll return for each caress
A hundredfold of tenderness!
Hearts like hers are made to bless!
    Tell her so!

You are hers, and hers alone—
Well you know she's all your own;
Don't wait to "carve it on a stone"—
    Tell her so!

Never let her heart grow cold—
Richer beauties will unfold;
She is worth her weight in gold!
    Tell her so!

A Health

by Edward Coate Pinkney (1802-1828)

A popular toast to a lady-love. The first or last
stanzas are often quoted.

I fill this cup to one made up
    Of loveliness alone,
A woman of her gentle sex
    The seeming paragon;
To whom the better elements
    And kindly stars have given
A form so fair, like the air
    'Tis less of earth than heaven.

Her very tone is music's own,
  Like those of morning birds,
And something more than melody
  Dwells ever in her words;
The coinage of her heart are they,
  And from her lips each flows
As one may see the burdened bee
  Forth issue from the rose.

Affections are as thought to her,
  The measure of her hours;
Her feelings have the fragrance,
  The freshness of young flowers;
And lovely passion, changing oft,
  So fill her, she appears
The image of themselves by turns,—
  The idol of past years!

Of her bright face one glance will trace
  A picture on the brain,
And of her voice in echoing hearts
  A sound must lay remain;
But memory, such as mine of her,
  So very much endears,
When death is nigh my latest sigh
  Will not be life's, but hers.

I fill this cup to one made up
  Of loveliness alone,
A woman, of her gentle sex
  The seeming paragon—
Her health! And would on earth there stood
  Some more of such a frame,
That life might be all poetry,
  And weariness a name.

A Certain Young Lady

by Washington Irving (1783-1859)

A very cleverly expressed tribute with a give
and take flavor.

> There's a certain young lady,
> Who's just in her hey-day,
> > And full of all mischief, I ween;
> > So teasing! so pleasing!
> > Capricious! delicious!
> And you know very well whom I mean.

> With an eye dark as night,
> Yet than noonday more bright,
> > Was ever a black eye so keen?
> > It can thrill with a glance,
> > With a beam can entrance,
> And you know very well whom I mean.

> With a stately step—such as
> You'd expect in a duchess—
> > And a brow might distinguish a queen,
> > With a mighty proud air,
> > That says "touch me who dare,"
> And you know very well whom I mean.

> With a toss of the head
> That strikes one quite dead,
> > But a smile to revive one again;
> > That toss so appalling!
> > That smile so enthralling!
> And you know very well whom I mean.

Confound her! de'll take her!—
A cruel heart-breaker—
     But hold! see that smile so serene.
     God love her! God bless her!
     May nothing distress her!
You know very well whom I mean.

Heaven help the adorer
Who happens to bore her,
The lover who wakens her spleen;
     But too blest for a sinner
     Is he who shall win her,
And you know very well whom I mean.

NATURE

A Little Dog-Angel
by Norah M. Holland

Real dog lovers will hear this angel bark, and
recognize it.

High up in the courts of heaven today
　　A little dog-angel waits,
With the other angels he will not play,
　　But he sits alone at the gates;
"For I know that my master will come," says he:
"And when he comes, he will call for me."

He sees the spirits that pass him by
　　As they hasten toward the Throne,
And he watches them with a wistful eye
　　As he sits at the gates alone;
"But I know if I just wait patiently
That some day my master will come," says he.

And his master far on the earth below,
　　As he sits in his easy chair,
Forgets sometimes, and he whistles low
　　For the dog that is not there;
And the little dog-angel cocks his ears,
And dreams that his master's call he hears.

And I know, when at length his master waits
　　Outside in the dark and cold
For the hand of Death to open the gates
　　That lead to those courts of gold,
The little dog-angel's eager bark
Will comfort his soul in the shivering dark.

The Little Cat Angel

by Leontine Stanfield

Cat lovers, you'll love it! The kids will too.

The ghost of a little white kitten
Crying mournfully, early and late,
Distracted St. Peter, the watchman,
As he guarded the heavenly gate.
"Say, what do you mean," said his Saintship,
"Coming here and behaving like that?"
"I want to see Nellie, my missus,"
Sobbed the wee little ghost of a cat.
"I know she's not happy without me,
Won't you open and let me go in?"
"Begone," gasped the horrified watchman,
"Why the very idea is a sin;
I open the gate to good angels,
Not to stray little beggars like you."
"All right," mewed the little white kitten,
"Though a cat I'm a good angel, too."
Amazed at so bold an assertion,
But aware that he must make no mistake,
In silence, St. Peter long pondered,
For his name and repute were at stake,
Then placing the cat in his bosom
With a "Whist now, and say all your prayers,"
He opened the heavenly portals
And ascended the bright golden stairs.
A little girl angel came flying,
"That's my kitty, St. Peter," she cried.
And seeing the joy of their meeting,
Peter let the cat angel abide.

This tale is the tale of a kitten
Dwelling now with the blessed above,
It vanquished grim Death and High Heaven
For the name of the kitten was Love.

Hark, The Herald Leaves of Spring

by Samuel N. Etheredge (1914-

Loving nature as I do, spending as much time as I do
in my garden, I had to add a little tribute of my own
to those lovely leaves.

Mother Nature may seem idly sleeping,
　　Just watching the world passing by.
But, season by season, she is keeping
　　A close eye as the years swiftly fly.

She stores up a great menu of each good thing,
　　And serves them up to us, deluxe, at her call.
Bringing all her vast brood to life in the spring,
　　And bidding them slow down and sleep in the fall.

Now the wise old lady has long been knowing
　　All the modern day marvels in sight,
And sees us control our coming and going
　　With a green, yellow and red traffic light.

It happens these tints are the dear lady's prime
　　So she keeps them always on call
First the pretty, bright green go leaves of springtime
　　Then the lovely yellow and red slow and stop leaves of fall.

She knows the green leaves say "No more freeze"
　　As things burst into life in the spring,
And the birds and the bees, the flowers and trees
　　Join the animals great estival fling.

Then after a long, hot, humid summer
　　The Lady thinks things should really slow down
So she sends out a nice warning rumor
　　As her yellow leaves start to abound.

When winter's icy winds become a bit churlish,
　　She knows her whole brood needs a rest,
So she takes out her brush with a flourish
　　And paints the leaves red with a zest.

So it is that we enjoy each season in rhyme,
Knowing what nature will bring to us all,
By the pretty, bright, green go leaves of springtime
And the lovely yellow and red slow leaves of fall.

A Thing of Beauty

by John Keats (1795-1821)

And beautifully stated.

A thing of beauty is a joy forever:
Its love increases; it will never
Pass into nothingness; but still will keep
A bower quiet for us, and a sleep
Full of sweet dreams, and health, and quiet breathing.
Therefore, on every morrow, we are wreathing
A flowery band to bind us to the earth,
Spite of despondence, of the inhuman dearth
Of noble natures, of the gloomy days,
Of all the unhealthy and o'er-darken'd ways
Made for our searching: yea, in spite of all,
Some shape of beauty moves away the pall
From our dark spirits. Such the sun, the moon,
Trees old and young, sprouting a shady boon
For simple sheep; and such are daffodils
With the green world they live in; and clear rills
That for themselves a cooling covert make
'Gainst the hot season; the mid forest brake,
Rich with a sprinkling of fair musk-rose blooms:
And such too is the grandeur of the dooms
We have imagined for the mighty dead;
All lovely tales that we have heard or read:
An endless fountain of immortal drink,
Pouring into us from the heaven's brink.

Bum

by W. Dayton Wedgefarth

Thank the Lord for Bums. If you haven't had one,
you haven't really lived. Bred dogs may be beautiful,
but Bums are special—real doggy dogs.

> He's a little dog, with a stubby tail, and a moth-eaten coat of tan,
> 　　And his legs are short, of the wabbly sort;
> I doubt if they ever ran;
> And he howls at night, while in broad daylight he sleeps like a
> 　　bloomin' log,
> And he likes the food of the gutter breed; he's a most irregular dog.
>
> I call him Bum, and in total sum he's all that his name implies,
> For he's just a tramp with a highway stamp that culture cannot
> 　　disguise;
> And his friends, I've found, in the streets abound, be they urchins
> 　　or dogs or men;
> Yet he sticks to me with a fiendish glee. It is truly beyond my ken.
>
> I talk to him when I'm lonesome-like, and I'm sure that he
> 　　understands
> When he looks at me so attentively and gently licks my hands;
> Then he rubs his nose on my tailored clothes, but I never say
> 　　nought thereat,
> For the good Lord knows I can buy more clothes, but never a friend
> 　　like that!

Under the Greenwood Tree
From "As you Like It"
by William Shakespeare (1564-1616)

The master playwright was a fine poet, too.

    Under the greenwood tree,
    Who loves to lie with me,
    And turn his merry note
    Unto the sweet bird's throat,
Come hither, come hither, come hither:
    Here shall he see
    No enemy
But winter and rough weather.

    Who doth ambition shun,
    And loves to live i' the sun,
    Seeking the food he eats,
    And pleased with what he gets,
Come hither, come hither, come hither:
    Here shall he see
    No enemy
But winter and rough weather.

The Fountain

by James Russell Lowell (1819-1891)

Getting a lift from a lovely fountain. Refreshing, as a shower should be.

Into the sunshine,
    Full of the light,
Leaping and flashing
    From morn till night!

Into the moonlight,
    Whiter than snow,
Waving so flower-like
    When the winds blow!

Into the starlight,
    Rushing in spray,
Happy at midnight,
    Happy by day!

Ever in motion,
    Blithesome and cheery,
Still climbing heavenward,
    Never aweary;

Glad of all weathers,
    Still seeming best,
Upward or downward
    Motion thy rest;

Full of a nature
    Nothing can tame,
Changed every moment,
    Ever the same;

Ceaseless aspiring,
    Ceaseless content,
Darkness or sunshine
    Thy element;

Glorious fountain!
    Let my heart be
Fresh, changeful, constant,
    Upward like thee!

The Wreck of the "Hesperus"

By Henry W. Longfellow (1807-1892)

A proud, boastful, headstrong skipper
would not listen to the pleas of his
daughter and a wise old sailor. Result—
catastrophe on December 17, 1839

It was the schooner *Hesperus*,
    That sailed the wintry sea;
And the skipper had taken his little daughter,
    To bear him company.

Blue were her eyes as the fairy-flax,
    Her cheeks like the dawn of day,
And her bosom white as the hawthorn buds
    That ope in the month of May.

The skipper he stood beside the helm,
    His pipe was in his mouth,
And he watched how the veering flaw did blow
    The smoke now West, now South.

Then up spake an old Sailor,
    Had sailed to the Spanish Main,
"I pray thee, put into yonder port,
    For I fear a hurricane.

"Last night, the moon had a golden ring,
    And to-night no moon we see!"
The skipper, he blew a whiff from his pipe,
    And a scornful laugh laughed he.

Colder and louder blew the wind,
    A gale from the Northeast,
The snow fell hissing in the brine,
    And the billows frothed like yeast.

Down came the storm, and smote amain
    The vessel in its strength;
She shuddered and paused, like a frighted steed,
    Then leaped her cable's length.

"Come hither! come hither! my little daughter,
    And do not tremble so;
For I can weather the roughest gale
    That ever wind did blow."

He wrapped her warm in his seaman's coat
    Against the stinging blast;
He cut a rope from a broken spar,
    And bound her to the mast.

"O father! I hear the church-bells ring,
    Oh say, what may it be?"
"'Tis a fog-bell on a rock-bound coast!"—
    And he steered for the open sea.

"O father! I hear the sound of guns,
    Oh say, what may it be?"
"Some ship in distress, that cannot live
    In such an angry sea!"

"O father! I see a gleaming light,
    Oh say, what may it be?"
But the father answered never a word,
    A frozen corpse was he.

Lashed to the helm, all stiff and stark,
    With his face turned to the skies,
The lantern gleamed through the gleaming snow
    On his fixed and glassy eyes.

The maiden clasped her hands and prayed
    That saved she might be;
And she thought of Christ, who stilled the wave,
    On the Lake of Galilee.

And fast through the midnight dark and drear,
Through the whistling sleet and snow,
Like a sheeted ghost, the vessel swept
Toward the reef of Norman's Woe.

And ever the fitful gusts between
A sound came from the land;
It was the sound of the trampling surf
On the rocks and the hard sea-sand.

The breakers were right beneath her bows,
She drifted a dreary wreck,
And a whooping billow swept the crew
Like icicles from her deck.

She struck where the white and fleecy waves
Looked soft as carded wool,
But the cruel rocks, they gored her side
Like the horns of an angry bull.

Her rattling shrouds, all sheathed in ice,
With the masts went by the board;
Like a vessel of glass, she stove and sank,—
Ho! ho! the breakers roared!

At daybreak, on the bleak sea-beach,
A fisherman stood aghast,
To see the form of a maiden fair,
Lashed close to a drifting mast.

The salt sea was frozen on her breast,
The salt tears in her eyes;
And he saw her hair, like the brown seaweed,
On the billows fall and rise.

Such was the wreck of the *Hesperus*,
In the midnight and the snow!
Christ save us all from a death like this,
On the reef of Norman's Woe!

A Wet Sheet and a Flowing Sea

by Allan Cunningham (1784-1842)

Climb aboard all you sailors; true sailors, that is.

A wet sheet and a flowing sea,
    A wind that follows fast,
And fills the white and rustling sail,
    And bends the gallant mast;
And bends the gallant mast, my boys,
    While, like the eagle free,
Away the good ship flies, and leaves
    Old England on the lee.

O for a soft and gentle wind!
    I heard a fair one cry;
But give to me the snoring breeze
    And white waves heaving high;
And white waves heaving high, my boys,
    The good ship tight and free—
The world of waters is our home,
    And merry men are we.

There's tempest in yon horned moon,
    And lightning in yon cloud;
And hark the music, mariners!
    The wind is piping loud;
The wind is piping loud, my boys,
    The lighting flashes free—
While the hollow oak our palace is,
    Our heritage the sea.

When the Frost is on the Punkin

by James Whitcomb Riley (1852-1926)

This will surely make you feel like, and like, autumn. Isn't it wonderful how you remember the sounds, smells, sights and textures of the season.

When the frost is on the punkin and the fodder's in the shock,
And you hear the kyouck and gobble of the struttin, turkey-cock,
And the clackin' of the guineys, and the cluckin' of the hens,
And the rooster's hallylooyer as he tiptoes on the fence;
O, it's then's the times a feller is a-feelin' at his best,
With the risin' sun to greet him from a night of peaceful rest,
As he leaves the house, bareheaded, and goes out to feed the stock,
When the frost is on the punkin and the fodder's in the shock.

They's something kindo' harty-like about the atmusfere
When the heat of summer's over and the coolin' fall is here—
Of course we miss the flowers, and the blossoms on the trees,
And the mumble of the hummin'-birds and buzzin' of the bees;
But the air's so appetizin'; and the landscape through the haze
Of a crisp and sunny morning of the airly autumn days
Is a pictur' that no painter has the colorin' to mock—
When the frost is on the punkin and the fodder's in the shock.

The husky, rusty russel of the tossels of the corn,
And the raspin' of the tangled leaves, as golden as the morn;
The stubble in the furries—kindo' lonesome-like, but still
A-preachin' sermuns to us of the barns they growed to fill;
The strawstack in the medder, and the reaper in the shed;
The hosses in theyr stalls below—the clover overhead!—
O, it sets my hart a-clickin' like the tickin' of a clock,
When the frost is on the punkin and the fodder's in the shock.

Then your apples all is getherd, and the ones a feller keeps
Is poured around the celler-floor in red and yeller heaps;
And your cider-makin's over, and your wimmern-folks is through
With their mince and apple-butter, and theyr souse and saussage,
    too!
I don't know how to tell it—but ef sich a thing could be
As the Angels wantin' boardin', and they'd call around on *me*—
I'd want to 'commodate 'em—all the whole-indurin' flock—
When the frost is on the punkin and the fodder's in the shock.

Out Fishin'

by Edgar A. Guest

Refreshing. I've had this hanging in my house for 25 years. I'm not much of a fisherman, but I love each stanza of this. I wonder why we can't relax like these guys when we are out golfin'! Maybe everybody should go out fishin', and I know some who should stay out there.

A feller isn't think' mean,
        Out fishin';
His thoughts are mostly good an' clean,
        Out fishin';
He doesn't knock his fellow men,
Or harbor any grudges then;
A feller's at his finest when
        Out fishin'.

The rich are comrades to the poor,
        Out fishin';
All brothers of a common lure
        Out fishin'.
The urchin with the pin an' string
Can chum with millionaire and king;
Vain pride is a forgotten thing,
        Out fishin'.

A feller gits a chance to dream,
    Out fishin',
He learns the beauties of a stream,
    Out fishin';
An' he can wash his soul in air
That isn't foul with selfish care,
An' relish plain and simple fare,
    Out fishin'.

A feller has no time for hate,
    Out fishin';
He isn't eager to be great,
    Out fishin'.
He isn't thinkin' thoughts of pelf,
Or goods stacked high upon a shelf,
But he is always just himself,
    Out fishin'.

A feller's glad to be a friend,
    Out fishin';
A helpin' hand he'll always lend,
    Out fishin'.
The brotherhood of rod an' line
An' sky and stream is always fine;
Men come real close to God's design,
    Out fishin'.

A feller isn't plotting schemes,
    Out fishin';
He's only busy with his dreams,
    Out fishin'.
His livery is a coat of tan,
His creed—to do the best he can;
A feller's always mostly man,
    Out fishin'.

(There, I feel better all over again!)

Plant a Tree

by Lucy Larcom (1824-1883)

You'll find how great a tree can be, in many
ways you may not have thought about.
Sorrowfully, the trend today is to cut them down,
even large sections of the great rain forests.

He who plants a tree
    Plants a hope.
Rootlets up through fibres blindly grope;
Leaves unfold into horizons free.
    So man's life must climb
    From the clods of time
    Unto heavens sublime.
Canst thou prophesy, thou little tree,
What the glory of thy boughs shall be?

He who plants a tree
    Plants a joy;
Plants a comfort that will never cloy;
Every day a fresh reality,
    Beautiful and strong,
    To whose shelter throng
    Creatures blithe with song.
If thou couldst but know, thou happy tree,
Of the bliss that shall inhabit thee!

He who plants a tree,—
    He plants peace.
Under its green curtains jargons cease.
Leaf and zephyr murmur soothingly;
    Shadows soft with sleep
    Down tired eyelids creep,
    Balm of slumber deep.
Never hast thou dreamed, thou blessed tree,
Of the benediction thou shalt be.

He who plants a tree,—
    He plants youth;
Vigor won for centuries in sooth;
Life of time, that hints eternity!
    Boughs their strength uprear;
    New shoots, every year,
    On old growths appear;
Thou shalt teach the ages, sturdy tree,
Youth of soul is immortality.

He who plants a tree,—
    He plants love,
Tents of coolness spreading out above
Wayfarers he may not live to see.
    Gifts that grow are best;
    Hands that bless are blest;
    Plant! life does the rest!
Heaven and earth help him who plants a tree,
And his work its own reward shall be.

Sea Fever

by John Masefield

For all Old Salts and Young Salts too. Don't take an
aspirin for this fever—it won't help.

I must go down to the seas again, to the lonely sea and the sky,
And all I ask is a tall ship and a star to steer her by;
And the wheel's kick and the wind's song and the white sail's shaking,
And a grey mist on the sea's face, and a grey dawn breaking.

I must go down to the seas again, for the call of the running tide
Is a wild call and a clear call that may not be denied;
And all I ask is a windy day with the white clouds flying,
And the flung spray and the blown spume, and the sea-gulls crying.

I must go down to the seas again, to the vagrant gypsy life,
To the gull's way and the whale's way, where the wind's like a
    whetted knife;
And all I ask is a merry yarn from a laughing fellow-rover,
And quiet sleep and a sweet dream when the long trick's over.

Woodman, Spare That Tree

by George Perkins Morris (1802-1864)

John Muir is smiling. And the Sierra Club is
laughing out loud.

Woodman, spare that tree!
　　Touch not a single bough!
In youth it sheltered me,
　　And I'll protect it now.
'Twas my forefather's hand
　　That placed it near his cot;
There, woodman, let it stand,
　　Thy axe shall harm it not!

That old familiar tree,
　　Whose glory and renown
Are spread o'er land and sea,
　　And wouldst thou hew it down?
Woodman, forbear thy stroke!
　　Cut not its earth-bound ties;
O, spare that aged oak,
　　Now towering to the skies!

When but an idle boy
　　I sought its grateful shade;
In all their gushing joy
　　Here too my sisters played.
My mother kissed me here;
　　My father pressed my hand—
Forgive this foolish tear,
　　But let that old oak stand!

My heart-strings round thee cling,
　　Close as thy bark, old friend!
Here shall the wild-bird sing,
　　And still thy branches bend.
Old tree! the storm still brave!
　　And, woodman, leave the spot;
While I've a hand to save,
　　Thy axe shall hurt it not.

The Lord God Planted a Garden

by Dorothy Frances Gurney

The bolded lines are probably the most used
quotation in gardens everywhere. I sincerely
believe those last two lines.

> The Lord God planted a garden
>   In the first white days of the world,
> And he set there an angel warden
>   In a garment of light enfurled.
>
> So near to the peace of Heaven,
>   That the hawk might nest with the wren,
> For there in the cool of the even'
>   God walked with the first of men.
>
> **The kiss of the sun for pardon,**
>   **The song of the birds for mirth—**
> **One is nearer God's heart in a garden**
>   **Than anywhere else on earth.**

Trees

by Sergeant Joyce Kilmer (1886-1918)

A beautiful poem, also made into a beautiful
song. The Trees and I thank you, Joyce, for
your lovely poem and your supreme sacrifice.
(Kilmer was 32 years old, a prominent poet,
author and journalist. Serving with the 165th
Infantry (69th New York) AEF in World War I, he was killed in action near
Seringes, France July 30, 1918.)

> **I think that I shall never see**
> **A poem lovely as a tree.**
>
> A tree whose hungry mouth is prest
> Against the earth's sweet flowing breast;
>
> A tree that looks at God all day,
> And lifts her leafy arms to pray;

A tree that may in Summer wear
A nest of robins in her hair,

Upon whose bosom snow has lain;
Who intimately lives with rain.

Poems are made by fools like me,
But only God can make a tree.

To a Waterfowl

by William Cullen Bryant (1794-1878)

A Naturalist's, and my, delight. Please don't miss the lesson taught in the last stanza. Remember he means you, as well as the goose. The wonder of waterfowl flying thousands of miles without maps, radar or other help and arriving at the same spots year after year.

Whither 'midst falling dew,
While glow the heavens with the last steps of day,
Far, through their rosy depths, dost thou pursue
Thy solitary way?

Vainly the fowler's eye
Might mark thy distant flight to do thee wrong,
As, darkly painted on the crimson sky,
Thy figure floats along.

Seek'st thou the plashy brink
Of weedy lake, or marge of river wide,
Or where the rocking billows rise and sink
On the chafed ocean's side?

There is a Power whose care
Teaches thy way along that pathless coast—
The desert and illimitable air—
Lone wandering, but not lost.

All day thy wings have fanned,
At that far height, the cold, thin atmosphere,
Yet stoop not weary, to the welcome land,
    Though the dark night is near.

And soon that toil shall end;
Soon shalt thou find a summer home, and rest,
And scream among thy fellows; reeds shall bend,
    Soon, O'er thy sheltered nest.

Thou'rt gone! the abyss of heaven
Hath swallowed up thy form; yet on my heart
Deeply hath sunk the lesson thou hast given,
    And shall not soon depart.

He who, from zone to zone,
Guides through the boundless sky thy certain flight,
In the long way that I must tread alone,
    Will lead my steps aright.

To a Skylark
by Percy Bysshe Shelley (1792-1822)

In my opinion, definitely Shelley's best. Long, but the 2
highlighted stanzas are worth all the build up. I do feel
that cut in half it would have been twice as great.

Hail to thee, blithe spirit!
    Bird thou never wert,
That from heaven, or near it,
    Pourest thy full heart
In profuse strains of unpremeditated art.

Higher still and higher
    From the earth thou springest,
Like a cloud of fire;
    The blue deep thou wingest,
And singing still dost soar, and soaring ever singest.

In the golden lightning
        Of the sunken sun,
    O'er which clouds are brightening,
        Thou dost float and run,
Like an unbodied joy whose race is just begun.

    The pale purple even
        Melts around thy flight;
    Like a star of heaven,
        In the broad daylight
Thou art unseen, but yet I hear thy shrill delight,

    Keen as are the arrows
        Of that silver sphere,
    Whose intense lamp narrows
        In the white dawn clear,
Until we hardly see, we feel that it is there.

    All the earth and air
        With thy voice is loud,
    As, when night is bare,
        From one lonely cloud
The moon rains out her beams, and heaven is overflowed.

    What thou art we know not;
        What is most like thee?
    From rainbow clouds there flow not
        Drops so bright to see,
As from thy presence showers a rain of melody.

    Like a poet hidden
        In the light of thought,
    Singing hymns unbidden,
        Till the world is wrought
To sympathy with hopes and fears it heeded not;

    Like a high-born maiden
        In a palace tower,
    Soothing her love-laden
        Soul in secret hour
With music sweet as love, which overflows her bower;

Like a glow-worm golden
　　　In a dell of dew,
　Scattering unbeholden
　　　Its aerial hue
Among the flowers and grass, which screen it from the view;

Like a rose embowered
　　　In its own green leaves,
　By winds deflowered,
　　　Till the scent it gives
Makes faint with too much sweet these heavy-wing'ed thieves.

Sound of vernal showers,
　　　On the twinkling grass,
　Rain-awakened flowers,
　　　All that ever was
Joyous and clear and fresh thy music doth surpass.

Teach us, sprite or bird,
　　　What sweet thoughts are thine!
　I have never heard
　　　Praise of love or wine
That panted forth a flood of rapture so divine.

Chorus hymeneal
　　　Or triumphal chant,
　Matched with thine, would be all
　　　But an empty vaunt,—
A thing wherein we feel there is some hidden want.

What objects are the fountains
　　　Of thy happy strain?
　What fields or waves or mountains?
　　　What shapes of sky or plain?
What love of thine own kind? what ignorance of pain?

With thy clear keen joyance
　　　Languor cannot be;
　Shadow of annoyance
　　　Never came near thee;
Thou lovest, but ne'er know love's sad satiety.

Waking or asleep,
Thou of death must deem
Things more true and deep
Than we mortals dream,
Or how could thy notes flow in such a crystal stream?

We look before and after,
And pine for what is not;
Our sincerest laughter
With some pain is fraught;
Our sweetest songs are those that tell of saddest thought.

Yet if we could scorn
Hate and pride and fear;
If we were things born
Not to shed a tear,
I know not how thy joy we ever should come near.

Better than all measures
Of delightful sound,
Better than all treasures
That in books are found,
Thy skill to poet were, thou scorner of the ground!

Teach me half the gladness
That thy brain must know,
Such harmonious madness
From my lips would flow,
The world should listen then, as I am listening now.

The World is Too Much with Us
by William Wordsworth (1770-1850)

Too many of us just don't bother to enjoy the wonderful pleasures of the land and the sea. Familiarity has almost built contempt.

The world is too much with us; late and soon,
Getting and spending, we lay waste our powers:
Little we see in Nature that is ours;
We have given our hearts away, a sordid boon!
The sea that bares her bosom to the moon,

The winds that will be howling at all hours,
And are up-gathered now like sleeping flowers;
For this, for everything, we are out of tune;
It moves us not—Great God! I'd rather be
A pagan suckled in a creed outworn;
So might I, standing on this pleasant lea,
Have glimpses that would make me less forlorn;
Have sight of Proteus rising from the sea;
Or hear old Triton blow his wreathed horn.

The Rhodora

On Being Asked Whence Is the Flower
by Ralph Waldo Emerson (1803-1882)

Remember from Elegy Written in a Country
Churchyard—"Full many a flower is born to
blush unseen, and waste its sweetness on the
desert air." Rhodora is a name for the plant
Rhododendron. The accented quote is often
used on garden plaques and could be used on many occasions.

In May, when sea-winds pierced our solitudes,
I found the fresh Rhodora in the woods,
Spreading its leafless blooms in a damp nook,
To please the desert and the sluggish brook.
The purple petals, fallen in the pool,
Made the black water with their beauty gay;
Here might the redbird come his plumes to cool,
And court the flower that cheapens his array.
Rhodora! if the sages ask thee why
This charm is wasted on the earth and sky,
Tell them, dear, that if eyes were made for seeing,
Then Beauty is its own excuse for being:
Why thou wert there, O rival of the rose!
I never thought to ask, I never knew:
But, in my simple ignorance, suppose
The self-same Power that brought me there brought you.

The Heart of the Tree
by Henry Cuyler Bunner (1855-1896)

If you were not convinced by Kilmer, read this. And
after you read this, you will enjoy and appreciate
trees even more. Plant a few and watch your
enjoyment grow with them.

What does he plant who plants a tree?
    He plants a friend of sun and sky;
    He plants the flag of breezes free;
    The shaft of beauty, towering high;
He plants a home to heaven anigh
    For song and mother-croon of bird
    In hushed and happy twilight heard—
    The treble of heaven's harmony—
These things be plants who plants a tree.

What does he plant who plants a tree?
    He plants cool shade and tender rain,
    And seed and bud of days to be,
    And years that fade and flush again;
He plants the glory of the plain;
    He plants the forest's heritage;
    The harvest of a coming age;
    The joy that unborn eyes shall see
These things he plants who plants a tree.

What does he plant who plants a tree?
    He plants, in sap and leaf and wood,
    In love of home and loyalty
    And far-cast thought of civic good—
His blessings on the neighborhood
    Who, in the hollow of His hand
    Holds all the growth of all our land—
    A nation's growth from sea to sea
Stirs in his heart who plants a tree.

The Daffodils
by William Wordsworth (1770-1850)

A must for any gardener or nature lover. Another
of my all-time most favorite poems. Go ahead and
read it twice—it's great! And read it again in the
spring when the daffys show their bright, shining
faces.

I wandered lonely as a cloud
    That floats on high o'er vales and hills,
When all at once I saw a crowd,
    A host, of golden daffodils,
Beside the lake, beneath the trees,
Fluttering and dancing in the breeze.

Continuous as the stars that shine
    And twinkle on the Milky Way,
They stretched in never-ending line
    Along the margin of a bay:
Ten thousand saw I at a glance,
Tossing their heads in sprightly dance.

The waves beside them danced, but they
    Outdid the sparkling waves in glee;
A poet could not but be gay
    In such a jocund company.
I gazed, and gazed, but little thought
What wealth the show to me had brought;

For oft, when on my couch I lie
    In vacant or in pensive mood,
They flash upon that inward eye
    Which is the bliss of solitude;
And then my heart with pleasure fills,
And dances with the daffodils.

Song of the Chattahoochee

by Sidney Lanier (1842-1881)

A cheerful little ditty that goes along like a
song being sung by the river. What a pleasant,
lovely and exciting ride. Can I borrow your canoe?
The Chattahoochee is an important river of Georgia, rising in the northern
county of Habersham, near the South Carolina border, and flowing
through the County of Hall, towards Atlanta. It then bends, joins the Flint
River to form the Apalachicola, and eventually enters the extensive
Tennessee River basin.

> Out of the hills of Habersham,
> Down the valleys of Hall,
> I hurry amain to reach the plain,
> > Run the rapid and leap the fall,
> > Split at the rock and together again,
> > Accept my bed, or narrow or wide,
> > And flee from folly on every side
> > With a lover's pain to attain the plain
> Far from the hills of Habersham,
> Far from the valleys of Hall.

> All down the hills of Habersham,
> All through the valleys of Hall,
> > The rushes cried *Abide, abide,*
> > The willful waterweeds held me thrall,
> > The laving laurel turned my tide,
> > The ferns and the fondling grass said Stay,
> > The dewberry dipped for to work delay,
> > And the little reeds sighed *Abide, abide,*
> Here in the hills of Habersham,
> Here in the valleys of Hall.

High o'er the hills of Habersham,
Veiling the valleys of Hall,
    The hickory told me manifold
    Fair tales of shade, the poplar tall
    Wrought me her shadowy self to hold,
    The chestnut, the oak, the walnut, the pine,
    Overleaning, with flickering meaning and sign,
    Said, Pass not, so cold, these manifold
Deep shades of the hills of Habersham,
These glades in the valleys of Hall.

And oft in the hills of Habersham,
And oft in the valleys of Hall,
    The white quartz shone, and the smooth brook-stone
    Did bar me of passage with friendly brawl,
    And many a luminous jewel lone—
    Crystals clear or a-cloud with mist,
    Ruby, garnet and amethyst—
    Made lures with the lights of streaming stone
In the clefts of the hills of Habersham,
In the beds of the valleys of Hall.

But oh, not the hills of Habersham,
And oh, not the valleys of Hall
    Avail: I am fain to water the plain.
    Downward the voices of Duty call—
    Downward, to toil and be mixed—with the main;
    The dry fields burn, and the mills are to turn,
    And a myriad flowers mortally yearn,
    And the lordly main beyond the plain
Calls o'er the hills of Habersham,
Calls through the valleys of Hall.

I Broke the Spell that Held Me Long

by William Cullen Bryant (1794-1878)

This expresses concisely my personal feeling of the pleasures of poetry and song and helps explain why I wanted to put this anthology together. Bryant's co-mingling of music and poetry is another expression of my statement in the introduction of this book; "Poetry - The Music of Literature. Music—The Poetry of Expression."

> I broke the spell that held me long,
>> The dear, dear witchery of song.
> I said, the poet's idle lore
>> Shall waste my prime of years no more,
> For poetry, though heavenly born
>> Consorts with poverty and scorn.
>
> I broke the spell—nor deemed the power
>> Could fetter me another hour.
> Ah, thoughtless! How could I forget
>> Its causes were around me yet?
> For whensoe'er I looked, the while
>> Was Nature's everlasting smile.
>
> Still came and lingered on my sight
>> Of flowers and streams the bloom and light
> And glory of the stars and sun;—
>> And these and poetry are one.
> They, ere the World had held me long,
>> Recalled me to the love of song.

To a Mouse

by Robert Burns (1759-1796)

Burns turned up the mouse's nest while plowing,
and according to the boy who was helping him, at
once became distracted. Immediately afterwards
he read to the helper this poem, obviously concocted
on the spot. A lot of lessons here!

Wee, sleekit, cow'rin', tim'rous beastie,
Oh, what a panic's in they breastie!
Thou needna start awa' sae hasty,
    Wi' bickering brattle!
I wad be laith to rin and chase thee,
    Wi' murd'ring pattle!

I'm truly sorry man's dominion
Has broken Nature's social union,
And justifies that ill opinion,
    Which makes thee startle
At me, thy poor earth-born companion
    And fellow-mortal!

I doubtna, whiles, but thou may thieve;
What then? poor beastie, thou maun live!
A daimen' icker² in a thrave
    'S a sma' request:
I'll get a blessin' wi' the lave,
    And never miss 'it!

Thy wee bit housie, too, in ruin!
Its silly wa's the win's are strewin'!
And naething now to big a new ane
    O' foggage³ green,
And bleak December winds ensuin',
    Baith snell and keen!

Thou saw the fields laid bare and waste
And weary winter comin' fast,
And cozie here, beneath the blast,
    Thou thought to dwell,
Till, crash! the cruel coulter passed
    Out through thy cell.

That wee bit heap o' leaves and stibble
Has cost thee monie a weary nibble!
Now thou's turned out for a' thy trouble,
    But house or hald,
To thole the winter's sleety dribble,
    And cranreuch[4] cauld!

But, Mousie, thou are no thy lane,
In proving foresight may be vain:
The best-laid schemes o' mice and men
    Gang aft a-gley,
And lea'e us naught but grief and pain,
    For promised joy.

Still thou are blest, compared wi' me!
The present only toucheth thee:
But, och! I backward cast my e'e
    On prospects drear!
And forward, though I canna see,
    I guess and fear.

[1] *daimen: rare*
[2] *icker: ear of corn*
[3] *foggage: long grass.*
[4] *cranreuch: hoar frost.*

To a Cricket
by William Cox Bennett (1820-1895)

Everyone wants a cricket, alive or metal, on their fireplace as a sign of good luck. The song, however, goes only with the live one.

> Voice of summer, keen and shrill,
>> Chirping round my winter fire,
>> Of thy song I never tire,
> Weary others as they will,
> For thy song with summer's filled—
>> Filled with sunshine, filled with June;
>> Firelight echo of that noon
> Heard in fields when all is stilled
>> In the golden light of May,
>> Bringing scents of new-mown hay,
>> Bees, and birds, and flowers away,
> Prithee, haunt my fireside still,
> Voice of summer, keen and shrill.

The Sea
by Bryan Waller Procter (1787-1874)

Salt must have gotten in his eyes—he couldn't see the land for the waves.

> The sea! the sea! the open sea!
> The blue, the fresh, the ever free!
> Without a mark, without a bound,
> It runneth the earth's wide regions round;
> It plays with the clouds; it mocks the skies;
> Or like a cradled creature lies.
>
> I'm on the sea! I'm on the sea!
> I am where I would ever be;
> With the blue above, and the blue below,
> And silence whereso'er I go;
> If a storm should come and awake the deep,
> What matter! I shall ride and sleep.

I love, O, how I love to ride
On the fierce, foaming, bursting tide,
When every mad wave drowns the moon
Or whistles aloft his tempest tune,
And tells how goeth the world below,
And why the sou'west blasts do blow.

I never was on the dull, tame shore,
But I loved the great sea more and more,
And backwards flow to her billowy breast,
Like a bird that seeketh its mother's nest;
And a mother she was, and is, to me;
For I was born on the open sea!

The waves were white, and red the morn,
In the noisy hour when I was born;
And the whale it whistled, the porpoise rolled,
And the dolphins bared their backs of gold;
And never was heard such an outcry wild
As welcomed to life the ocean-child!

I've lived since then, in calm and strife,
Full fifty summers, a sailor's life,
With wealth to spend and a power to range,
But never have sought nor sighed for change;
And Death, whenever he comes to me,
Shall come on the wild, unbounded sea!

The Rime of the Ancient Mariner
by Samuel Taylor Coleridge (1772-1834)

This is a truly great poem, but very long. Please don't start it unless you are sitting down and have about 20 minutes to read it slowly and really enjoy it. Follow the ship as it works its way down the eastern coast of South America and then struggles up the west coast. Then the dire results of the senseless killing of the albatross. The Mariner finds, at voyage's end, that he gets a severe pain of guilt from the deed, that is only relieved by telling his whole story to someone who will listen; in this case to a Wedding-Guest. The stirring message and lesson of the poem is summarized in the two highlighted stanzas at the end.

It is an ancient Mariner,
And he stoppeth one of three.
"By thy long gray beard and glittering eye,
Now wherefore stopp'st thou me?

"The Bridegroom's doors are opened wide,
And I am next of kin;
The guests are met, the feast is set:
May'st hear the merry din."

He holds him with his skinny hand,
"There was a ship," quoth he,
"Hold off! unhand me, gray-beard loon!"
Eftsoons his hand dropped he.

He holds him with his glittering eye—
The Wedding-Guest stood still,
And listens like a three year's child:
The Mariner hath his will.

The Wedding-Guest sat on a stone:
He cannot choose but hear;
And thus spake on that ancient man,
The bright-eyed Mariner.

"The ship was cheered, the harbor cleared,
Merrily did we drop
Below the kirk, below the hill,
Below the lighthouse top.

"The Sun came up upon the left,
Out of the sea came he!
And he shone bright, and on the right
Went down into the sea.

"Higher and higher every day,
Till over the mast at noon—"
The Wedding-Guest here beat his breast,
For he heard the loud bassoon.

The bride hath paced into the hall,
Red as a rose is she;
Nodding their heads before her goes
The merry minstrelsy.

The Wedding-Guest he beat his breast,
Yet he cannot choose but hear;
And thus spake on that ancient man,
The bright-eyed Mariner.

"And now the Storm-blast came, and he
Was tyrannous and strong:
He struck with his o'ertaking wings,
And chased us south along.

"With sloping masts and dipping prow,
As who pursued with yell and blow
Still treads the shadow of his foe,
And forward bends his head,
The ship drove fast, loud roared the blast,
And southward aye we fled.

"And now there came both mist and snow,
And it grew wondrous cold:
And ice, mast-high, came floating by,
As green as emerald.

"And through the drifts the snowy clifts
Did send a dismal sheen:
Nor shapes of men, nor beasts we ken—
The ice was all between.

"The ice was here, the ice was there,
The ice was all around:
It cracked and growled, and roared and howled,
Like noises in a swound!

"At length did cross an Albatross,
Through the fog it came;
As if it had been a Christian soul,
We hailed it in God's name.

"It ate the food it ne'er had eat,
And round and round it flew:
The ice did split with a thunder-fit;
The helmsman steered us through!

"And a good south wind sprung up behind;
The Albatross did follow,
And every day, for food or play,
Came to the mariners' hollo!

"In mist or cloud, on mast or shroud,
It perched for vespers nine;
Whiles all the night, through fog-smoke white,
Glimmered the white moonshine."

"God save thee, ancient Mariner,
From the fiends, that plague thee thus!—
Why look'st thou so?" "With my crossbow
I shot the Albatross.

Part II

"The Sun now rose upon the right:
Out of the sea came he,
Still hid in mist, and on the left
Went down into the sea.

"And the good south wind still blew behind,
But no sweet bird did follow,
Nor any day for food or play
Came to the mariners' hollo!

"And I had done a hellish thing,
And it would work 'em woe:
For all averred I had killed the bird
That made the breeze to blow,
Ah wretch! said they, the bird to slay,
That made the breeze to blow!

"Nor dim nor red, like God's own head,
The glorious Sun uprist:
Then all averred I had killed the bird
That brought the fog and mist.
'Twas right, said they, such birds to slay,
That bring the fog and mist.

"The fair breezes blew, the white foam flew,
The furrow followed free;
We were the first that ever burst
Into that silent sea.

"Down dropped the breeze, the sails dropped down,
'Twas sad as sad could be;
And we did speak only to break
The silence of the sea!

"All in a hot and copper sky,
The bloody Sun, at noon,
Right up above the mast did stand,
No bigger than the Moon.

"**Day after day, day after day,
We stuck, nor breath nor motion;
As idle as a painted ship
Upon a painted ocean.**

"**Water, water, everywhere,
And all the boards did shrink;
Water, water, everywhere,
Nor any drop to drink.**

"The very deep did rot: O Christ!
That ever this should be!
Yea, slimy things did crawl with legs
Upon the slimy sea.

"About, about, in reel and rout
The death-fires danced at night;
The water, like a witch's oils,
Burnt green, and blue, and white.

"And some in dreams assured were
Of the spirit that plagued us so;
Nine fathom deep he had followed us
From the land of mist and snow.

"And every tongue, through utter drought,
Was withered at the root;
We could not speak, no more than if
We had been choked with soot.

"Ah! well-a-day! what evil looks
Had I from old and young!
Instead of the cross, the Albatross
About my neck was hung.

Part III

"There passed a weary time. Each throat
Was parched, and glazed each eye.
A weary time! a weary time!
How glazed each weary eye!
When looking westward, I beheld
A something in the sky.

"At first it seemed a little speck,
And then it seemed a mist;
It moved and moved, and took at last
A certain shape, I wist.

"A speck, a mist, a shape, I wist!
And still it neared and neared:
As if it dodged a water-sprite,
It plunged, and tacked, and veered.

"With throats unslaked, with black lips baked,
We could nor laugh nor wail;
Through utter drought all dumb we stood!
I bit my arm, I sucked the blood,
And cried, A sail! a sail!

"With throats unslaked, with black lips baked,
Agape they heard me call:
Gramercy! they for joy did grin,
And all at once their breath drew in,
As they were drinking all.

"See! See! (I cried) she tacks no more
Hither to work us weal—
Without a breeze, without a tide,
She steadies with upright keel!

"The western wave was all aflame,
The day was wellnigh done!
Almost upon the western wave
Rested the broad, bright Sun;
When that strange shape drove suddenly
Betwixt us and the Sun.

"And straight the Sun was flecked with bars
(Heaven's Mother send us grace!),
As if through a dungeon-grate he peered
With broad and burning face.

"Alas! (thought I, and my heart beat loud)
How fast she nears and nears!
Are those her sails that glance in the Sun,
Like restless gossameres?

"Are those her ribs through which the Sun
Did peer, as through a grate?
And is that Woman all her crew?
Is that a Death? and are there two?
Is Death that Woman's mate?

"Her lips were red, her looks were free,
Her locks were yellow as gold:
Her skin was as white as leprosy,
The Nightmare Life-in-Death was she,
Who thicks man's blood with cold.

"The naked hulk alongside came,
And the twain were casting dice;
'The game is done! I've won! I've won!'
Quoth she, and whistles thrice.

"The Sun's rim dips; the stars rush out
At one stride comes the dark;
With far-heard whisper, o'er the sea,
Off shot the specter-bark.

"We listened and looked sideways up!
Fear at my heart, as at a cup,
My life-blood seemed to sip!
The stars were dim, and thick the night,
The steersman's face by his lamp gleamed white;
From the sails the dew did drip—
Till clomb above the eastern bar
The horned Moon, with one bright star
Within the nether tip.

"One after one, by the star-dogged Moon,
Too quick for groan or sigh,
Each turned his face with a ghastly pang,
And cursed me with his eye.

"Four times fifty living men
(And I heard nor sigh nor groan),
With heavy thump, a lifeless lump,
They dropped down one by one.

"The souls did from their bodies fly—
They fled to bliss or woe!
And every soul, it passed me by
Like the whizz of my crossbow!"

Part IV

"I fear thee, ancient Mariner!
I fear thy skinny hand!
And thou art long, and lank, and brown,
As is the ribbed sea-sand.

"I fear thee and thy glittering eye,
And thy skinny hand so brown."—
"Fear not, fear not, thou Wedding-Guest!
This body dropped not down.

"Alone, alone, all, all alone,
Alone on a wide, wide sea!
And never a saint took pity on
My soul in agony.

"The many men, so beautiful!
And they all dead did lie:
And a thousand thousand slimy things
Lived on; and so did I.

"I looked upon the rotting sea,
And drew my eyes away;
I looked upon the rotting deck,
And there the dead men lay.

"I looked to heaven, and tried to pray;
But or ever a prayer had gushed,
A wicked whisper came, and made
My heart as dry as dust.

"I closed my lids, and kept them close,
And the balls like pulses beat;
For the sky and the sea, and the sea and the sky,
Lay like a load on my weary eye,
And the dead were at my feet.

"The cold sweat melted from their limbs,
Nor rot nor reek did they:
The look with which they looked on me
Had never passed away.

"An orphan's curse would drag to hell
A spirit from on high;
But oh! more horrible that that
Is a curse in a dead man's eye!
Seven days, seven nights, I saw that curse,
And yet I could not die.

"The moving Moon went up the sky,
And nowhere did abide;
Softly she was going up,
And a star or two beside—

"Her beams bemocked the sultry main,
Like April hoar-frost spread;
But where the ship's huge shadow lay,
The charmed water burnt alway
A still and awful red.

"Beyond the shadow of the ship,
I watched the water-snakes:
They moved in tracks of shining white,
And when they reared, the elfish light
Fell off in hoary flakes.

"Within the shadow of the ship
I watched their rich attire:
Blue, glossy green, and velvet black,
They coiled and swam; and every track
Was a flash of golden fire.

"O happy living things! no tongue
Their beauty might declare:
A spring of love gushed from my heart,
And I blessed them unaware:
Sure my kind saint took pity on me,
And I blessed them unaware.

"The selfsame moment I could pray;
And from my neck so free
The Albatross fell off, and sank
Like lead into the sea.

Part V

"O sleep! it is a gentle thing,
Beloved from pole to pole!
To Mary Queen the praise be given!
She sent the gentle sleep from Heaven,
That slid into my soul.

"The silly buckets on the deck,
That had so long remained,
I dreamt that they were filled with dew;
And when I awoke, it rained.

"My lips were wet, my throat was cold,
My garments all were dank;
Sure I had drunken in my dreams,
And still my body drank.

"I moved, and could not feel my limbs;
I was so light—almost
I thought that I had died in sleep,
And was a blessed ghost.

"And soon I heard a roaring wind:
It did not come anear;
But with its sound it shook the sails,
That were so thin and sere.

"The upper air burst into life;
And a hundred fire-flags sheen;
To and fro they were hurried about;
And to and fro, and in and out,
The wan stars danced between.

"And the coming wind did roar more loud,
And the sails did sigh like sedge;
And the rain poured down from one black cloud;
The Moon was at its edge.

"The thick black cloud was cleft, and still
The Moon was at its side;
Like waters shot from some high crag,
The lightning fell with never a jag,
A river steep and wide.

"The loud wind never reached the ship,
Yet now the ship moved on!
Beneath the lightning and the Moon
The dead men gave a groan.

"They groaned, they stirred, they all uprose,
Nor spake, nor moved their eyes;
It had been strange, even in a dream,
To have seen those dead men rise.

"The helmsman steered, the ship moved on;
Yet never a breeze up-blew;
The mariners all 'gan work the ropes,
Where they were wont to do;
They raised their limbs like lifeless tools—
We were a ghastly crew.

"The body of my brother's son
Stood by me, knee to knee:
The body and I pulled at one rope,
But he said naught to me."

"I fear thee, ancient Mariner!"
"Be calm, thou Wedding-Guest:
'Twas not those souls that fled in pain,
Which to their corses came again,
But a troop of spirits blest:

"For when it dawned—they dropped their arms,
And clustered round the mast;
Sweet sounds rose slowly through their mouths,
And from their bodies passed.

"Around, around, flew each sweet sound,
Then darted to the Sun;
Slowly the sounds came back again,
Now mixed, now one by one.

"Sometimes a-dropping from the sky
I heard the skylark sing;
Sometimes all little birds that are,
How they seemed to fill the sea and air
With their sweet jargoning!

"And now 'twas like all instruments,
Now like a lonely flute;
And now it is an angel's song
That makes the Heavens be mute.

"It ceased: yet still the sails made on
A pleasant noise till noon,
A noise like that of a hidden brook
In the leafy month of June,
That to the sleeping woods all night
Singeth a quiet tune.

"Till noon we quietly sailed on,
Yet never a breeze did breathe:
Slowly and smoothly went the ship,
Moved onward from beneath.

"Under the keel nine fathom deep,
From the land of mist and snow,
The Spirit slid: and it was he
That made the ship to go.
The sails at noon left off their tune,
And the ship stood still also.

"The Sun, right up above the mast,
Had fixed her to the ocean:
But in a minute she 'gan stir,
With a short uneasy motion—
Backwards and forwards half her length
With a short uneasy motion.

"Then like a pawing horse let go,
She made a sudden bound:
It flung the blood into my head,
And I fell down in a swound.

"How long in that same fit I lay,
I have not to declare;
But ere my living life returned,
I heard, and in my soul discerned
Two voices in the air.

"'Is it he?' quoth one, 'is this the man?
By Him who died on cross,
With his cruel bow he laid full low
The harmless Albatross.

"'The Spirit who bideth by himself
In the land of mist and snow,
He loved the bird that loved the man
Who shot him with his bow.'

"The other was a softer voice,
As soft as honey-dew:
Quoth he, 'The man hath penance done,
And penance more will do.'

Part VI

First Voice:
"'But tell me, tell me! speak again,
Thy soft response renewing—
What makes that ship drive on so fast?
What is the Ocean doing?'

Second Voice:
"'Still as a slave before his lord,
The Ocean hath no blast;
His great bright eye most silently
Up to the Moon is cast—

"'If he may know which way to go;
For she guides him smooth or grim.
See, brother, see! how graciously
She looketh down on him.'

First Voice:
"'But why drives on that ship so fast,
Without or wave or wind?'

Second Voice:
"'The air is cut away before,
And closes from behind.

"'Fly, brother, fly! more high, more high!
Or we shall be belated:
For slow and slow that ship will go,
When the Mariner's trance is abated."

"I woke, and we were sailing on
As in a gentle weather:
'Twas night, calm night, the Moon was high;
The dead men stood together.

"All stood together on the deck,
For a charnel-dungeon fitter:
All fixed on me their stony eyes,
That in the Moon did glitter.

"The pang, the curse, with which they died,
Had never passed away:
I could not draw my eyes from theirs,
Nor turn them up to pray.

"And now this spell was snapped: once more
I viewed the ocean green,
And looked far forth, yet little saw
Of what had else had been seen—

"Like one that on a lonesome road
Doth walk in fear and dread,
And having once turned round, walks on,
And turns no more his head;
Because he knows a frightful fiend
Doth close behind him tread.

"But soon there breathed a wind on me,
Nor sound nor motion made:
Its path was not upon the sea,
In ripple or in shade.

"It raised my hair, it fanned my cheek
Like a meadow-gale of spring—
It mingled strangely with my fears,
Yet it felt like a welcoming.

"Swiftly, swiftly flew the ship,
Yet she sailed softly too:
Sweetly, sweetly blew the breeze—
On me alone it blew.

"O dream of joy! is this indeed
The lighthouse top I see?
Is this the hill? is this the kirk?
Is this mine own countree?

"We drifted o'er the harbor-bar,
And I with sobs did pray—
O let me be awake, my God!
Or let me sleep away.

"The harbor-bay was clear as glass,
So smoothly it was strewn!
And on the bay the moonlight lay,
And the shadow of the Moon.

"The rock shone bright, the kirk no less,
That stands above the rock:
The moonlight steeped in silentness
The steady weathercock.

"And the bay was white with silent light
Till rising from the same,
Full many shapes, that shadows were
In crimson colors came.

"A little distance from the prow
Those crimson shadows were;
I turned my eyes upon the deck—
O Christ! what saw I there!

"Each corse lay flat, lifeless and flat,
And, by the holy rood!
A man all light, a seraph-man,
On every corse there stood.

"This seraph-band, each waved his hand:
It was a heavenly sight!
They stood as signals to the land,
Each one a lovely light;

"This seraph-band, each waved his hand,
No voice did they impart—
No voice; but O, the silence sank
Like music on my heart.

"But soon I heard the dash of oars,
I heard the Pilot's cheer;
My head was turned perforce away,
And I saw a boat appear.

"The Pilot and the Pilot's boy,
I heard them coming fast:
Dear Lord in Heaven! it was a joy
The dead men could not blast.

"I saw a third—I heard his voice:
It was the Hermit good!
He singeth loud his godly hymns
That he makes in the wood.
He'll shrieve my soul, he'll wash away
The Albatross's blood.

Part VII

"This Hermit good lives in that wood
Which slopes down to the sea.
How loudly his sweet voice he rears!
He loves to talk with marineres
That come from a far countree.

"He kneels at morn, and noon, and eve—
He hath a cushion plump:
It is the moss that wholly hides
The rotted old oak-stump.

"The skiff-boat neared: I heard them talk,
'Why, this is strange, I trow!
Where are those lights so many and fair,
That signal made but now?'

"'Strange, by my faith!' the Hermit said—
'And they answered not our cheer!
The planks look warped! and see those sails,
How thin they are and sere!
I never saw aught like to them,
Unless perchance it were

"'Brown skeletons of leaves that lag
My forest-brook along;
When the ivy-tod is heavy with snow,
And the owlet whoops to the wolf below,
That eats the she-wolf's young.'

"'Dear Lord! it hath a fiendish look—
(The Pilot made reply)
I am a-feared.'—'Push on, push on!'
Said the Hermit cheerily.

"The boat came closer to the ship,
But I nor spake nor stirred;
The boat came close beneath the ship,
And straight a sound was heard.

"Under the water it rumbled on,
Still louder and more dread:
It reached the ship, it split the bay;
The ship went down like lead.

"Stunned by that loud and dreadful sound,
Which sky and ocean smote,
Like one that hath been seven days drowned
My body lay afloat;
But swift as dreams, myself I found
Within the Pilot's boat.

"Upon the whirl, where sank the ship,
The boat spun round and round;
And all was still, save that the hill
Was telling of the sound.

"I moved my lips—the Pilot shrieked
And fell down in a fit;
The holy Hermit raised his eyes,
And prayed where he did sit:

"I took the oars: the Pilot's boy,
Who now doth crazy go,
Laughed loud and long, and all the while
His eyes went to and fro.
'Ha! ha!' quoth he, 'full plain I see
The Devil knows how to row.'

"And now, all in my own countree,
I stood on the firm land!
The Hermit stepped forth from the boat,
And scarcely he could stand.

"'O shrieve me, shrieve me, holy man!'
The Hermit crossed his brow,
'Say quick,' quoth he, 'I bid thee say—
What manner of man art thou?'

"Forthwith this frame of mine was wrenched
With a woeful agony,
Which forced me to begin my tale;
And then it left me free.

"Since then, at an uncertain hour,
That agony returns:
And till my ghastly tale is told,
This heart within me burns.

"I pass, like night, from land to land;
I have strange power of speech;
That moment that his face I see,
I know the man that must hear me:
To him my tale I teach.

"What loud uproar bursts from that door!
The wedding-guests are there:
But in the garden-bower the bride
And bride-maids singing are:
And hark, the little vesper bell,
Which biddeth me to prayer!

"O Wedding-Guest! this soul hath been
Alone on a wide, wide sea:
So lonely 'twas, that God Himself
Scarce seemed there to be.

"O sweeter than the marriage-feast,
'Tis sweeter far to me,
To walk together to the kirk
With a goodly company!—

"To walk together to the kirk,
And all together pray,
While each to his great Father bends,
Old men, and babes, and loving friends,
And youths and maidens gay!

"Farewell, farewell! but this I tell
To thee, thou Wedding-Guest!
He prayeth well, who loveth well
Both man and bird and beast.

"He prayeth best, who loveth best
All things both great and small;
For the dear God, who loveth us,
He made and loveth all."

The Mariner, whose eye is bright,
Whose beard with age is hoar,
Is gone: and now the Wedding-Guest
Turned from the bridegroom's door.

He went like one that hath been stunned,
And is of sense forlorn:
A sadder and wiser man
He rose the morrow morn.

The poor Wedding-Guest surely paid a great price to learn the above
lesson and give the poor Mariner at least temporary relief again.

The Raven
by Edgar Allan Poe (1809-1849)

Logo of the Raven Society

A truly great poem. It is felt that Poe wrote, or at least envisioned *The Raven* while attending the University of Virginia and living at 13 West Range, which is a part of Mr. Jefferson's original "Academic Village." 100 years later, as a medical student, I lived for 4 years opposite from Poe's room at 20 East Range, in a an identical room. It surely makes it easy for me to picture the black bird sitting in the poorly lit room, on the shutters which are still there, and finding Poe in one of his very low moods, while mourning the loss of his beloved *Lenore*, or *Annabel Lee*. Incidentally, each room has a small, usable fireplace. The University of Virginia, proud of its ill-starred poet alumnus, has an honor society named after this poem, The Raven Society. Membership is voted on the combined features of scholarship and service to the University. Instead of a pin or a ring, the recipients received a key for admission to 13 West Range, Poe's old room. I highly treasure my key. Unfortunately the keys are no longer given.

> Once upon a midnight dreary, while I pondered, weak and weary,
> Over many a quaint and curious volume of forgotten lore,
> While I nodded, nearly napping, suddenly there came a tapping,
> As of someone gently rapping, rapping at my chamber door.
> "'Tis some visitor," I muttered, "tapping at my chamber door;
>   Only this, and nothing more."
>
> Ah, distinctly I remember, it was in the bleak December,
> And each separate dying ember wrought its ghost upon the floor.
> Eagerly I wished the morrow; vainly I had sought to borrow
> From my books surcease of sorrow, sorrow for the lost Lenore,
> For the rare and radiant maiden whom the angels name Lenore,
>   Nameless here forevermore.
>
> And the silken sad uncertain rustling of each purple curtain
> Thrilled me—filled me with fantastic terrors never felt before;
> So that now, to still the beating of my heart, I stood repeating,
> "'Tis some visitor entreating entrance at my chamber door,
> Some late visitor entreating entrance at my chamber door
>   This it is, and nothing more."

Presently my soul grew stronger; hesitating then no longer,
"Sir," said I, "or madam, truly your forgiveness I implore;
But the fact is, I was napping, and so gently you came rapping,
And so faintly you came tapping, tapping at my chamber door,
That I scarce was sure I heard you." Here I opened wide the door;—
    Darkness there, and nothing more.

Deep into the darkness peering, long I stood there, wondering, fearing,
Doubting, dreaming dreams no mortals ever dared to dream before;
But the silence was unbroken, and the stillness gave no token,
And the only word there spoken was the whispered word, "Lenore?"
This I whispered, and an echo murmured back the word, "Lenore!"
    Merely this, and nothing more.

Back into the chamber turning, all my soul within me burning,
Soon again I heard a tapping, something louder than before,
"Surely," said I, "surely, that is something at my window lattice
Let me see, then, what thereat is, and this mystery explore;
Let my heart be still a moment, and this mystery explore;
    'Tis the wind, and nothing more."

Open-here I flung the shutter, when, with many a flirt and flutter,
In there stepped a stately raven, of the saintly day of yore.
Not the least obeisance made he; not a minute stopped or stayed he;
But with mien of lord or lady, perched above my chalice door;
Perched upon a bust of Pallas, just above my chamber door,
    Perched, and sat, and nothing more.

Then this ebony bird beguiling my sad fancy into smiling,
By the grave and stern decorum of the countenance it wore,
"Though thy crest be shorn and shaven, thou," I said, "art sure no craven,
Ghastly, grim, and ancient raven, wandering from the nightly shore.
Tell me what thy lordly name is on the Night's Plutonian shore."
    Quoth the raven, "Nevermore."

Much I marvelled this ungainly fowl to hear discourse so plainly,
Though its answer little meaning, little relevancy bore;
For we cannot help agreeing that no living human being
Ever yet was blessed with seeing bird above his chamber door,
Bird or beast upon the sculptured bust above his chamber door,
     With such name as "Nevermore."

But the raven, sitting lonely on that placid bust, spoke only
That one word, as if his soul in that one word he did outpour.
Nothing further then he uttered; not a feather then he fluttered;
Till I scarcely more than muttered, "Other friends have flown before;
On the morrow he will leave me, as my hopes have flown before."
     Then the bird said, "Nevermore."

Startled at the stillness broken by reply so aptly spoken,
"Doubtless," said I, "what it utters is its only stock and store,
Caught from some unhappy master, from unmerciful disaster
Followed fast and followed faster, till his songs one burden bore,—
Till the dirges of his hope that melancholy burden bore
     Of Never-nevermore."

But the raven still beguiling all my fancy into smiling,
Straight I wheeled a cushioned seat in front of bird and bust and door;
Then, upon the velvet sinking, I betook myself to linking
Fancy unto fancy, thinking what this ominous bird of yore,
What this grim, ungainly, ghastly, gaunt, and ominous bird of yore
     Meant in croaking, "Nevermore."

Thus I sat engaged in guessing, but no syllable expressing
To the fowl, whose fiery eyes now burned into my bosom's core
This and more I sat divining with my head at ease reclining
On the cushion's velvet lining that the lamplight gloated o'er
But whose velvet violet lining with the lamplight gloat'ing o'er
     She shall press, ah, nevermore.

Then, methought, the air grew denser, perfumed from an unseen censer
Swung by seraphim whose footfalls tinkled on the tufted floor.
"Wretch," I cried, "thy God hath lent thee—by these angels he hath
    sent thee
Respite—respite and nepenthe from thy memories of Lenore!
Quaff, O quaff this kind nepenthe, and forget this lost Lenore!"
        Quoth the raven, "Nevermore!"

"Prophet!" said I, "thing of evil!—prophet still, if bird or devil!
Whether Tempter sent, or whether tempest tossed thee here ashore,
Desolate, yet all undaunted, on this desert land enchanted
On this home by horror haunted—tell me truly, I implore:
Is there—is there balm in Gilead?—tell me—tell me I implore!"
        Quoth the raven, "Nevermore."

"Prophet!" said I, "thing of evil-prophet still, if bird or devil!
By that heaven that bends above us,—by that God we both adore—
Tell this soul with sorrow laden, if, within the distant Aidenn,
It shall clasp a sainted maiden, whom the angels name Lenore—
Clasp a rare and radiant maiden, whom the angels name Lenore?"
        Quoth the raven, "Nevermore."

"Be that word our sign of parting, bird or fiend!" I shrieked, upstarting—
"Get thee back into the tempest and the Night's Plutonian shore!
Leave no black plume as a token of that lie thy soul hath spoken!
Leave my loneliness unbroken!—quit the bust above my door!
Take thy beak from out my heart, and take thy form from off my door!"
        Quoth the raven, "Nevermore."

And the raven, never flitting, still is sitting, still is sitting
On the pallid bust of Pallas just above my chamber door;
And his eyes have all the seeming of a demon's that is dreaming;
And the lamplight o'er him streaming throws the shadow on the floor;
And my soul from out that shadow that lies floating on the floor
        Shall be lifted—nevermore!

The Inchcape Rock
by Robert Southey (1774-1843)

Wickedness reaps a very just and appropriate reward. The Inchcape Rock, in the North Sea off Scotland, is submerged at high tide.

No stir in the air, no stir in the sea,
The ship was still as she could be;
Her sails from Heaven received no motion,
Her keel was steady in the ocean.

Without either sign or sound of their shock,
The waves flowed over the Inchcape Rock;
So little they rose, so little they fell,
They did not move the Inchcape Bell.

The holy Abbot of Aberbrothok
Had placed that bell on the Inchcape Rock;
On a buoy in the storm it floated and swung,
And over the waves its warning rung.

When the rock was hid by the surges' swell,
The mariners heard the warning bell;
And then they knew the perilous Rock,
And blessed the Abbot of Aberbrothok.

The Sun in heaven was shining gay,
All things were joyful on that day;
The sea-birds screamed as they wheeled around,
And there was joyance in their sound.

The buoy on the Inchcape Rock was seen,
A darker speck on the ocean green;
Sir Ralph, the Rover, walked his deck,
And he fixed his eye on the darker speck.

He felt the cheering power of spring,
It made him whistle, it made him sing;
His heart was mirthful to excess;
But the Rover's mirth was wickedness.

His eye was on the Inchcape float;
Quoth he, "My men, put out the boat;
And row me to the Inchcape Rock,
And I'll plague the Abbot of Aberbrothok."

The boat is lowered, the boatmen row,
And to the Inchcape Rock they go;
Sir Ralph bent over from the boat,
And cut the Bell from the Inchcape float.

Down sank the Bell with a gurgling sound;
The bubbles rose, and burst around.
Quoth Sir Ralph, "The next who comes to the Rock
Will not bless the Abbot of Aberbrothok."

Sir Ralph, the Rover, sailed away,
He scoured the seas for many a day;
And now, grown rich with plundered store,
He steers his course for Scotland's shore.

So thick a haze o'erspreads the sky
They cannot see the Sun on high;
The wind hath blown a gale all day;
At evening it hath died away.

On the deck the Rover takes his stand;
So dark it is they see no land.
Quoth Sir Ralph, "It will be lighter soon,
For there is the dawn of the rising Moon."

"Canst hear," said one, "the breakers roar?
For yonder, methinks, should be the shore."
"Now where we are I cannot tell,
But I wish we could hear the Inchcape Bell."

They hear no sound; the swell is strong;
Though the wind hath fallen, they drift along,
Till the vessel strikes with a shivering shock,—
"O Christ! it is the Inchcape Rock."

Sir Ralph, the Rover, tore his hair;
He cursed himself in his despair.
The waves rush in on every side;
The ship is sinking beneath the tide.

But, even in his dying fear,
One dreadful sound he seemed to hear,—
A sound as if, with the Inchcape Bell,
The Devil below was ringing his knell.

The Green Little Shamrock of Ireland

by Andrew Cherry (1762-1812)

Irish eyes can start smiling. Legend has it that St. Patrick
picked the 3-leaf shamrock to represent the trinity of the
Church. The myth continues that, with it as a symbol, he
drove the snakes out of Ireland.

There's a dear little plant that grows in our isle,
　　'Twas Saint Patrick himself sure that set it;
And the sun on his labor with pleasure did smile,
　　And with dew from his eye often wet it.
It thrives through the bog, through the brake, and the mireland;
And he called it the dear little shamrock of Ireland—
　　The sweet little shamrock, the dear little shamrock,
　　The sweet little, green little, shamrock of Ireland!

This dear little plant still grows in our land,
　　Fresh and fair as the daughters of Erin,
Whose smiles can bewitch, whose eyes can command,
　　In each climate that they may appear in;
And shine through the bog, through the brake, and the mireland,
Just like their own dear little shamrock of Ireland,
　　The sweet little shamrock, the dear little shamrock,
　　The sweet little, green little, shamrock of Ireland!

This dear little plant that springs from our soil,
　　When its three little leaves are extended,
Denotes on one stalk we together should toil,
　　And ourselves by ourselves be befriended;
And still through the bog, through the brake, and the mireland,
From one root should branch, like the shamrock of Ireland,
　　The sweet little shamrock, the dear little shamrock,
　　The sweet little, green little, shamrock of Ireland!

The Cricket

by William Cowper (1731-1800)

Real pleasure from that perky critter. I bet you think you're hearing one as you read this.

Little inmate, full of mirth,
Chirping on my kitchen hearth,
Whereso'er be thine abode
Always harbinger of good,
Pay me for thy warm retreat
With a song more soft and sweet;
In return thou shalt receive
Such a strain as I can give.

Thus thy praise shall be expressed,
Inoffensive, welcome guest!
While the rat is on the scout,
And the mouse with curious snout,
With what vermin else infest
Every dish, and spoil the best;
Frisking thus before the fire,
Thou hast all thy heart's desire.

Though in voice and shape they be
Formed as if akin to thee,
Thou surpassest, happier far,
Happiest grasshoppers that are;
Theirs is but a summer's song,
Thine endures the winter long,
Unimpaired, and shrill, and clear
Melody throughout the year.

Neither night nor dawn of day
Puts a period to thy play:
Sing then—and extend thy span
Far beyond the date of man;
Wretched man, whose years are spent
In repining discontent,
Lives not, aged though he be,
Half a span, compared with thee.

Where the Bee Sucks

From "The Tempest"
by William Shakespeare (1564-1616)

> Where the bee sucks, there suck I;
> In a cowslip's bell I lie:
> There I couch, when owls do cry.
> On the bat's back I do fly,
> After summer, merrily:
> Merrily, merrily, shall I live now
> Under the blossom that hangs on the bough.

The Death of the Flowers

by William Cullen Bryant (1794-1878)

He relates the death of all the pretty flowers to the
death of his pretty young sister.

> **The melancholy days are come, the saddest of the year,**
> Of wailing winds, and naked woods, and meadows brown and sere.
> Heaped in the hollows of the grove, the autumn leaves lie dead;
> They rustle to the eddying gust, and to the rabbit's tread;
> The robin and the wren are flown, and from the shrubs the jay,
> And from the wood-top calls the crow through all the gloomy day.

> Where are the flowers, the fair young flowers, that lately sprang and stood
> In brighter light and softer airs, a beauteous sisterhood?
> Alas! They all are in their graves, the gentle race of flowers
> Are lying in their lowly beds, with the fair and good of ours.
> The rain is falling where they lie, but the cold November rain
> Calls not from out the gloomy earth the lovely ones again.

> The wind-flower and the violet, they perished long ago,
> And the brier-rose and the orchis dies amid the summer glow;
> But on the hill the golden-rod, and the aster in the wood,
> And the yellow sun-flower by the brook, in autumn beauty stood,
> Till fell the frost from the clear cold heaven, as falls the plague on men,
> And the brightness of their smile was gone, from upland, glade and glen.

And now, when comes the calm mild day, as still such days will come,
To call the squirrel and the bee from out their winter home;
When the sound of dropping nuts is heard, though all the trees are still,
And twinkle in the smoky light, the waters of the rill,
The south wind searches for the flowers whose fragrance late he bore,
And sighs to find them in the wood and by the stream no more.

And then I think of one who in her youthful beauty died,
The fair meek blossom that grew up and faded by my side.
In the cold moist earth we laid her, when the forest cast the leaf,
And we wept that one so lovely should have a life so brief;
Yet not unmeet it was that one like that young friend of ours,
So gentle and so beautiful, should perish with the flowers.

The Brook's Song
by Alfred Lord Tennyson (1809-1892)

Come take a pleasant ride down a happy
stream. Sounds like a ride down the
Chattahoochee, too.

I come from haunts of coot and hern,
    I make a sudden sally,
And sparkle out among the fern,
    To bicker down a valley.

By thirty hills I hurry down,
    Or slip between the ridges,
By twenty thorps, a little town,
    And half a hundred bridges.

Till last by Philip's farm I flow
    To join the brimming river,
For men may come and men may go,
    But I go on for ever.

I chatter over stony ways,
    In little sharps and trebles,
I bubble into eddying bays,
    I babble on the pebbles.

With many a curve my banks I fret
  By many a field and fallow,
And many a fairy foreland set
  With willow-weed and mallow.

I chatter, chatter, as I flow
  To join the brimming river,
For men may come and men may go,
  But I go on for ever.

I wind about, and in and out,
  With here a blossom sailing,
And here and there a lusty trout,
  And here and there a grayling.

And here and there a foamy flake
  Upon me, as I travel
With many a silvery water-break
  Above the golden gravel.

And draw them all along, and flow
  To join the brimming river,
For men may come and men may go,
  But I go on for ever.

I steal by lawns and grassy plots,
  I slide by hazel covers;
I move the sweet forget-me-nots
  That grow for happy lovers.

I slip, I slide, I gloom, I glance,
  Among my skimming swallows;
I make the netted sunbeam dance
  Against my sandy shallows.

I murmur under moon and stars
  In brambly wildernesses;
I linger by my shingly bars;
  I loiter round my cresses;

And out again I curve and flow
  To join the brimming river,
**For men may come and men may go,
  But I go on for ever.**

Robert of Lincoln

by William Cullen Bryant (1794-1878)

Everyone who has heard the "bob-o-link" echo in the field will love this poem. Those who haven't have really missed a treat. If you're lucky, catch him in his 'spring fling'. The bob-o-link is a very gregarious, migratory bird. Large flocks travel from North America to South America every winter. As the poem relates, the male is gaily dressed in spring and summer, and gaily sings all day, on the ground or in flight. After the nest is empty, he dons a somber coat and sings more sedately.

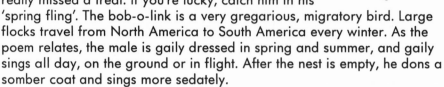

Merrily swinging on brier and weed,
    Near to the nest of his little dame,
Over the mountain-side or mead,
    Robert of Lincoln is telling his name.
        Bob-o'-link. bob-o'-link,
        Spink, spank, spink,
Snug and safe is this nest of ours,
Hidden among the summer flowers.
        Chee, chee, chee.

Robert of Lincoln is gayly dressed,
    Wearing a bright, black wedding-coat;
White are his shoulders, and white his crest,
    Hear him call in his merry note,
        Bob-o'-link, bob-o'-link,
        Spink, spank, spink,
Look what a nice, new coat is mine;
Sure there was never a bird so fine.
        Chee, chee, chee.

Robert of Lincoln's Quaker wife,
    Pretty and quiet, with plain brown wings,
Passing at home a patient life,
    Broods in the grass while her husband sings
        Bob-o'-link, bob-o'-link,
        Spink, spank, spink,
Brood, kind creature, you need not fear
Thieves and robbers while I am here.
        Chee, chee, chee.

Modest and shy as a nun is she;
 One weak chirp is her only note;
Braggart, and prince of braggarts is he,
  Pouring boasts from his little throat,
   Bob-o'-link, bob-o'-link,
   Spink. spank, spink,
Never was I afraid of man,
Catch me, cowardly knaves, if you can.
   Chee, chee, chee.

Six white eggs on a bed of hay,
 Flecked with purple, a pretty sight:
There as the mother sits all day,
  Robert is singing with all his might,
   Bob-o'-link, bob-o'-link,
   Spink, spank, spink,
Nice good wife that never goes out,
Keeping house while I frolic about.
   Chee, chee, chee.

Soon as the little ones chip the shell,
 Six wide mouths are open for food;
Robert of Lincoln bestirs him well,
  Gathering seeds for the hungry brood:
   Bob-o'-link, bob-o'-link,
   Spink, spank, spink,
This new life is likely to be
Hard for a gay young fellow like me.
   Chee, chee, chee.

Robert of Lincoln at length is made
 Sober with work, and silent with care,
Off is his holiday garment laid,
  Half forgotten that merry air,
   Bob-o'-link, bob-o'-link,
   Spink, spank, spink,
Nobody knows but my mate and I,
Where our nest and our nestlings lie.
   Chee, chee, chee.

Summer wanes, the children are grown;
    Fun and frolic no more he knows,
Robert of Lincoln's a hum-drum drone;
    Off he flies, and we sing as he goes,
      Bob-o'-link, bob-o'-link,
      Spink, spank, spink,
When you can pipe that merry old strain,
Robert of Lincoln, come back again.
      Chee, chee, chee.

Old Winter

by Thomas Noel (1790-1861)

'Tis the season to dream of a White Christmas,
by a cozy fireside.

Old Winter sad, in snow yclad,
    Is making a doleful din;
But let him howl till he crack his jowl,
    We will not let him in.

Ay, let him lift from the billowy drift
    His hoary, haggard form,
And scowling stand, with his wrinkled hand
    Outstretching to the storm.

And let his weird and sleety beard
    Stream loose upon the blast,
And, rustling, chime to the tinkling rime
    From his bald head falling fast.

Let his baleful breath shed blight and death
    On herb and flower and tree;
And brooks and ponds in crystal bonds
    Bind fast, but what care we?

Let him push at the door,—in the chimney roar,
    And rattle the window-pane;
Let him in at us spy with his icicle eye,
    But he shall not entrance gain.

Let him gnaw, forsooth, with his freezing tooth,
　　On our roof-tiles, till he tire;
But we care not a whit, as we jovial sit
　　Before our blazing fire.

Come, lads, let's sing, till the rafters ring;
　　Come, push the can about;—
From our snug fire-side this Christmas-tide
　　We'll keep old Winter out.

June

by James Russell Lowell (1819-1891)

The birds, the bees, the flowers, the trees—the
hormones—all break out in June.

What is so rare as a day in June?
　　Then, if ever, come perfect days;
Then Heaven tries the earth if it be in tune,
　　And over it softly her warm ear lays:
Whether we look, or whether we listen,
　　We hear life murmur, or see it glisten;
Every clod feels a stir of might,
　　An instinct within it that reaches and towers,
And, groping blindly above it for light,
　　Climbs to a soul in grass and flowers;
The flush of life may well be seen
　　Thrilling back over hills and valleys;
The cowslip startles in meadows green,
　　The buttercup catches the sun in its chalice,
And there's never a leaf nor a blade too mean
　　To be some happy creature's palace;
The little bird sits at his door in the sun
　　Atilt like a blossom among the leaves,
And lets his illumined being o'errun
　　With the deluge of summer it receives;
His mate feels the eggs beneath her wings,
　　And the heart in her dumb breast flutters and sings;
He sings to the wide world, and she to her nest,—
　　In the nice ear of Nature which song is the best?

❧ BRAVERY ❧

Casabianca

by Felicia Hermans (1743-1835)

A little hard to believe, but touching. Louis de Casabianca (1762-1798) was put in command of the ship *Orient* at the Battle of the Nile in August, 1798. Casabianca, though badly wounded, fought the burning ship to the end, and perished with most of the crew. His son, 10 year-old Giacomo Jocante, the hero of this story, refused to leave his duty on the ship and

died in the conflagration. The English fleet under Lord Nelson destroyed Napoleon's French fleet in the Battle of the Nile, and firmly entrenched England in Egypt and the Mediterranean. The French battleship Orient, described in this poem, was the largest ship in the battle. The remains of this ship and much further wreckage were found by undersea explorers in the summer of 1998.

> The boy stood on the burning deck,
>   Whence all but him had fled;
> The flame that lit the battle's wreck
>   Shone round him o'er the dead.
>
> Yet beautiful and bright he stood,
>   As born to rule the storm;
> A creature of heroic blood,
>   A proud though childlike form.
>
> The flames rolled on—he would not go
>   Without his father's word;
> That father, faint in death below,
>   His voice no longer heard.

He called aloud, "Say, father, say
    If yet my task is done?"
He knew not that, the chieftain lay
    Unconscious of his son.

"Speak, father!" once again he cried,
    "If I may yet be gone! "
And but the booming shots replied,
    And fast the flames rolled on.

Upon his brow he felt their breath,
    And in his waving hair;
And looked from that lone post of death,
    In still, yet brave despair.

And shouted but once more aloud
    "My father! must I stay?"
While o'er him fast, through sail and shroud.
    The wreathing fires made way.

They wrapt the ship in splendour wild,
    They caught the flag on high,
And streamed above the gallant child
    Like banners in the sky.

Then came a burst of thunder sound—
    The boy—oh! where was he?
Ask of the winds that far around
    With fragments strew the sea;

With mast, and helm, and pennon fair,
    That well had borne their part—
But the noblest thing that perished there
    Was that young, faithful heart.

The Leak in the Dike

by Phœbe Cary (1824-1871)

Sorry it's so long, but the story is such a classic
when told in detail that we just couldn't shorten it
or omit it. Who hasn't heard of that famous little
Dutch boy and his finger in the dike. The lesson
is stupendous; great for any youngster to learn.
The occurrence of this incident in Holland, or
The Netherlands, is of extreme importance, since
an estimated 2/5 of the country lies below sea
level and depends entirely on the system of dikes and canals. It is all too
true that a small leak can become a catastrophic disaster in hours.

> The good dame looked from her cottage
>   At the close of the pleasant day,
> And cheerily called to her little son
>   Outside the door at play:
> "Come, Peter, come! I want you to go,
>   While there is yet light to see,
> To the hut of the blind old man who lives
>   Across the dike, for me;
> And take these cakes I made for him—
>   They are hot and smoking yet;
> You have time enough to go and come
>   Before the sun is set."
>
> Then the good wife turned to her labor,
>   Humming a simple song,
> And thought of her husband, working hard
>   At the sluices all day along;
> And set the turf a-blazing,
>   And brought the coarse, black bread,
> That he might find a fire at night,
>   And see the table spread.
>
> And Peter left the brother
>   With whom all day he had played,
> And the sister who had watched their sports
>   In the willow's tender shade;

And told them they'd see him back before
    They saw a star in sight!—
Though he wouldn't be afraid to go
    In the very darkest night!
For he was a brave, bright fellow,
    With eye and conscience clear;
He could do whatever a boy might do,
    And he had not learned to fear.
Why, he wouldn't have robbed a bird's nest,
    Nor brought a stork to harm,
Though never a law in Holland
    Had stood to stay his arm!

And now, with his face all glowing,
    And eyes as bright as the day
With the thoughts of his pleasant errand,
    He trudged along the way;
And soon his joyous prattle
    Made glad a lonesome place—
Alas! If only the blind old man
    Could have seen that happy face!
Yet he somehow caught the brightness
    Which his voice and presence lent;
And he felt the sunshine come and go
    As Peter came and went.

And now, as the day was sinking,
    And the winds began to rise,
The mother looked from her door again,
    Shading her anxious eyes,
And saw the shadows deepen,
    And birds to their homes come back,
But never a sign of Peter
    Along the level track.
But she said, "He will come at morning,
    So I need not fret or grieve—
Though it isn't like my boy at all
    To stay without my leave."

But where was the child sleeping?
    On the homeward way was he,
And across the dike while the sun was up
    An hour above the sea.
He was stooping now to gather flowers;
    Now listening to the sound,
As the angry waters dashed themselves
    Against their narrow bound.
"Ah! well for us," said Peter,
    "That the gates are good and strong,
And my father tends them carefully,
    Or they would not hold you long!
You're a wicked sea," said Peter;
    "I know why you fret and chafe;
You would like to spoil our lands and homes;
    But our sluices keep you safe!"

But hark! through the noise of waters
    Comes a low, clear, trickling sound;
And the child's face pales with terror,
    As his blossoms drop to the ground.
He is up to the bank in a moment,
    And, stealing through the sand,
He sees a stream not yet so large
    As his slender, childish hand.
'Tis a leak in the dike! He is but a boy,
    Unused to fearful scenes;
But, young as he is, he has learned to know
    The dreadful thing that means.
A *leak in the dike!* The stoutest heart
    Grows faint that cry to hear,
And the bravest man in all the land
    Turns white with mortal fear.
For he knows the smallest leak may grow
    To a flood in a single night;
And he knows the strength of the cruel sea
    When loosed in its angry might.

And the boy! He has seen the danger,
　　And, shouting a wild alarm,
He forces back the weight of the sea
　　With the strength of his single arm!
He listens for the joyful sound
　　Of a footstep passing nigh;
And lays his ear to the ground, to catch
　　The answer to his cry,—
And he hears the rough winds blowing,
　　And the waters rise and fall,
But never an answer comes to him
　　Save the echo of his call.

He sees no hope, no succor,
　　His feeble voice is lost;
Yet what shall he do but watch and wait,
　　Though he perish at his post!
So, faintly calling and crying
　　Till the sun is under the sea;
Crying and moaning till the stars
　　Come out for company;
He thinks of his brother and sister,
　　Asleep in their safe, warm bed;
He thinks of dear father and mother;
　　Of himself as dying and dead;
And of how, when the night is over,
　　They must come and find him at last;
But he never thinks he can leave the place
　　Where duty holds him fast.

The good dame in the cottage
　　Is up and astir with the light,
For the thought of her little Peter
　　Has been with her all the night.
And now she watches the pathway,
　　As yester-eve she had done;
But what does she see so strange and black
　　Against the rising sun?

Her neighbors are bearing between them
    Something straight to her door;
Her child is coming home, but not
    As he ever came before!

"He is dead!" she cries; "my darling!"
    And the startled father hears,
And comes and looks the way she looks,
    And fears the thing she fears;
Till a glad shout from the bearers
    Thrills the stricken man and wife—
"Give thanks, for your son has saved our land,
    And God has saved his life!"
So, there in the morning sunshine
    They knelt about the boy;
And every head was bared and bent
    In tearful, reverent joy.

'Tis many a year since then; but still,
    When the sea roars like a flood,
Their boys are taught what a boy can do
    Who is brave and true and good.
For every man in that country
    Takes his son by the hand,
And tells him of little Peter,
    Whose courage saved the land.

They have many a valiant hero,
    Remembered through the years;
But never one whose name so oft
    Is named with loving tears.
And his deed shall be sung by the cradle,
    And told to the child on the knee,
So long as the dikes of Holland
    Divide the land from the sea!

How Did You Die

by Edmund Vance Cooke

A very thoughtful dissertation on a rather touchy
subject.

Did you tackle the trouble that came your way
    With a resolute heart and cheerful?
Or hide your face from the light of day
    With a craven soul and fearful?
Oh, a trouble's a ton, or a trouble's an ounce,
    Or a trouble is what you make it.
And it isn't the fact that you're hurt that counts,
    But only how did you take it?

You are beaten to earth? Well, well, what's that?
    Come up with a smiling face.
It's nothing against you to fall down flat,
    But to lie there—that's disgrace.
The harder you're thrown, why, the higher you bounce;
    Be proud of your blackened eye!
It isn't the fact that you're licked that counts;
    It's how did you fight—and why?

And though you be done to the death, what then?
    If you battled the best you could,
If you played your part in the world of men,
    Why, the Critic will call it good.
Death comes with a crawl, or comes with a pounce,
    And whether he's slow or spry,
It isn't the fact that you're dead that counts,
    But only how did you die?

The Battle of Blenheim

by Robert Southey (1774-1843)

This was included mainly to stress the futility of many unnecessary wars. No reason for this war, and nothing gained. But, it was "a great victory!" but what a price!. The Battle of Blenheim, August 12-13, 1704, occurred at that small town on the Danube River in Bavaria, Germany. A force of Austrians under Prince Eugene and the British under the Duke of Marlborough, decisively defeated a combined force of French, under Gallard, and Bavarians under Marsin. Losses were heavy on both sides, but much worse for the French, in particular. In appreciation, the British built a castle for the Duke and appropriately named it "Blenheim."

It was a summer's evening
       Old Kaspar's work was done,
And he before his cottage door
       Was sitting in the sun;
And by him sported on the green
His little grandchild, Wilhelmine.

She saw her brother Peterkin
       Roll something large and round,
Which he, beside the rivulet,
       In playing there, had found.
He came to ask what he had found,
That was so large, and smooth, and round.

Old Kaspar took it from the boy,
       Who stood expectant by;
And then the old man shook his head,
       And, with a natural sigh,
"'Tis some poor fellow's skull," said he,
"Who fell in the great victory!

"I find them in the garden,
       For there's many hereabout;
And often when I go to plow,
       The plowshare turns them out;
For many thousand men," said he,
"Were slain in that great victory!"

"Now tell us what 'twas all about,"
    Young Peterkin he cries;
And little Wilhelmine looks up
    With wonder-waiting eyes;
"Now tell us all about the war,
And what they killed each other for."

"It was the English," Kaspar cried,
    "Who put the French to rout;
But what they killed each other for
    I could not well make out.
But everybody said," quoth he,
"That 'twas a famous victory!

"My father lived at Blenheim then,
    Yon little stream hard by:
They burned his dwelling to the ground
    And he was forced to fly;
So with his wife and child he fled,
Nor had he where to rest his head.

"With fire and sword the country round
    Was wasted far and wide;
And many a childing mother then
    And new-born baby died.
But things like that, you know, must be
At every famous victory.

"They say it was a shocking sight
    After the field was won;
For many thousand bodies here
    Lay rotting in the sun.
But things like that, you know, must be
After a famous victory.

"Great praise the Duke of Marlborough won
    And our good Prince Eugene."
"Why, 'twas a very wicked thing!"
    Said little Wilhelmine.
"Nay, nay, my little girl," quoth he,
"It was a famous victory!

"And everybody praised the Duke
        Who this great fight did win."
"But what good came of it at last?"
        Quoth little Peterkin.
"Why, that I cannot tell," said he,
"But 'twas a famous victory."

The Ballad of East and West
by Rudyard Kipling (1865-1936)

A rollicking tale of one of England's border struggles, this one in Pakistan.
Told in true Kiplingesque. Long, but well worth the time. A very intriguing
finish to a thrilling ride.

> Oh, East is East, and West is West, and never the twain shall meet,
> Till Earth and Sky stand presently at God's great Judgment Seat:
> But there is neither East nor West, Border, nor Breed, nor Birth,
> When two strong men stand face to face, though they come from the ends
>   of the earth!

Kamal is out with twenty men to raise the Border-side,
And he has lifted the Colonel's mare that is the Colonel's pride:
He has lifted her out of the stable-door between the dawn and the day,
And turned the calkins' upon her feet, and ridden her far away.
Then up and spoke the Colonel's son that led a troop of the Guides:
"Is there never a man of all my men can say where Kamal hides?"
Then up and spoke Mohammed Khan, the son of the Ressaldar:
"If ye know the track of the morning-mist, ye know where his pickets are.
At dusk he harries the Abazai—at dawn he is into Bonair,
But he must go by Fort Bukloh to his own place to fare,
So if ye gallop to Fort Bukloh as fast as a bird can fly,
By the favor of God ye may cut him off ere he win to the Tongue of Jagai,
But if he be past the Tongue of Jagai, right swiftly turn ye then,

For the length and the breadth of the grisly plain is sown with
  Kamal's men.
There is rock to the left, and rock to the right, and low lean thorn
  between,
And ye may hear a breech-bolt snick where never a man is seen."
The Colonel's son has taken a horse, and a raw rough dun was he,
With the mouth of a bell and the heart of Hell and the head of a
  gallows-tree.
The Colonel's son to the Fort has won, they bid him stay to eat—
Who rides at the tail of a Border thief, he sits not long at his meat.
He's up and away from Fort Bukloh as fast as he can fly,
Till he was aware of his father's mare in the gut of the Tongue of Jagai,
Till he was aware of his father's mare with Kamal upon her back,
And when he could spy the white of her eye, he made the pistol crack.
He has fired once, he has fired twice, but the whistling ball went wide.
"Ye shoot like a soldier," Kamal said. "Show now if ye can ride."
It's up and over the Tongue of Jagai, as blown dust-devils go.
The dun he fled like a stag of ten, but the mare like a barren doe.
The dun he leaned against the bit and slugged his head above,
But the red mare played with the snaffle-bars, as a maiden plays with
  a glove.
There was rock to the left and rock to the right, and low lean thorn
  between,
And thrice he heard a breech-bolt snick though never a man was seen.
They have ridden the low moon out of the sky, their hoofs drum up
  the dawn,
The dun he went like a wounded bull, but the mare like a new-
  roused fawn.
The dun he fell at a water-course—in a woeful heap fell he,
And Kamal has turned the red mare back, and pulled the rider free.
He has knocked the pistol out of his hand—small room was there to
  strive,
"'Twas only by favor of mine," quoth he, "ye rode so long alive:
There was not a rock for twenty mile, there was not a clump of tree,
But covered a man of my own men with his rifle cocked on his knee.
If I had raised my bridle-hand, as I have held it low,
The little jackals that flee so fast were feasting all in a row:
If I had bowed my head on my breast, as I have held it high,
The kite that whistles above us now were gorged till she could not fly."

Lightly answered the Colonel's son: "Do good to bird and beast,
But count who come for the broken meats before thou makest a
feast.
If there should follow a thousand swords to carry my bones away,
Belike the price of a jackal's meal were more than a thief could pay.
They will feed their horse on the standing crop, their men on the
garnered grain.
The thatch of the byres will serve their fires when all the cattle are slain.
But if thou thinkest the price be fair,—thy brethren wait to sup,
The hound is kin to the jackal-spawn,—howl, dog, and call them up!
And if thou thinkest the price be high, in steer and gear and stack,
Give me my father's mare again, and I'll fight my own way back!"
Kamal has gripped him by the hand and set him upon his feet.
"No talk shall be of dogs," said he, "when wolf and gray wolf meet.
May I eat dirt if thou hast hurt of me in deed or breath;
What dam of lances brought thee forth to jest at the dawn with Death?"
Lightly answered the Colonel's son: "I hold by the blood of my clan:
Take up the mare for my father's gift—by God, she has carried a man!"
The red mare ran to the Colonel's son, and nuzzled against his breast;
"We be two strong men," said Kamal then, "but she loveth the
younger best.
So she shall go with a lifter's dower, my turquoise-studded rein,
My broidered saddle and saddle-cloth, and silver stirrups twain."
The Colonel's son a pistol drew, and held it muzzle-end,
"Ye have taken the one from a foe," said he; "will ye take the mate
from a friend?"
"A gift for a gift," said Kamal straight; "a limb for the risk of a limb.
Thy father has sent his son to me, I'll send my son to him!"
With that he whistled his only son, that dropped from a mountain-
crest—
He trod the ling like a buck in spring, and he looked like a lance in
rest.
"Now here is thy master," Kamal said, "who leads a troop of the
Guides,
And thou must ride at his left side as shield on shoulder rides.
Till Death or I cut loose the tie, at camp and board and bed,
Thy life is his—thy fate it is to guard him with thy head.
So thou must eat the White Queen's meat, and all her foes are thine,

And thou must harry thy father's hold for the peace of the Border-line,
And thou must make a trooper tough and hack thy way to power—
Belike they will raise thee to Ressaldar when I am hanged in Peshawur."

They have looked each other between the eyes, and there they found
no fault,
They have taken the Oath of the Brother-in-Blood on leavened bread
and salt:
They have taken the Oath of the Brother-in-Blood on fire and fresh-
cut sod,
On the hilt and the haft of the Khyber knife, and the Wonderous
Names of God.
The Colonel's son he rides the mare and Kamal's boy the dun,
And two have come back to Fort Bukloh where there went forth but
one.
And when they drew to the Quarter-Guard, full twenty swords flew
clear—
There was not a man but carried his feud with the blood of the
mountaineer.
"Ha' done! Ha' done!" said the Colonel's son. "Put up the steel at your
sides!
Last night ye had struck at a Border thief—to-night 'tis a man of the
Guides!"

Oh, East is East, and West is West, and never the twain shall meet,
Till Earth and Sky stand presently at God's great Judgment Seat:
But there is neither East nor West, Border, nor Breed, nor Birth,
When two strong men stand face to face, though they come from the ends
of the earth!

¹ Calkin - A projection on the horse shoe to prevent slipping. In the poem they
were apparently turned around to make it look as if the mare was going the
opposite way.

Gunga Din

by Rudyard Kipling (1865-1936)

England fighting again, this time in India. The
hero is the humble, fearless, water carrier who
does everything for everybody. His final words, as he lay dying, "'I 'ope
you liked your drink.' sez Gunga Din," I think makes one of the greatest
quotes of all poetry.

You may talk o' gin an' beer
When you're quartered safe out 'ere,
An' you're sent to penny-fights an' Aldershot it;
But when it comes to slaughter
You will do your work on water,
An' you'll lick the bloomin' boots of 'im that's got it.
Now in Injia's sunny clime,
Where I used to spend my time
A-servin' of 'Er Majesty the Queen,
Of all them black-faced crew
The finest man I knew
Was our regimental *bhisti¹*, Gunga Din.
　　　　He was "Din! Din! Din!
　　　You limpin' lump o' brick-dust, Gunga Din!
　　　　　Hi! *slippey hitherao!*
　　　　　Water! get it! *Panee lao!*
　　　You squidgy-nosed old idol, Gunga Din!"

The uniform 'e wore
Was nothin' much before,
An' rather less than 'arf o' that be'ind,
For a piece of twisty rag
An' a goatskin water-bag
Was all the field equipment 'e could find.
When the sweatin' troop-train lay
In a sidin' through the day,
Where the 'eat would make your bloomin' eye-brows crawl,
We shouted "*Harry By!*"
Till our throats were bricky-dry,
Then we wopped 'im cause 'e couldn't serve us all.
　　　　It was "Din! Din! Din!

You 'eathen, where the mischief 'ave you been?
    You put some *juldee* in it
    Or I'll *marrow* you this minute,
If you don't fill up my helmet, Gunga Din!"

'E would dot an' carry one
Till the longest day was done;
An' 'e didn't seem to know the use o' fear.
If we charged or broke or cut,
You could bet your bloomin' nut,
'E'd be waitin' fifty paces right flank rear.
With 'is *mussick*² on 'is back,
'E would skip with our attack,
An' watch us till the bugles made "Retire,"
An' for all 'is dirty 'ide
'E was white, clear white, inside
When 'e went to tend the wounded under fire!
    It was "Din! Din! Din!"
    With the bullets kickin' dust-spots on the green.
    When the cartridges ran out,
    You could 'ear the front-files shout,
    "Hi! Ammunition-mules an' Gunga Din!"

I sha'n't forgit the night
When I dropped be'ind the fight
With a bullet where my belt-plate should 'a' been.
I was chokin' mad with thirst,
An' the man that spied me first
Was our good old grinnin', gruntin' Gunga Din.
'E lifted up my 'ead,
An' 'e plugged me where I bled,
An' 'e guv me 'arf-a-pint o' water—green:
It was crawlin' an' it stunk,
But of all the drinks I've drunk,
I'm gratefullest to one from Gunga Din.
    It was "Din! Din! Din!
    'Ere's a beggar with a bullet through 'is spleen;
    'E's chawin' up the ground,
    An' 'e's kickin' all around:
    For Gawd's sake git the water, Gunga Din!"

'E carried me away
To where a *dooli*³ lay,
An' a bullet come an' drilled the beggar clean.
'E put me safe inside,
An' just before 'e died:
"I 'ope you liked your drink," sez Gunga Din.
So I'll meet 'im later on
At the place where 'e is gone—
Where it's always double drill an' no canteen;
'E'll be squattin' on the coals,
Givin' drink to pore damned souls,
An' I'll git a swig in hell from Gunga Din!
        Yes, Din! Din! Din!
    You Lazarushian-leather Gunga Din!
        Though I've belted you an' flayed you,
        By the livin' God that made you,
    You're a better man than I am, Gunga Din!

¹ *bhisti: a water carrier*
² *mussick: a goat skin water-bag*
³ *dooli: a litter*

(The description of the drink of water that Gunga Din brought certainly reminds me of some I had during our Marine invasion of Bougainville. And surprisingly, it tasted just that good to me in that hot jungle.)

Fuzzy-Wuzzy

by Rudyard Kipling (1865-1936)

A delightful, heart-felt tribute to the native fighters
of Sowdan (Sudan). Despite using only their long
swords against the rifles of the British Sudan
Expeditionary Force of 1889, they were able,
through their fierce bravery, to "bruk the square."
To defend themselves from attacks from all
directions at once, the British in Africa fought in a
square formation. They took great pride in
bragging that the square couldn't be broken; but Fuzzy did it!

> We've fought with many men acrost the seas,
>   An' some of em' was brave an' some was not;
> The Paythan an' the Zulu an' Burmese;
>   But the Fuzzy was the finest o' the lot.
> We never got a ha' porth's change of 'im:
>   'E squatted in the scrub an' 'ocked our 'orses,
> 'E cut our sentries up at Suakim,
>   An 'e played the cat an' banjo with our forces.
>   So 'ere's to you, Fuzzy-Wuzzy, at your 'ome in the Sowdan;
>   You're a pore benighted 'eathen but a first-class fightin' man;
>   We gives you your certifikit, an' if you want it signed
>   We'll come an' 'ave a romp with you whenever you're inclined.
>
> We took our chanst among the Kyber 'ills,
>   The Boers knocked us silly at a mile,
> The Burman guv us Irriwaddy chills,
>   An' a Zulu impi dished us up in style:
> But all we ever got from such as they
>   Was pop to what the Fuzzy made us swaller;
> We 'eld our bloomin' own, the papers say,
>   But man for man the Fuzzy knocked us 'oller.
>   Then 'ere's to you, Fuzzy-Wuzzy, an' the missis and the kid;
>   Our orders was to break you, an' of course we went and did.
>   We sloshed you with Martinis, an' it wasn't 'ardly fair;
>   But for all the odds agin you, Fuzzy-Wuz, you bruk the square.

'E 'asn't got no papers of 'is own,
    'E 'asn't got no medals nor rewards,
So we most certify the skill 'e's shown
    In usin' of 'is long two-'anded swords:
When 'e's 'oppin' in an' out among the bush
    With 'is coffin-'eaded shield an' shovel-spear,
A 'appy day with Fuzzy on the rush
    Will last a 'ealthy Tommy for a year.
      So 'ere's to you, Fuzzy-Wuzzy, an' your friends which is no more.
      If we 'adn't lost some messmates we would 'elp you to deplore;
      But give an' take's the gospel, an' we'll call the bargain fair,
      For if you 'ave lost more than us, you crumpled up the square!

'E rushes at the smoke when we let drive,
    An', before we know, 'e's 'ackin' at our 'ead;
'E's all 'ot sand an' ginger when alive,
    An' 'e's generally shammin' when 'e's dead.
'E's a daisy, 'e's a ducky, 'e's a lamb!
    'E's a injia-rubber idiot on the spree,
E's the only thing that doesn't give a damn
    For the Regiment o' British Infantree.
      So here's to you, Fuzzy-Wuzzy, at your 'ome in the Sowdan;
      You're a pore benighted 'eathen but a first -class fightin' man;
      An' 'ere's to you, Fuzzy-Wuzzy, with your 'ayrick 'ead of hair—
      You big black boundin' beggar—for you bruk a British square.

The Spires of Oxford

(as seen from the train)
by Winifred M. Letts

A touching tribute to the brave men who left
Oxford to fight in World War I. And remember
there were many 'Oxfords'. Unfortunately even
more again in World War II.

I saw the spires of Oxford
  As I was passing by,
The gray spires of Oxford
  Against a pearl-gray sky.
My heart was with the Oxford men
  Who went abroad to die.

The years go fast in Oxford,
  The golden years and gay,
The hoary Colleges look down
  On careless boys at play.
But when the bugles sounded war
  They put their games away.

They left the peaceful river,
  The cricket-field, the quad,
The shaven lawn of Oxford
  To seek a bloody sod—
They gave their merry youth away
  For country and for God.

God rest you, happy gentlemen,
  Who laid your good lives down,
Who took the khaki and the gun
  Instead of cap and gown.
God bring you to a fairer place
  Than even Oxford town.

❧ PATRIOTISM ❧

America

by Samuel Francis Smith (1808-1895)

A wonderful song; a wonderful poem; a wonderful
country. When did you last hear or read the last
three verses? Aren't they great?

My country 'tis of thee
Sweet land of liberty:
Of thee I sing.
Land where my fathers died
Land of the Pilgrims' pride
From every mountainside
Let freedom ring.

My native country—thee
Land of the noble free
Thy name I love:
I love thy rocks and rills
Thy woods and templed hills
My heart with rapture thrills
Like that above.

Let music swell the breeze
And ring from all the trees
Sweet freedom's song.
Let all that breathe partake
Let mortal tongues awake
Let rocks their silence break
The sound prolong.

Our fathers' God to thee
Author of liberty
To thee we sing.
Long may our land be bright
With freedom's holy light
Protect us by thy might
Great God, our King.

America for Me
by Henry van Dyke

Every dyed-in-the-wool American will feel
good after reading this.

'Tis fine to see the Old World, and travel up and down
Among the famous palaces and cities of renown,
To admire the crumbly castles and the statues of the kings,—
But now I think I've had enough of antiquated things.

So it's home again, and home again, America for me!
My heart is turning home again, and there I long to be,
In the land of youth and freedom beyond the ocean bars,
Where the air is full of sunlight and the flag is full of stars.

Oh, London is a man's town, there's power in the air;
And Paris is a woman's town, with flowers in her hair;
And it's sweet to dream in Venice, and it's great to study Rome;
But when it comes to living, there is no place like home.

I like the German fir-woods, in green battalions drilled;
I like the gardens of Versailles with flashing fountains filled;
But, oh, to take your hand, my dear, and ramble for a day
In the friendly western woodland where Nature has her way!

I know that Europe's wonderful, yet something seems to lack:
The Past is too much with her, and the people looking back.
But the glory of the Present is to make the Future free,
We love our land for what she is and what she is to be.

Oh, it's home again, and home again, America for me!
I want a ship that's westward bound to plough the rolling sea,
To the blessed Land of Room Enough beyond the ocean bars,
Where the air is full of sunlight and the flag is full of stars.

America, The Beautiful

by Katharine Lee Bates

You will feel proud after reading this, even though you've heard it many, many times. There's no question—God did bountifully shed his grace on us.

O beautiful for spacious skies,
　　For amber waves of grain,
For purple mountain majesties
　　Above the fruited plain!!
America! America!
　　God shed His grace on thee
And crown thy good with brotherhood
　　From sea to shining sea!

O beautiful for pilgrim feet,
　　Whose stern, impassioned stress
A thoroughfare for freedom beat
　　Across the wilderness!
America! America!
　　God mend thine every flaw,
Confirm thy soul in self-control,
　　Thy liberty in law!

O beautiful for heroes proved
　　In liberating strife,
Who more than self their country loved,
　　And mercy more than life!
America! America!
　　May God thy gold refine,
Till all success be nobleness
　　And every gain divine!

O beautiful for patriot dream
　　That sees beyond the years
Thine alabaster cities gleam
　　Undimmed by human tears!
America! America!
　　God shed His grace on thee,
And crown thy good with brotherhood
　　From sea to shining sea!

My Land

by Thomas Osborne Davis (1814-1845)

Doesn't hurt to be reminded just how great.

She is a rich and rare land;
Oh! she's a fresh and fair land,
She is a dear and rare land—
      This native land of mine.

No men than hers are braver—
Her women's hearts ne'er waver;
I'd freely die to save her,
      And think my lot divine.

She's not a dull or cold land;
No! she's a warm and bold land;
Oh! she's a true and old land—
      This native land of mine.

Could beauty ever guard her,
And virtue still reward her,
No foe would cross her border—
      No friend within it pine.

Oh! she's a fresh and fair land,
Oh! she's a true and rare land!
Yes, she's a rare and fair land—
      This native land of mine.

My Native Land

by Sir Walter Scott

From *The Lay of the Last Minstrel*, CANTO VI. The powerful drive of patriotism which should be so much stronger than ego.

> **Breathes there the man with soul so dead**
> **Who never to himself hath said,**
> **This is my own, my native land!**
> Whose heart hath ne'er within him burned,
> As home his footsteps he hath turned
> From wandering on a foreign strand?
> If such there breathe, go, mark him well;
> For him no minstrel raptures swell;
> High though his titles, proud his name,
> Boundless his wealth as wish can claim,
> Despite those titles, power, and pelf,
> The wretch, concentred all in self,
> Living, shall forfeit fair renown,
> And, doubly dying, shall go down
> To the vile dust from whence he sprung,
> Unwept, unhonored, and unsung.

The Star-Spangled Banner
by Sir Francis Scott Key (1780-1843)

I consider myself a tough old Marine, but when this bursts forth, and particularly if well sung, I still find myself with my hand brushing my eyes—and I don't mind admitting it. Key was a successful lawyer in Washington, D.C. During the War of 1812, he had gone aboard a British warship in an effort to secure the release of a friend who had been captured. He was still aboard when the British fleet shelled Fort McHenry, one of the many defenses of Baltimore. Key watched the flag flying during the night, and when it was still there in the morning, began putting together these lines to the Star Spangled Banner. Congress waited, as usual, until 1931 to make this officially our National Anthem. The additional verses just are not heard enough, especially the second and fourth. For my money, he could have skipped the third. I strongly feel that it is criminal what some singers do to our National Anthem when performing before large audiences. All to bring special attention to themselves.

> O! say, can you see, by the dawn's early light,
> What so proudly we hailed at the twilight's last gleaming—
> Whose broad stripes and bright stars, through the perilous fight,
> O'er the ramparts we watched were so gallantly streaming!
> And the rocket's red glare, the bombs bursting in air,
> Gave proof through the night that our flag was still there:
> O! say, does that star-spangled banner yet wave
> O'er the land of the free, and the home of the brave
>
> On that shore dimly seen through the mists of the deep,
> Where the foe's haughty host in dread silence reposes,
> What is that which the breeze, o'er the towering steep,
> As it fitfully blows, now conceals, now discloses?
> Now it catches the gleam of the morning's first beam,
> In full glory reflected now shines on the stream;
> 'Tis the star-spangled banner; O long may it wave
> O'er the land of the free, and the home of the brave!

And where is that band who so vauntingly swore
That the havoc of war and the battle's confusion
A home and a country should leave us no more?
Their blood has washed out their foul footsteps' pollution.
No refuge could save the hireling and slave
From the terror of or the gloom of the grave;
And the star-spangled banner in triumph doth wave
O'er the land of the free, and the home of the brave.

O! thus be it ever, when freemen shall stand
Between their loved homes and the war's desolation!
Blest with victory and peace, may the heav'n-rescued land
Praise the power that hath made and preserved us a nation.
Then conquer we must, for our cause it is just,
And this be our motto—"In God is our trust";
And the star-spangled banner in triumph shall wave
O'er the land of the free, and the home of the brave.

The Flag Goes By

by Henry Holcomb Bennett

A rededication to the honor of our flag. Probably a reflection on noting the recent drop in proper respect for Old Glory, and all it stands for. Come on—get those hats off.

> Hats off
> Along the street there comes
> A blare of bugles, a ruffle of drums,
> A flash of color beneath the sky:
> Hats off!
> The flag is passing by!

> Blue and crimson and white it shines,
> Over the steel-tipped, ordered lines.
> Hats off!
> The colors before us fly;
> But more than the flag is passing by.

> Sea-fights and land-fights, grim and great,
> Fought to make and to save the State:
> Weary marches and sinking ships;
> Cheers of victory on dying lips;

> Days of plenty and years of peace;
> March of a strong land's swift increase;
> Equal justice, right and law,
> Stately honor and reverend awe;

> Sign of a nation, great and strong
> To ward her people from foreign wrong:
> Pride and glory and honor,—all
> Live in the colors to stand or fall.

> Hats off!
> Along the street there comes
> A blare of bugles, a ruffle of drums;
> And loyal hearts are beating high:
> Hats off!
> The flag is passing by!

The War Inevitable

March 23, 1775
by Patrick Henry (1736-1799)

Stirring speech delivered by Patrick Henry in St. John's Church in Richmond, Virginia on March 23, 1775. The church still stands. I have stood at the spot—what a feeling! We needed a Patrick Henry in 1941. It took all the bombs of Pearl Harbor to silence the ever-present Peaceniks and wake up America. Great as he was, I hope we never need him again. Like the shot at Concord heard 'round the world, these brave and powerful words were heard 'round the world and will be resounding forever. Again, I strayed from true poetry, but this speech is so strong and fluid that I have thrilled every time I read it—which has been very many times. Remember that this was treason to the English crown, punishable by death, and Henry was putting his own life on the line when he said these magnificent words.

They tell us, Sir, that we are weak,—unable to cope with so formidable an adversary. But when shall we be stronger? Will it be the next week, or the next year? Will it be when we are totally disarmed, and when a British guard shall be stationed in every house? Shall we gather strength by irresolution and inaction? Shall we acquire the means of effectual resistance by lying supinely on our backs, and hugging the delusive phantom of hope, until our enemies shall have bound us hand and foot? Sir, we are not weak, if we make a proper use of those means which the God of nature hath placed in our power.

Three millions of People, armed in the holy cause of liberty, and in such a country as that which we possess, are invincible by any force which our enemy can send against us. Beside, Sir, we shall not fight our battles alone. There is a just God who presides over the destinies of Nations, and who will raise up friends to fight our battles for us. The battle, Sir, is not to the strong alone; it is to the vigilant, the active, the brave. Besides, Sir, we have no election. If we were base enough to desire it, it is now too late to retire from the contest. There is no retreat but in submission and slavery! Our chains are forged! Their clanking may be heard on the plains of Boston! The war is inevitable; and let it come! I repeat, Sir, let it come!

It is in vain, Sir, to extenuate the matter. **Gentlemen may cry, Peace, Peace!–but there is no peace. The war is actually begun! The next gale that sweeps from the North will bring to our ears the clash of resounding arms! Our brethren are already in the field! Why stand we here idle? What is it that Gentlemen wish? What would they have? Is life so dear, or peace so sweet, as to be purchased at the price of chains and slavery? Forbid it, Almighty God! I know not what course others may take; but as for me, GIVE ME LIBERTY OR GIVE ME DEATH!**

Paul Revere's Ride
by Henry Wadsworth Longfellow (1807-1892)

What a pleasant way to learn history. Stirring, dramatic and beautifully expressed. A thrilling horse ride and a call to arms that echoed around the world, and still does more than 200 years later. Revere woke us up in 1775 like Pearl Harbor did in 1941.

Listen, my children, and you shall hear
Of the midnight ride of Paul Revere,
On the eighteenth of April, in Seventy-five;
Hardly a man is now alive
Who remembers that famous day and year.

He said to his friend, "If the British march
By land or sea from the town to-night,
Hang a lantern aloft in the belfry arch
Of the North Church tower as a signal light,–
One if by land, and two if by sea;
And I on the opposite shore will be,
Ready to ride and spread the alarm
Through every Middlesex village and farm,
For the country folk to be up and to arm."

Then he said "Good-night!" and with muffled oar
Silently rowed to the Charlestown shore,
Just as the moon rose over the bay,
Where swinging wide at her moorings lay
The Somerset, British man-of-war;
A phantom ship, with each mast and spar

Across the moon like a prison bar,
And a huge black hulk, that was magnified
By its own reflection in the tide.

Meanwhile, his friend through alley and street
Wanders and watches, with eager ears,
Till in the silence around him he hears
The muster of men at the barrack door,
The sound of arms, and the tramp of feet,
And the measured tread of the grenadiers,
Marching down to their boats on the shore.

Then he climbed the tower of the Old North Church,
By the wooden stairs, with stealthy tread,
To the belfry chamber overhead,
And startled the pigeons from their perch
On the sombre rafters, that round him made
Masses and moving shapes of shade,—
By the trembling ladder, steep and tall,
To the highest window in the wall,
Where he paused to listen and look down
A moment on the roofs of the town
And the moonlight flowing over all.

Beneath, in the churchyard, lay the dead,
In their night encampment on the hill,
Wrapped in silence so deep and still
That he could hear, like a sentinel's tread,
The watchful night-wind, as it went
Creeping along from tent to tent,
And seeming to whisper, "All is well!"
A moment only he feels the spell,
Of the place and the hour, and the secret dread
Of the lonely belfry and the dead;
For suddenly all his thoughts are bent
On a shadowy something far away,
Where the river widens to meet the bay,—
A line of black that bends and floats
On the rising tide like a bridge of boats.

Meanwhile, impatient to mount and ride,
Booted and spurred, with a heavy stride
On the opposite shore walked Paul Revere.
Now he patted his horse's side,
Now he gazed at the landscape far and near,
Then, impetuous, stamped the earth,
And turned and tightened his saddle girth;
But mostly he watched with eager search—
The belfry tower of the Old North Church,
As it rose above the graves on the hill,
Lonely and spectral and sombre and still.
And lo! as be looks, on the belfry's height
A glimmer, and then a gleam of light!
He springs to the saddle, the bridle he turns,
But lingers and gazes, till full on his sight
A second lamp in the belfry burns.

A hurry of hoofs in a village street,
A shape in the moonlight, a bulk in the dark,
And beneath, from the pebbles, in passing, a spark
Struck out by a steed flying fearless and fleet;
That was all! And yet, through the gloom and the light,
The fate of a nation was riding that night;
And the spark struck out by that steed, in his flight,
Kindled the land into flame with its heat.

He has left the village and mounted the steep,
And beneath him, tranquil and broad and deep,
Is the Mystic, meeting the ocean tides;
And under the alders that skirt its edge,
Now soft on the sand, now loud on the ledge,
Is heard the tramp of his steed as he rides.

It was twelve by the village clock
When he crossed the bridge into Medford town.
He heard the crowing of the cock,
And the barking of the farmer's dog,
And felt the damp of the river fog,
That rises after the sun goes down.
It was one by the village clock,

When he galloped into Lexington.
He saw the gilded weathercock
Swim in the moonlight as he passed,
And the meeting-house windows, black and bare,
Gaze at him with a spectral glare,
As if they already stood aghast
At the bloody work they would look upon.

It was two by the village clock,
When he came to the bridge in Concord town.
He heard the bleating of the flock,
And the twitter of birds among the trees,
And felt the breath of the morning breeze
Blowing over the meadow brown.
And one was safe and asleep in his bed
Who at the bridge would be first to fall,
Who that day would be lying dead,
Pierced by a British musket ball.

You know the rest. In the books you have read
How the British Regulars fired and fled,—
How the farmers gave them ball for ball,
From behind each fence and farmyard wall,
Chasing the redcoats down the lane,
Then crossing the fields to emerge again
Under the trees at the turn of the road,
And only pausing to fire and load.

So through the night rode Paul Revere;
And so through the night went his cry of alarm
To every Middlesex village and farm,—
A cry of defiance, and not of fear,
A voice in the darkness, a knock at the door,
And a word that shall echo for evermore!
For, borne on the night-wind of the Past,
Through all our history, to the last,
In the hour of darkness and peril and need,
The people will waken and listen to hear
The hurrying hoof-beats of that steed,
And the midnight message of Paul Revere.

Concord Hymn

by Ralph Waldo Emerson (1803-1892)

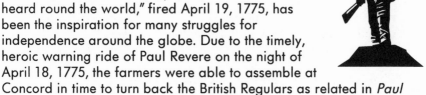

Given at the dedication of the Battle Monument at Concord, Massachusetts, April 19, 1836. The "shot heard round the world," fired April 19, 1775, has been the inspiration for many struggles for independence around the globe. Due to the timely, heroic warning ride of Paul Revere on the night of April 18, 1775, the farmers were able to assemble at Concord in time to turn back the British Regulars as related in *Paul Revere's Ride*. The Revolutionary War was on.

> By the rude bridge that arched the flood,
>> Their flag to April's breeze unfurled,
> Here once the embattled farmers stood,
>> And fired the shot heard round the world.

> The foe long since in silence slept;
>> Alike the conqueror silent sleeps;
> And Time the ruined bridge has swept
>> Down the dark stream which seaward creeps.

> On this green bank, by this soft stream,
>> We set today a votive stone;
> That memory may their deed redeem,
>> When, like our sires, our sons are gone.

> Spirit, that made those spirits dare
>> To die, and leave their children free,
> Bid Time and Nature gently spare
>> The shaft we raise to them and thee.

Song of Marion's Men

by William Cullen Bryant (1794-1878)

Brigadier-General Francis Marion was best
known as the "Swamp Fox." Born and raised in
South Carolina, he led small groups of guerrillas
in lightning attacks on the British during the
Revolution, with often spectacular results.

Our band is few, but true and tried,
    Our leader frank and bold;
The British soldier trembles
    When Marion's name is told.
Our fortress is the good greenwood,
    Our tent the cypress-tree;
We know the forest round us,
    As seamen know the sea.
We know its walls of thorny vines,
    Its glades of reedy grass,
Its safe and silent islands
    Within the dark morass.

Woe to the English soldiery
    That little dread us near!
On them shall light at midnight
    A strange and sudden fear:
When, waking to their tents on fire,
    They grasp their arms in vain,
And they who stand to face us
    Are beat to earth again;
And they who fly in terror deem
    A mighty host behind,
And hear the tramp of thousands
    Upon the hollow wind.

Then sweet the hour that brings release
    From danger and from toil;
We talk the battle over,
    We share the battle's spoil.

The woodland rings with laugh and shout
    As if a hunt were up,
And woodland flowers are gathered
    To crown the soldier's cup.
With merry songs we mock the wind
    That in the pine-top grieves,
And slumber long and sweetly
    On beds of oaken leaves.

Well knows the fair and friendly moon
    The band that Marion leads—
The glitter of their rifles,
    The scampering of their steeds.
'Tis life to guide the fiery barb
    Across the moonlight plain;
'Tis life to feel the night-wind
    That lifts his tossing mane.
A moment in the British camp—
    A moment—and away,
Back to the pathless forest
    Before the peep of day.

Grave men there are by broad Santee,
    Grave men with hoary hairs;
Their hearts are all with Marion,
    For Marion are their prayers.
And lovely ladies greet our band
    With kindliest welcoming,
With smiles like those of summer,
    And tears like those of spring.
For them we wear these trusty arms,
    And lay them down no more
Till we have driven the Briton,
    Forever, from our shore.

Old Ironsides

by Oliver Wendell Holmes (1809-1894)

The great warship, Constitution; never defeated in battle. She was launched in 1799 at a total cost of around $300,000. That amount today would probably buy a medium sized landing craft. She earned the name of *Old Ironsides* from her sailors, who watched the cannon balls bounce off her sturdy oak timbers when she defeated the British *Guerriere* during the War of 1812. The ship was saved from destruction when Holmes wrote this poem and stirred up nationwide patriotic fervor. As a result, she was completely restored. She is moored in Boston Harbor, and is now the oldest ship afloat. A commemorative sail was carried out in 1997 to celebrate her 200th birthday.

Ay, tear her tattered ensign down!
    Long has it waved on high,
And many an eye has danced to see
    That banner in the sky;
Beneath it rung the battle shout,
    And burst the cannon's roar;—
The meteor of the ocean air
    Shall sweep the clouds no more.

Her deck, once red with heroes' blood,
    Where knelt the vanquished foe,
When winds were hurrying o'er the flood,
    And waves were white below,
No more shall feel the victor's tread,
    Or know the conquered knee;
The harpies of the shore shall pluck
    The eagle of the sea!

O, better that her shattered hulk
    Should sink beneath the wave;
Her thunders shook the mighty deep,
    And there should be her grave;
Nail to the mast her holy flag,
    Set every threadbare sail,
And give her to the god of storms,
    The lightning and the gale!

The Charge of the Light Brigade

by Alfred Lord Tennyson (1809-1892)

A badly bungled episode of a badly handled war, The Crimean War of 1853-1856 between Great Britain, France and Turkey against Russia. Someone blundered and the Light Brigade was ordered in the wrong direction, straight into the Russian guns. The Brigade knew that the ordered charge was deadly wrong, but the honor of the Brigade carried it out with the expected terrible result. The only good that came out of this unnecessary war was Florence Nightingale and the greatly improved care and nursing of battle casualties.

> Half a league, half a league,
> Half a league onward,
> All in the valley of Death
>   Rode the six hundred.
>   "Forward, the Light Brigade!
> Charge for the guns!" he said—.
> Into the valley of Death
>   Rode the six hundred.
>
> "Forward, the Light Brigade!"
> Was there a man dismayed?
> Not tho' the soldiers knew
>   Some one had blundered:
> Theirs not to make reply,
> Theirs not to reason why,
> Theirs but to do and die.
> Into the valley of Death
>   Rode the six hundred.
>
> Cannon to right of them,
> Cannon to left of them,
> Cannon in front of them
>   Volleyed and thunder'd;
> Storm'd at with shot and shell,
> Boldly they rode and well,
> Into the jaws of Death,
> Into the mouth of Hell,
>   Rode the six hundred.

Flashed all their sabres bare,
Flashed as they turned in air,
Sab'ring the gunners there,
Charging an army, while
    All the world wondered:
Plunged in the battery smoke,
Right through the line they broke;
Cossack and Russian
Reeled from the sabre-stroke
    Shattered and sundered.
Then they rode back, but not—
    Not the six hundred.

Cannon to right of them,
Cannon to left of them
Cannon behind them
    Volleyed and thundered;
Stormed at with shot and shell,
While horse and hero fell,
They that had fought so well
Came thro' the jaws of Death,
Back from the mouth of Hell,
All that was left of them,
    Left of six hundred.

When can their glory fade?
Oh, the wild charge they made!
    All the world wondered.
Honor the charge they made!
Honor the Light Brigade,
    Noble Six Hundred!

A Georgia Volunteer

by Mary Ashley Townsend (1832-1901)

This was a great favorite of mine in grammar school days, and it still is. It was such a favorite of mine, that in college, when we had to submit a poem to write a critique on, I chose this one. The professor liked my report so well he gave me an A+ and an extra statement of how impressed he was. I think he sensed my thorough pleasure in reading these touching words, which I think he enjoyed too. (I have to confess I only remembered the first two stanzas. However, Ms. Nielsen of the University of Georgia library staff was kind enough to send me the full edition plus other information.)

> Far up the lonely mountain-side
>   My wandering footsteps led;
> The moss lay thick beneath my feet,
>   The pine sighed overhead.
> The trace of a dismantled fort
>   Lay in the forest nave,
> And in the shadow near my path
>   I saw a soldier's grave.
>
> The bramble wrestled with the weed
>   Upon the lowly mound,
> The simple headboard, rudely writ
>   Had rotted to the ground;
> I raised it with a reverent hand,
>   From dust its words to clear,
> But time had blotted all but these—
>   "A Georgia Volunteer."
>
> I saw the toad and scaly snake
>   From tangled covert start,
> And hide themselves among the weeds
>   Above the dead man's heart;
> But undisturbed, in sleep profound,
>   Unheeding, there he lay;
> His coffin but the mountain soil,
>   His shroud Confederate gray.

I heard the Shenandoah roll
    Along the vale below,
I saw the Alleghenies rise
    Towards the realms of snow.
The "Valley Campaign" rose to mind,—
    Its leader's name—and then
I knew the sleeper had been one
    Of Stonewall Jackson's men.

Yet whence he came, what lip shall say?
    Whose tongue will ever tell
What desolated hearths and hearts
    Have been because he fell?
What sad-eyed maiden braids her hair,
    Her hair which he held dear?
One lock of which, perchance, lies with
    The Georgia Volunteer!

What mother, with long watching eyes
    And white lips cold and dumb,
Waits with appalling patience for
    Her darling boy to come?
Her boy! whose mountain grave swells up
    But one of many a scar
Out in the face of our fair land
    By gory-handed war.

What fights he fought, what wounds he wore
    Are all unknown to fame;
Remember, on his lonely grave
    There is not e'en a name!
That he fought well and bravely, too,
    And held his country dear,
We know, or else he had never been
    A Georgia Volunteer.

He sleeps—what need to question now
    If he were wrong or right?
He knows ere this whose cause was just
    In God the Father's sight.
He wields no warlike weapons now,
    Returns no foeman's thrust,—
Who but a coward would revile
    An honest soldier's dust?

Roll, Shenandoah, proudly roll,
    Adown thy rocky glen,
Above thee lies the grave of one
    Of Stonewall Jackson's men.
Beneath the cedar and the pine,
    In solitude austere,
Unknown, unnamed, forgotten, lies
    A Georgia Volunteer.

The Blue and the Gray

by Francis Miles Finch (1827-1907)

A beautiful, conciliatory tribute to the dead of the North and South in our deadliest war; 498,000 killed, more Americans than were lost in World War II. Just think—brother against brother, and cousin against cousin, for four long years, and on home soil.

By the flow of the inland river,
    Whence the fleets of iron have fled,
Where the blades of the grave grass quiver,
    Asleep are the ranks of the dead;—
      Under the sod and the dew,
        Waiting the judgment day;—
      Under the one, the Blue;
        Under the other, the Gray.

These in the robings of glory,
    Those in the gloom of defeat,
All with the battle blood gory,
    In the dusk of eternity meet;—
      Under the sod and the dew,
        Waiting the judgment day;—
      Under the laurel, the Blue;
        Under the willow, the Gray.

From the silence of sorrowful hours
    The desolate mourners go,
Lovingly laden with flowers
    Alike for the friend and the foe,—
      Under the sod and the dew,
        Waiting the judgment day;—
      Under the roses, the Blue;
        Under the lilies, the Gray.

So with an equal splendor
    The morning sun rays fall,
With a touch, impartially tender,
    On the blossoms blooming for all;—
      Under the sod and the dew,
        Waiting the judgment day;—
      Broidered with gold, the Blue;
        Mellowed with gold, the Gray.

So when the summer calleth,
    On forest and field of grain
With an equal murmur falleth
    The cooling drip of the rain;—
      Under the sod and the dew,
        Waiting the judgment day;—
      Wet with the rain, the Blue;
        Wet with the rain, the Gray.

Sadly, but not with upbraiding,
    The generous deed was done;
In the storm of the years that are fading,
    No braver battle was won;—
      Under the sod and the dew,
        Waiting the judgment day;—
      Under the blossoms, the Blue;
        Under the garlands, the Gray.

No more shall the war cry sever,
    Or the winding rivers be red;
They banish our anger forever
    When they laurel the graves of our dead!
      Under the sod and the dew,
        Waiting the judgment day;—
      Love and tears for the Blue;
        Tears and love for the Gray.

Gettysburg Address
by Abraham Lincoln (1809-1865)

What a speech! Speech at the Dedication of the National Cemetery at Gettysburg, Pennsylvania, November 19, 1863. Not a poem, but words so carefully chosen and eloquently combined that Lincoln was able to express, in some 2 minutes, what the noted orator, Edward Everett, couldn't get across in 2 hours of boredom at the same dedication. Everett wrote Lincoln the next day and paid him this compliment. "I wish that I could flatter myself that I had come as near to the central idea of this occasion in two hours, as you did in two minutes."

"Fourscore and seven years ago our fathers brought forth upon this continent a new nation, conceived in liberty, and dedicated to the proposition that all men are created equal. Now we are engaged in a great civil war, testing whether that nation, or any nation so conceived and so dedicated, can long endure. We are met on a great battlefield of that war. We have come to dedicate a portion of that field as a final resting-place for those who here gave their lives that that nation might live. It is altogether fitting and proper that we should do this. But in a larger sense we cannot dedicate, we cannot consecrate, we cannot hallow this ground. The brave men, living and dead, who struggled here, have consecrated it far above our poor power to add or detract. The world will little note, nor long remember, what we say here; but it can never forget what they did here. It is for us, the living, rather to be dedicated here to the unfinished work which they who fought here have thus far so nobly advanced. It is rather for us to be here dedicated to the great task remaining before us, that from these honored dead we take increased devotion to that cause for which they gave the last full measure of devotion; that we here highly resolve that these dead shall not have died in vain; that this nation, under God, shall have a new birth of freedom, and that government of the people, by the people, and for the people, shall not perish from the earth."

How wrong Lincoln was in that sentence "The world will little note, nor long remember what we say here" concerning his speech. But that sentence certainly described Everett's long harangue.

Barbara Frietchie

by John Greenleaf Whittier (1807-1892)

An unmatched story of patriotic bravery and
deep respect of friend and foe. During the Civil
War, due to a marked shortage of transportation
and supplies, Robert E. Lee and Stonewall
Jackson were able to invade the North on only a
very few occasions. On one of these trips, this
episode was said to have occurred in Frederick, Maryland.

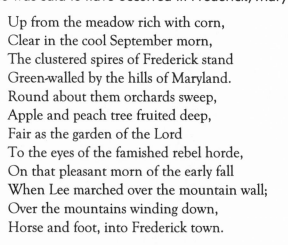

Up from the meadow rich with corn,
Clear in the cool September morn,
The clustered spires of Frederick stand
Green-walled by the hills of Maryland.
Round about them orchards sweep,
Apple and peach tree fruited deep,
Fair as the garden of the Lord
To the eyes of the famished rebel horde,
On that pleasant morn of the early fall
When Lee marched over the mountain wall;
Over the mountains winding down,
Horse and foot, into Frederick town.

Forty flags with their silver stars,
Forty flags with their crimson bars,
Flapped in the morning wind: the sun
Of noon looked down, and saw not one.
Up rose old Barbara Frietchie then,
Bowed with her fourscore years and ten;
Bravest of all in Frederick town,
She took up the flag the men hauled down;
In her attic window the staff she set,
To show that one heart was loyal yet.

Up the street came the rebel tread,
Stonewall Jackson riding ahead.
Under his slouched hat left and right
He glanced; the old flag met his sight.
"Halt"—the dust-brown ranks stood fast.
"Fire"—out blazed the rifle blast.
It shivered the window, pane and sash;

It rent the banner with seam and gash.
Quick, as it fell, from the broken staff
Dame Barbara snatched the silken scarf.
She leaned far out on the windowsill,
And shook it forth with a royal will.
"Shoot, if you must, this old gray head,
But spare your country's flag," she said.

A shade of sadness, a blush of shame,
Over the face of the leader came;
The nobler nature within him stirred
To life at that woman's deed and word;
"Who touches a hair on yon gray head
Dies like a dog! March on!" he said.
All day long through Frederick street
Sounded the tread of marching feet:
All day long that free flag tossed
Over the heads of the rebel host.
Ever its torn folds rose and fell
On the loyal winds that loved it well;
And through the hill gaps sunset light
Shone over it with a warm good night.

Barbara Frietchie's work is o'er,
And the Rebel rides on his raids no more.
Honor to her! and let a tear
Fall, for her sake, on Stonewall's bier.
Over Barbara Frietchie's grave
Flag of Freedom and Union, wave!
Peace and order and beauty draw
Round thy symbol of light and law;
And ever the stars above look down
On thy stars below in Frederick town!

O Captain! My Captain!

By Walt Whitman (1819-1892)

The exultation of the Union at the ending of the bloody
Civil War was immediately dampened by the tragic
assassination of Abraham Lincoln, "My Captain."
Although born and raised a devout and proud
Southerner, I will always believe that, if Lincoln had
survived, the South would never have gone through the
terrible Reconstruction Period with Carpetbagging and other disgraceful
embarrassments which I think set race relations back 100 years. I have no
doubt that he would have been as fair to the defeated enemy as he was to
the cause of slavery. This is a moving tribute to Lincoln in death. The
assassin, John Wilkes Booth, an actor, was certainly no friend of the South
when he shot Lincoln.

> O Captain! my Captain! our fearful trip is done;
> The ship has weather'd every rack, the prize we sought is won;
> The port is near, the bells I hear, the people all exulting,
> While follow eyes the steady keel, the vessel grim and daring:
>
>> But O heart! heart! heart!
>> O the bleeding drops of red,
>>> Where on the deck my Captain lies,
>>> Fallen cold and dead.
>
> O Captain! my Captain! rise up and hear the bells;
> Rise up—for you the flag is flung—for you the bugle trills;
> For you bouquets and ribbon'd wreaths for you the shores a-crowding;
> For you they call, the swaying mass, their eager faces turning:
>
>> Here Captain! dear father!
>> This arm beneath your head;
>>> It is some dream that on the deck
>>> You've fallen cold and dead.
>
> My Captain does not answer, his lips are pale and still;
> My father does not feel my arm, he has no pulse or will;
> The ship is anchor'd safe and sound, its voyage closed and done;
> From fearful trip the victor ship comes in with object won:
>
>> Exult, O shores, and ring, O bells!
>> But I, with mournful tread,
>>> Walk the deck my Captain lies,
>>> Fallen cold and dead.

Boots
by Rudyard Kipling (1865-1936)

As far as I am concerned, this poem, along with Poe's *Bells*, comprise the best examples of alliteration in the literature. This gives a great description of a British soldier's life in far off, hot Africa, and the monotony of those ever-marching Boots, Boots, Boots.

> We're foot slog-slog-slog-sloggin' over Africa,
>   Foot-foot-foot-foot-sloggin' over Africa—
> (Boots-boots-boots-boots-movin' up and down again!)
>   There's no discharge in the war!
>
> Seven-six-eleven-five-nine-an'-twenty mile to-day—
>   Four-eleven-seventeen-thirty-two the day before—
> (Boots-boots-boots-boots-movin' up and down again!)
>   There's no discharge in the war!
>
> Don't-don't-don't-don't-look at what's in front of you.
>   (Boots-boots-boots-boots-movin' up and down again),
> Men-men-men-men-men go mad with watchin' 'em,
>   An' there's no discharge in the war!
>
> Try-try-try-try-to think o' something different—
>   Oh-my-God-keep-me from goin' lunatic!
> (Boots-boots-boots-boots-movin' up and down again!)
>   There's no discharge in the war!
>
> Count-count-count-count-the bullets in the bandoliers.
>   If-your-eyes-drop-they will get atop o' you.
> (Boots-boots-boots-boots-movin' up and down again!) —
>   There's no discharge in the war!
>
> We-can-stick-out-'unger, thirst, an' weariness,
>   But-not-not-not-not the chronic sight of 'em—
> Boots-boots-boots-boots-movin' up and down again,
>   An' there's no discharge in the war!

'Tain't-so-bad-by-day because o' company,
    But-night-brings-long-strings-o' forty thousand million
Boots-boots-boots-boots-movin' up and down again.
    There's no discharge in the war!

I-'ave-marched-six-weeks in 'Ell an' certify
    It-is-not-fire-devils-dark or anything,
But boots-boots-boots-boots-movin' up and down again,
    There's no discharge in the war!

Recessional
by Rudyard Kipling (1865-1936)

Published in the late 1890's, but read as a tribute at Queen Victoria's 60th Jubilee in 1903. Undoubtedly the best of Kipling's many works. I have read that the Queen took great offense at the reference to power, boasting, and loss of awe to the Almighty, which Kipling so cleverly pointed out. The repeated "Lest we forget" must have really gotten under her skin.

God of our fathers, known of old—
    Lord of our far-flung battle line—
Beneath Whose awful hand we hold
    Dominion over palm and pine'—
Lord God of Hosts, be with us yet,
    Lest we forget—lest we forget!

The tumult and the shouting dies;
    The captains and the kings depart:
Still stands Thine ancient Sacrifice,
    An humble and contrite heart.
Lord God of Hosts, be with us yet,
    Lest we forget—lest we forget!

Far-called, our navies melt away;
    On dune and headland sinks the fire:
Lo, all our pomp of yesterday
    Is one with Nineveh and Tyre!
Judge of the Nations, spare us yet,
    Lest we forget—lest we forget!

If, drunk with sight of power, we loose
      Wild tongues that have not Thee in awe—
Such boasting as the Gentiles use
      Or lesser breeds without the Law—
Lord God of Hosts, be with us yet,
      Lest we forget—lest we forget!

For heathen heart that puts her trust
      In reeking tube and iron shard—
All valiant dust that builds on dust,
      And guarding, calls not Thee to Guard—
For frantic boast and foolish word,
      Thy mercy on Thy people, Lord!
Amen.

[1] *Palm and pine: refers to India and Canada*

The Unknown Soldier
by Billy Rose

If you haven't visited the Grave of the
Unknown Soldier, don't miss a chance to
see it. Very moving, as is this poem. The
graves of the Unknown Soldiers rest in
Arlington National Cemetery, just outside
Washington, D.C. in Northern Virginia.
Arlington Mansion was the home of Robert E. Lee and was occupied by
the North shortly after the start of the Civil War. Many casualties of that
war were buried on the grounds, and later it was established as a
National Cemetery. The graves of the Unknown Soldiers, bodies that
could not be identified, are buried there for each war, so that families can
at least honor them as possibly their lost loved ones. A very somber, but
colorful and impressive guard marching service is in place there, with its
methodical "Changing of the Guard" procedure. In addition to the section
for the Unknown Soldier are some 262,000 graves (increasing by 15 a
day) of servicemen dating back to the Revolution. President John Kennedy
has a very impressive grave there with an eternal flame. This poem raises
good questions from the graveyard, and the answers are not always
good.

> There's a Graveyard near the White House
>> Where the Unknown Soldier lies,
> And the flowers there are sprinkled
>> With the tears from mother's eyes.
>
> I stood there not so long ago
>> With roses for the brave,
> And suddenly I heard a voice
>> Speak from out the grave:
>
> "I am the Unknown Soldier,"
>> The spirit voice began,
> "And I think I have the right
>> To ask some questions man to man.
>
> "Are my buddies taken care of?
>> Was their victory so sweet?
> Is that big reward you offered
>> Selling pencils on the street?

"Did they really win the freedom
        They battled to achieve?
Do you still respect that Croix de Guerre
        Above that empty sleeve?

"Does a gold star in the window
        Now mean anything at all?
I wonder how my old girl feels
        When she hears a bugle call.

"And that baby who sang
        'Hello, Central, give me no man's land—'
Can they replace her daddy
        With a military band?

"I wonder if the profiteers
        Have satisfied their greed?
I wonder if a soldier's mother
        Ever is in need?

"I wonder if the kings, who planned it all
        Are really satisfied?
They played their game of checkers
        And eleven million died.

"I am the Unknown Soldier
        And maybe I died in vain,
But if I were alive and my country called,
        I'd do it all over again."

In Flanders Fields
by Lt.-Col. John McCrae - Canadian Army (1872-1918)

A moving plea by the author who must have sensed his own death in combat in 1918, after four long years in fighting on the Western Front.

> In Flanders fields the poppies blow
> Between the crosses, row on row,
>> That mark our place; and in the sky
>> The larks, still bravely singing, fly
> Scarce heard amid the guns below.
>
> We are the Dead. Short days ago
> We lived, felt dawn, saw sunset glow,
>> Loved and were loved, and now we lie
>> In Flanders fields.
>
> Take up our quarrel with the foe;
> To you from failing hands we throw
>> The torch; be yours to hold it high.
>> If ye break faith with us who die
> We shall not sleep, though poppies grow
>> In Flanders fields.

America's Answer
by R. W. Lilliard

Regretfully the lesson of World War I lasted only 21 years to the start of World War II, an even bloodier holocaust, but, as promised, we took up the quarrel and held the torch high, not once, but twice.

> Rest ye in peace, ye Flanders dead.
> The fight that ye so bravely led
> We've taken up. And we will keep
> True faith with you who lie asleep
> With each a cross to mark his bed,
>> In Flanders fields.

Fear not that ye have died for naught.
The torch ye threw to us we caught.
Ten million hands will hold it high,
And Freedom's light shall never die!
We've learned the lesson that ye taught
        In Flanders fields.

Marine's Hymn

At a parade or other military occurrence, when the band strikes up *The Caissons go Rolling Along, Wild Blue Yonder,* or *Anchors Aweigh,* there is always a loud cheer. But when the *Marine's Hymn* breaks forth, there is usually a deafening roar of approval. There just seems to be a special aura about the Marines.

From the halls of Montezuma[1], to the shores of Tripoli[2],
We fight our country's battles in the air, on land and sea.
First to fight for right and freedom, and to keep our honor clean;
We are proud to claim the title of United States Marine.

Our flag's unfurled to every breeze from dawn to setting sun.
We have fought in every clime and place, where we could take a gun.
In the snow of far off northern lands and in sunny tropic scenes,
You will find us always on the job, The United States Marines.

Here's health to you and to our Corps which we are proud to serve.
In many a strife we've fought for life and never lost our nerve.
If the Army and the Navy ever look on heaven's scenes,
They will find the streets are guarded by United States Marines.

[1] *Montezuma: refers to the Marines' part in the Mexican War 1846-1848*
[2] *Tripoli: refers to the Marine action in the wars with the Barbary Pirates in the Tripolitan War 1801-1805*

Hate Comes to Paradise

by Samuel Norfleet Etheredge (1914-

In the early days of the Pacific War, the Marine Corps sent troops to various islands for the dual purpose of garrison and training for combat. We arrived on Samoa in February, 1943 as the 10th Replacement Battalion. Although an M.D., I was forced to go thru all the jungle training of combat patrol, crawling under barb wire with overhead firing, and simulated night assaults over jungle covered mountains. This was tough, but necessary, and not our big problem. The big problems, as described in the poem, were the boredom of the majority of the time, the poor contact with loved ones back home, the limited use of the magnificent local terrain, the concern about the dread Mumu, and of course, the threatening movement up to actual combat, which wasn't going very well at that time. Our battalion moved on up to join the Third Marine Division and its attacks on Bougainville, Guam, and Iwo Jima.

> South Sea Island Paradise was all we'd ever heard about it.
> The strangest part about it was, we'd never stopped to doubt it.
> Land of lazy waving palms, metropolis of Pago¹,
> Land where dusky maidens civa-civa² the native tango;
> Land where blue Pacific waves dash on a coral shore;
> Oh, freely nature had bestowed from all her wondrous store.
>
> That's the way we pictured it, and don't think us alone,
> 'Til cruel Fate's disrobing brush painted a different tone.
> "Detached, proceed beyond the seas," our orders read as one.
> With such a spot to train, we thought our first stop would be fun.
> But you're not here long 'ere you know every song, that tells of such
>   tropical bliss
> Was written by guys, 'neath far away skies, who never lived south of
>   St. Louis.

No urge of greed, nor lustful creed, had driven us so far.
We heard the call for patriots all; we answered, "here we are."
But time and tide can pierce the hide of the toughest, there's no
doubt.
Tho' each will smile a creaky smile, the truth is seeping out.
For our time is many long months of hell, our tide this damn
stagnation
Of tropic clime that eats the mind of men of every station.

Now they've seen us grin, when we've been in such rains, that
should they hap,
To pelter down on our home town they'd wash it off the map.
And, with oceans of water, you'd think that we ought to get
frequent nice swims it appears.
But the trim barracuda is a most grim intruder, and the fungus will
grow in your ears.
Yes, the fungus grows in your ears and your toes, and eats the soles
off your feet.
The way it has grown on all that we own is a most unbelievable feat.

We've fussed and we've cussed, as good marines must, at millions of
damn mosquitoes.
If it wasn't for the bugs they bore, we'd simply let them eat us.
But grotesque elephantiasis, the doc says filariasis, and the natives
call it "mu-mu"
Has plagued half their bodies, and lots of our buddies, and soon will
get most of us too.
Oh! we've bungled thru jungle, we've clomped through the swamp,
we've slept in six inches of mud.
We've gone without water, had stomach disorder, you wouldn't
believe what we've stood.

Now, I've watched the men dream, both the crud and the cream,
with that homesick look in their eye.
You can tell they're far away, in the dear U.S.A.; you could guess all
the rest if you try.
There's Joe whose brunette is the very best yet, and Bill proud of his
unseen son;
And Rosy's cute daughters, Red's bachelors' quarters, and Mike has
just socked a home run.

Young Chicken misses his mother, and Bob his kid brother, it's been a long time now you know.

The Colonel dreams of fishing; and the Major is wishing for another week-end in Diego.

But the smile on each face is quickly erased, as the now slams the door on the past.

There's a glint in each eye, as they all figure why, such pleasures could not always last.

Seeds of hate that were sown, as each ship was blown to hell on the bay at Pearl Harbor,

Have lain quiet, sprouted, and then upward spouted, one flame to a huge candelabra.

Mr. Moto, you'll pay, for each single day you've kept us from loved ones back there.

With your tainted blood you will sign, upon the dotted line, for the heart-break you've spread everywhere.

Hirohito, we're coming, to your own den we're coming, break out your white flag Tokyo.

Hate has stung us that hard, we won't stop, Praise the Lord, 'til these things we promise are so.

When you are rewarded for what you have started, and you gaze on your own Nippon's scenes

You will see your schemes thwarted and all your streets guarded BY THE UNITED STATES MARINES.

---

[1] *Pago-Pago: in Samoa, this was pronounced as Pango-Pango. The capital of American Samoa.*

[2] *civa-civa: the native dance*

Father Land and Mother Tongue

by Samuel Lover (1797-1868)

Tough questions—simple answers, at least as
good as any.

Our Father Land! and wouldst thou know
    Why we should call it Father Land?
It is that Adam here below
    Was made of earth by Nature's hand;
And he, our father made of earth,
    Hath peopled earth on every hand;
And we, in memory of his birth,
    Do call our country Father Land.

At first, in Eden's bowers, they say,
    No sound of speech had Adam caught,
But whistled like a bird all day,—
    And maybe 'twas for want of thought:
But Nature, with resistless laws,
    Made Adam soon surpass the birds;
She gave him lovely Eve because
    If he'd a wife they must *have words*.

And so the native land, I hold,
    By male descent is proudly mine;
The language, as the tale hath told,
    Was given in the female line.
And thus we see on either hand
    We name our blessings whence they've sprung;
We call our country Father Land,
    We call our language Mother Tongue.

The Bivouac of the Dead

by Theodore O'Hara (1820-1867)

Perfect for Arlington National Cemetery where some 262,000 casualties of all our wars are buried. The cemetery was established at the end of the Civil War, but casualties of even the Revolution are buried there. The poem is also carved on a monument on a Crimean battlefield.

The muffled drum's sad roll has beat
    The soldier's last tattoo!
No more on life's parade shall meet
    The brave and fallen few.
On Fame's eternal camping ground
    Their silent tents are spread,
And glory guards with solemn round
    The bivouac of the dead.

No rumor of the foe's advance
    Now swells upon the wind,
Nor troubled thought of midnight haunts,
    Of loved ones left behind;
No vision of the morrow's strife
    The warrior's dreams alarms,
No braying horn or screaming fife
    At dawn to call to arms.

Their shivered swords are red with rust,
    Their plumed heads are bowed,
Their haughty banner, trailed in dust,
    Is now their martial shroud—
And plenteous funeral tears have washed
    The red stains from each brow,
And the proud forms by battle gashed
    Are free from anguish now.

The neighing troop, the flashing blade,
    The bugle's stirring blast,
The charge,—the dreadful cannonade,
    The din and shout, are passed;
Nor war's wild notes, nor glory's peal
    Shall thrill with fierce delight
Those breasts that nevermore shall feel
    The rapture of the fight.

Like the fierce Northern hurricane
    That sweeps the great plateau,
Flushed with the triumph yet to gain,
    Come down the serried foe,
Who heard the thunder of the fray
    Break o'er the field beneath,
Knew the watchword of the day
    Was "Victory or death!"

Rest on, embalmed and sainted dead,
    Dear is the blood you gave—
No impious footstep here shall tread
    The herbage of your grave.
Nor shall your glory be forgot
    While Fame her record keeps,
Or honor points the hallowed spot
    Where valor proudly sleeps.

Yon marble minstrel's voiceless stone
    In deathless song shall tell,
When many a vanquished year hath flown,
    The story how you fell.
Nor wreck nor change, nor winter's blight,
    Nor time's remorseless doom,
Can dim one ray of holy light
    That gilds your glorious tomb.

Bougainville

by Samuel Norfleet Etheredge (1914-

Bougainville is the Northwesternmost and largest of the Solomon Islands. The purpose of the Bougainville campaign was not to conquer the entire island but to obtain and secure an area large enough for a couple of airstrips, sufficient to get air control over Rabaul, the largest Japanese base in the general area of the Western Pacific. The end result was so effective that a very major, and probably very costly, attack on Kavieng, New Ireland was called off at the last second by Nimitz and MacArthur, and the big sweep up to Saipan and Guam saved a great deal of time and unquestionably many lives.

> We've come from far
> And here we are
> All set to start to kill,
>> For the day is D, the hour is H,
>>> And the place is Bougainville.

> Our cannons roar
> And smash the shore
> To break the deathly still,
>> For the day is D, the hour is H,
>>> And the place is Bougainville.

> Yes, some are young
> And came along
> Just for this very thrill,
>> For the day is D, the hour is H,
>>> And the place is Bougainville.

> But we are old
> And not so bold
> And we feel a bone-deep chill,
>> For the day is D, the hour is H,
>>> And the place is Bougainville.

Now when we come back
There's many a "Mac"
Who won't be with us still,
     For the day is D, the hour is H,
          And the place is Bougainville.

I'm telling you, matey
If I live to be eighty
I'll remember each split second still,
     When the day was D, the hour was H,
          And the place was Bougainville.

I have kept my promise. I have lived to past eighty—and I remember it like it was yesterday, especially the H + 8 minutes when I landed with the second wave. This patch (gold on a red field) is the emblem of the 3rd Marine Division, the main attacking force at Bougainville. It was designed by a Navy Corpsman when the division was formed.

UNIQUE AND

❧ INTERESTING PLACES ❧

For sure I'll skip the first two. Mandalay sounds inviting and the Yukon sounds exciting, but I would, and did, opt for "Out Where the West Begins."

Hell in Texas

by Unknown

Unknown must have lived there—and maybe just be afraid to give his name?

The devil, we're told, in hell was chained,
And a thousand years he there remained,
And he never complained, nor did he groan,
But determined to start a hell of his own
Where he could torment the souls of men
Without being chained to a prison pen.

So he asked the Lord if He had on hand
Anything left when He made the land.
The Lord said, "Yes, I had plenty on hand,
But I left it down on the Rio Grande.
The fact is, old boy, the stuff is so poor,
I don't think you could use it in hell any more."

But the devil went down to look at the truck,
And said if it came as a gift, he was stuck;
For after examining it careful and well
He concluded the place was too dry for hell.
So in order to get it off His hands
God promised the devil to water the lands.

For he had some water, or rather some dregs,
A regular cathartic that smelt like bad eggs.
Hence the deal was closed and the deed was given,
And the Lord went back to His place in Heaven.
And the devil said, "I have all that is needed
To make a good hell," and thus he succeeded.

He began to put thorns on all the trees,
And he mixed the sand with millions of fleas,
He scattered tarantulas along all the roads,
Put thorns on the cacti and horns on the toads;
He lengthened the horns of the Texas steers
And put an addition on jack rabbits' ears.

He put little devils in the broncho steed
And poisoned the feet of the centipede.
The rattlesnake bites you, the scorpion stings,
The mosquito delights you by buzzing his wings.
The sand burrs prevail, so do the ants,
And those that sit down need half soles on their pants.

The devil then said that throughout the land
He'd manage to keep up the devil's own brand,
And all would be mavericks unless they bore
The marks of scratches and bites by the score.
The heat in the summer is a hundred and ten,
Too hot for the devil and too hot for men.

The wild boar roams through the black chaparral,
It's a hell of a place he has for a hell;
The red pepper grows by the bank of the brook,
The Mexicans use it in all that they cook.
Just dine down there one night and then you will shout,
"I've a hell on the inside as well as without."

Owed to New York

by Byron Rufus Newton

There will be lots of debate about this from you know whom. Maybe the Texans were debating the New Yorkers in poetry. My personal vote goes to California or Virginia.

Vulgar of manner, overfed,
Overdressed and underbred,
Heartless, Godless, hell's delight,
Rude by day and lewd by night;
Bedwarfed the man, o'ergrown the brute,
Ruled by boss and prostitute:
Purple-robed and pauper-clad,
Raving, rotting, money-mad;
A squirming herd in Mammon's mesh,
A wilderness of human flesh;
Crazed by avarice, lust and rum,
New York, thy name's "Delirium."

Mandalay

by Rudyard Kipling (1865-1936)

If you like Kipling, and I do, you can't help but
enjoy his flowery, rhythmic description of life in
Burma during the British occupation. Geographically, Mandalay lies near
the center of Burma, several hundred miles up the Irrawaddy River from
Rangoon on the coast. The smaller Moulmein lies to the east across an
arm of the Bay of Bengal.

By the old Moulmein Pagoda, lookin' eastward to the sea,
There's a Burma girl a-settin', an' I know she thinks o' me;
For the wind is in the palm trees, an' the temple bells they say:
"Come you back, you British soldier; come you back to Mandalay!"
    Come you back to Mandalay,
    Where the old Flotilla lay:
    Can't you 'ear their paddles chunkin' from Rangoon to Mandalay?
    On the road to Mandalay,
    Where the flyin'-fishes play,
    An' the dawn comes up like thunder outer China 'crost the Bay!

'Er petticut was yaller an' 'er little cap was green,
An' 'er name was Supi-yaw-lat—jes' the same as Theebaw's Queen,
An' I seed her fust a-smokin' of a whackin' white cheroot,
An' a-wastin' Christian kisses on an 'eathen idol's foot:
    Bloomin' idol made o' mud—
    Wot they called the Great Gawd Budd—
    Plucky lot she cared for idols when I kissed 'er where she stud!
    On the road to Mandalay—

When the mist was on the rice-fields an' the sun was droppin' slow,
She'd git 'er little banjo an' she'd sing "*Kulla-lo-lo!*"
With 'er arm upon my shoulder, an' 'er cheek agin my cheek,
We useter watch the steamers an' the *hathis* pilin' teak.
    Elephints a-pilin' teak
    In the sludgy, squdgy creek,
    Where the silence 'ung that 'eavy you was 'arf afraid to speak!
    On the road to Mandalay—

But that's all shove be'ind me—long ago an' fur away,
An' there ain't no 'buses running' from the Benk to Mandalay;
An' I'm learnin' 'ere in London what the ten-year sodger tells:
"If you've 'eard the East a-callin', why, you won't 'eed nothin' else."
    No! You won't 'eed nothin' else
    But them spicy garlic smells
    An' the sunshine an' the palm trees an' the tinkly temple bells!
    On the road to Mandalay—

I am sick o' wastin' leather on these gritty pavin'-stones,
An' the blasted Henglish drizzle wakes the fever in my bones;
Though I walks with fifty 'ousemaids outer Chelsea to the Strand,
An' they talks a lot o' lovin', but wot do they understand?
    Beefy face an' grubby 'and—
    Law! wot *do* they understand?
    I've a neater, sweeter maiden in a cleaner, greener land!
    On the road to Mandalay—

Ship me somewhere east of Suez where the best is like the worst,
Where there aren't no Ten Commandments, an' a man can raise a thirst;
For the temple bells are callin', an' it's there that I would be—
By the old Moulmein Pagoda, lookin' lazy at the sea—
    On the road to Mandalay—
    Where the old Flotilla lay,
    With our sick beneath the awnings when we went to Mandalay!
    Oh, the road to Mandalay,
    Where the flyin'-fishes play,
    An' the dawn comes up like thunder outer China crost the Bay!

The Spell of the Yukon
by Robert Service (1874-1958)

You will feel like you've been there after you read this—Beware of the spell, it could be catching. This is a terrific poem. You can tell it is truly heart-felt..

I wanted the gold, and I sought it;
    I scrabbled and mucked like a slave.
Was it famine or scurvy—I fought it;
    I hurled my youth into a grave.
I wanted the gold, and I got it—
    Came out with a fortune last fall,—
Yet somehow life's not what I thought it,
    And somehow the gold isn't all.

No! There's the land. (Have you seen it?)
    It's the cussedest land that I know,
From the big, dizzy mountains that screen it
    To the deep, deathlike valleys below.
Some say God was tired when He made it;
    Some say it's a fine land to shun;
Maybe; but there's some as would trade it
    For no land on earth—and I'm one.

You come to get rich (damned good reason);
    You feel like an exile at first;
You hate it like hell for a season,
    And then you are worse than the worst.
It grips you like some kinds of sinning;
    It twists you from foe to a friend;
It seems it's been since the beginning;
    It seems it will be to the end.

I've stood in some mighty-mouthed hollow
    That's plumb-full of hush to the brim;
I've watched the big, husky sun wallow
    In crimson and gold, and grow dim,
Till the moon set the pearly peaks gleaming,
    And the stars tumbled out, neck and crop;
And I've thought that I surely was dreaming,
    With the peace o' the world piled on top.

The summer—no sweeter was ever;
    The sunshiny woods all athrill;
The grayling aleap in the river,
    The bighorn asleep on the hill.
The strong life that never knows harness;
    The wilds where the caribou call;
The freshness, the freedom, the fairness—
    O God! how I'm stuck on it all.

The winter! the brightness that blinds you,
    The white land locked tight as a drum,
The cold fear that follows and finds you,
    The silence that bludgeons you dumb.
The snows that are older than history,
    The woods where the weird shadows slant;
The stillness, the moonlight, the mystery,
    I've bade 'em good-by—but I can't.

There's a land where the mountains are nameless,
    And the rivers all run God knows where;
There are lives that are erring and aimless,
    And deaths that just hang by a hair;
There are hardships that nobody reckons;
    There are valleys unpeopled and still;
There's a land—oh, it beckons and beckons,
    And I want to go back—and I will.

They're making my money diminish;
    I'm sick of the taste of champagne.
Thank God! when I'm skinned to a finish
    I'll pike to the Yukon again.
I'll fight—and you bet it's no sham-fight;
    It's hell!—but I've been there before;
And it's better than this by a damsite—
    So me for the Yukon once more.

There's gold, and it's haunting and haunting;
    It's luring me on as of old;
Yet it isn't the gold that I'm wanting
    So much as just finding the gold.
It's the great, big, broad land 'way up yonder,
    It's the forests where silence has lease;
It's the beauty that thrills me with wonder,
    It's the stillness that fills me with peace.

Out Where the West Begins

by Arthur Chapman

Come West, young man. And bring the ladies with you.

> Out where the handclasp's a little stronger,
> Out where the smile dwells a little longer,
>> That's where the West begins;
> Out where the sun is a little brighter,
> Where the snows that fall are a trifle whiter,
> Where the bonds of home are a wee bit tighter,
>> That's where the West begins;
>
> Out where the skies are a trifle bluer,
> Out where friendship's a little truer,
>> That's where the West begins;
> Out where a fresher breeze is blowing,
> Where there's laughter in every streamlet flowing,
> Where there's more of reaping and less of sowing,
>> That's where the West begins;
>
> Out where the world is in the making,
> Where fewer hearts in despair are aching,
>> That's where the West begins;
> Where there's more of singing and less of sighing,
> Where there's more of giving and less of buying,
> And a man makes friends without half trying—
>> That's where the West begins;

⊶ LOOKING BACK ⊷

To Critics
by Walter Leonard

Sounds mighty familiar.

> When I was seventeen I hear
> 　From each censorious tongue,
> "I'd not do that if I were you;
> 　You see you're rather young."
>
> Now that I number forty years,
> 　I'm quite as often told
> Of this or that I shouldn't do
> 　Because I'm quite too old.
>
> O carping world! If there's an age
> 　Where youth and manhood keep
> An equal poise, alas! I must
> 　Have passed it in my sleep.

Recompense
by Nixon Waterman

After the dark clouds and rain; the rainbow.

> The gifts that to our breasts we fold
> 　Are brightened by our losses.
> The sweetest joys a heart can hold
> 　Grow up between its crosses.
> And on life's pathway many a mile
> 　Is made more glad and cheery,
> Because, for just a little while,
> 　The way seemed dark and dreary.

Growing Older
by R. G. Wells

How did he read my mind so closely?

A little more tired at the close of day,
A little more anxious to have our way,
A little less ready to scold and blame,
A little more care for a brother's name;
And so we are nearing the journey's end,
Where time and eternity meet and blend.

A little less care for bonds or gold,
A little more zeal for the days of old.
A broader view and a saner mind,
And a little more love for all mankind;
And so we are faring down the way
That leads to the gates of a better day.

A little more love for the friends of youth,
A little more zeal for established truth,
A little more charity in our views,
A little less thirst for the daily news;
And so we are folding our tents away
And passing in silence at close of day.

A little more leisure to sit and dream,
A little more real the things unseen,
A little nearer to those ahead,
With visions of those long loved and dead;
And so we are going where all must go—
To the place the living may never know.

A little more laughter, a few more tears,
And we shall have told our increasing years.
The book is closed and the prayers are said,
And we are part of the countless dead;
Thrice happy, then, if some soul can say,
"I live because of their help on the way."

The Old Oaken Bucket

by Samuel Woodworth (1770-1850)

A country boy's fond memories.

How dear to my heart are the scenes of my childhood,
　　When fond recollection presents them to view!
The orchard, the meadow, the deep tangled wildwood,
　　And every loved spot which my infancy knew,
The wide-spreading pond and the mill that stood by it,
　　The bridge and the rock where the cataract fell;
The cot of my father, the dairy house nigh it,
　　And e'en the rude bucket that hung in the well.

That moss-covered bucket I hailed as a treasure,
　　For often at noon, when returned from the field,
I found it the source of an exquisite pleasure,
　　The purest and sweetest that nature can yield.
How ardent I seized it, with hands that were glowing,
　　And quick to the white-pebbled bottom it fell.
Then soon, with the emblem of truth overflowing,
　　And dripping with coolness, it rose from the well.

How sweet from the green, mossy brim to receive it,
　　As, poised on the curb, it inclined to my lips!
Not a full, blushing goblet could tempt me to leave it,
　　Tho' filled with the nectar that Jupiter sips.
And now, far removed from the loved habitation,
　　The tear of regret will intrusively swell,
As fancy reverts to my father's plantation,
　　And sighs for the bucket that hung in the well.

The Old Oaken Bucket

by *Unknown*

The callous retort of a country-boy, turned city-boy.

With what anguish of mind I remember my childhood,
    Recalled in the light of knowledge since gained,
The malarious farm, the wet, fungus-grown wildwood,
    The chills then contracted that since have remained;
The scum-covered duck-pond, the pigsty close by it,
    The ditch where the sour-smelling house drainage fell,
The damp, shaded dwelling, the foul barnyard nigh it—
    But worse than all else was that terrible well,
And the old oaken bucket, the mold-crusted bucket,
    The moss-covered bucket that hung in the well.

Just think of it! Moss on the vessel that lifted
    The water I drank in the days called to mind,
Ere I knew what professors and scientist gifted
    In the waters of wells by analysis find;
The rotting wood-fiber, the oxide of iron,
    The algae, the frog of unusual size,
The water as clear as the verses of Byron,
    Are things I remember with tears in my eyes.

Oh, had I but realized in time to avoid them
    The dangers that lurked in that pestilent draft,
I'd have tested for organic germs and destroyed them
    With potassic permanganate ere I had quaffed.
Or perchance I'd have boiled it, and afterward strained it
    Through filters of charcoal and gravel combined;
Or, after distilling, condensed and regained it
    In potable form with its filth left behind.

How little I knew of the enteric fever
    Which lurked in the water I ventured to drink;
But since I've become a devoted believer
    In the teachings of science, I shudder to think.
And now, far removed from the scenes I'm describing,
    The story of warning to others I tell,
As memory reverts to my youthful imbibing
    And I gag at the thought of that horrible well,
And the old oaken bucket, the fungus-grown bucket—
    In fact, the slop bucket—that hung in the well.

Oft in the Stilly Night

by Thomas Moore (1779-1852)

A great retrospective tribute to all the good
things that happened along the way. If you
don't enjoy it now, just you wait.

> Oft in the stilly night,
>   Ere slumber's chain has bound me,
> Fond memory brings the light
>   Of other days around me;
>   The smiles, the tears,
>   Of boyhood's years,
>   The words of love then spoken;
>   The eyes that shone,
>   Now dimmed and gone,
>   The cheerful hearts now broken!
> Thus, in the stilly night,
>   Ere slumber's chain has bound me,
> Sad Memory brings the light
>   Of other days around me.
>
> When I remember all
>   The friends, so linked together,
> I've seen around me fall,
>   Like leaves in wintry weather,
>   I feel like one
>   Who treads alone
>   Some banquet-hall deserted,
>   Whose lights are fled,
>   Whose garlands dead,
>   And all but he departed!
> Thus, in the stilly night,
>   Ere Slumber's chain has bound me,
> Sad Memory brings the light
>   Of other days around me.

The Pessimist
by Ben King (1857-1894)

They never find the sunny side of the street, much
less the end of the rainbow.

> Nothing to do but work,
>   Nothing to eat but food;
> Nothing to wear but clothes
>   To keep one from going nude.
>
> Nothing to breathe but air,
>   Quick as a flash 'tis gone;
> Nowhere to fall but off,
>   Nowhere to stand but on.
>
> Nothing to comb but hair,
>   Nowhere to sleep but in bed;
> Nothing to weep but tears,
>   Nothing to bury but dead.
>
> Nothing to sing but songs;
>   Ah, well, alas! alack!
> Nowhere to go but out,
>   Nowhere to come but back.
>
> Nothing to see but sights,
>   Nothing to quench but thirst;
> Nothing to have but what we've got;
>   Thus thro' life we are cursed.
>
> Nothing to strike but a gait;
>   Everything moves that goes.
> Nothing at all but common sense
>   Can ever withstand these woes.

Diana, A Special Kind of Shooting Star

by Samuel N. Etheredge (1914-

> *"Thy day without a cloud hath pass'd*
> *And thou went lovely to the last;*
> *Extinguish'd, not decay'd!*
> *As stars that shoot along the sky*
> *Shine brightest as they fall from high."*
>
> *From Byron, And Thou Are Dead*

Princess Di, I salute you and your meteoric career, and mourn your most
untimely death.

When you think of shooting stars, and other heavenly sights,
　　Like full moons, gold sunsets or eerie Northern Lights.
You recall the sun, the moon, and well known stars
　　All pass in precise rotation
While those fast moving streaks that quickly come and go
　　Have a special fascination.

A true shooting star doesn't go very far,
　　And flames out, without trace, in seconds.
While a comet's great show will come back we know,
　　As plainly shown in our records.
The third star-like shooter, well known as a meteor,
　　May well be of very great girth
And when it flames down, and smashes the ground
　　It leaves a great hole in the earth.
(If you have doubts about their power
　　We suggest you quiz a dinosaur.)

Comparing these in our own human race,
　　Bright stars have shone and burned out without trace.
Such as movie stars whose only claim to fame,
　　Was a figure like Venus, or a real handsome face.
And sadly this group includes names that bring shudders,
　　Since they all strove for the top, by stepping on others.

But a meteor, as stated, makes a very great impression
    And we know one of this type who fit the bill despite some
        indiscretion.
Her noble nature rose far above her regal name and station,
    For true royalty are only such, as how they rule their nation.

She touched the sick, the poor, the maimed and made them know
    she cared.
        She raised her king and princely sons, as no one else had
            dared.
And then, with happiness near, one step from her Nirvana,
    O' cruel fate—Are tears too late? Princess of Wales, our Queen
        of Hearts, Diana

Unlike the sky-borne meteors that leave their mark when they fall,
    Our queenly lady had already made her mark with each and all.
And with her charm, her elan and her dash,
    She became the first meteor to mark before its crash.
Now a heartbroken world sends a heartfelt, Hosanna!
    To our star of stars, our Queen of Hearts, Diana.

Little by Little
by Unknown

Reminds me of that great song *Little Things Mean a Lot.*

Little by little the time goes by—
    Short, if you sing through it, long, if you sigh.
Little by little—an hour a day,
    Gone with the years that have vanished away.
Little by little the race is run;
    Trouble and waiting and toil are done!

Little by little the skies grow clear;
    Little by little the sun comes near;
Little by little the days smile out,
    Gladder and brighter on pain and doubt;
Little by little the seed we sow
    Into a beautiful yield will grow.

Little by little the world grows strong,
     Fighting the battle of Right and Wrong;
Little by little the Wrong gives way—
     Little by little the Right has sway.
Little by little all longing souls
     Struggle up nearer the shining goals.

Little by little the good in men
     Blossoms to beauty, for human ken;
Little by little the angels see
     Prophecies better of good to be;
Little by little the God of all
     Lifts the world nearer the pleading call.

The Old Man Dreams
by Oliver Wendell Holmes (1809-1894)

Reflections of a wise old man's lifetime. The rollicking pleasures
of youth are replaced by the more serious blessings of old age.

Oh for one hour of youthful joy!
     Give back my twentieth spring!
I'd rather laugh, a bright-haired boy,
     Then reign, a gray-beard king.

Off with the spoils of wrinkled age!
     Away with Learning's crown!
Tear out life's Wisdom-written page,
     And dash its trophies down!

One moment let my life-blood stream
     From boyhood's fount of flame!
Give me one giddy, reeling dream
     Of life all love and fame!

My listening angel heard the prayer,
     And calmly smiling, said,
"If I but touch thy silvered hair,
     Thy hasty wish hath sped.

"But is there nothing in thy track
    To bid thee fondly stay,
While the swift seasons hurry back
    To find the wished-for day?"

"Ah, truest soul of womankind!
    Without thee what were life?
One bliss I cannot leave behind:
    I'll take—my—precious—wife!"

The angel took a sapphire pen
    And wrote in rainbow dew,
The Man would be a boy again,
    And be a husband, too!

"And is there nothing yet unsaid,
    Before the change appears?
Remember, all their gifts have fled
    With those dissolving years."

"Why, yes:" for memory would recall
    My fond paternal joys;
"I could not bear to leave them all—
    I'll take—my—girl—and—boys."

The smiling angel dropped his pen,—
    "Why, this will never do;
The man would be a boy again,
    And be a father, too!"

———

And so I laughed,—my laughter woke
    The household with its noise,—
And wrote my dream, when morning broke,
    To please the gray-haired boys.

The Barefoot Boy

by John Greenleaf Whittier (1807-1892)

The similarities of the young lives of Hiawatha and the
barefoot boy are very startling, enjoying all the fascinating
delights of nature. Who among us, past middle-age,
wouldn't love to trade places with the Barefoot Boy. And
sure there will still be a bit of the barefoot boy in every
80-year old.

> Blessings on thee, little man,
> Barefoot boy, with cheek of tan!
> With thy turned-up pantaloons,
> And thy merry whistled tunes;
> With thy red lip, redder still,
> Kissed by strawberries on the hill;
> With the sunshine on thy face,
> Through thy torn brim's jaunty grace,
> From my heart I give thee joy,—
> I was once a barefoot boy.
> Prince thou art,—the grown-up man
> Only is republican.
> Let the million-dollared ride!
> Barefoot, trudging at his side,
> Thou hast more than he can buy,
> In the reach of ear and eye—
> Outward sunshine, inward joy;
> Blessings on thee, barefoot boy!
>
> Oh, for boyhood's painless play,
> Sleep that wakes in laughing day,
> Health that mocks the doctor's rules,
> Knowledge never learned of schools,
> Of the wild bee's morning chase,
> Of the wild flower's time and place,
> Flight of fowl and habitude
> Of the tenants of the wood;
> How the tortoise bears his shell,
> How the woodchuck digs his cell,
> And the groundmole sinks his well;
> How the robin feeds her young,

How the oriole's nest is hung,
Where the whitest lilies blow,
Where the freshest berries grow,
Where the ground-nut trails its vine,
Where the wood-grape's clusters shine,

Of the black wasp's cunning way,—
Mason of his walls of clay,—
And the architectural plans
Of gray-hornet artisans!
For, eschewing books and tasks,
Nature answers all he asks,
Hand in hand with her he walks,
Face to face with her he talks,
Part and parcel of her joy,—
Blessings on the barefoot boy!

Oh, for boyhood's time of June,
Crowding years in one brief moon,
When all things I heard or saw,
Me, their master, waited for.
I was rich in flowers and trees,
Humming-birds and honeybees,
For my sport the squirrel played,
Plied the snouted mole his spade;
For my task the blackberry cone
Purpled over hedge and stone;
Laughed the brook for my delight
Through the day and through the night,—
Whispering at the garden wall,
Talked with me from fall to fall;
Mine the sand-rimmed pickerel pond,
Mine the walnut slopes beyond,
Mine, on bending orchard trees,
Apples of Hesperides!
Still, as my horizon grew,
Larger grew my riches too;
All the world I saw or knew
Seemed a complex Chinese toy
Fashioned for a barefoot boy.

Oh, for festal dainties spread,
Like my bowl of milk and bread,—
Pewter spoon and bowl of wood,
On the doorstone, gray and rude!
O'er me, like a regal tent,
Cloudy-ribbed, the sunset bent,
Purple-curtained, fringed with gold,
Looped in many a wind-swung fold,
While for music came the play
Of the pied frog's orchestra,
And, to light the noisy choir,
Lit the fly his lamp of fire.
I was monarch: pomp and joy
Waited on thee, barefoot boy!

Cheerily, then, my little man,
Live and laugh as boyhood can!
Though the flinty slopes be hard,
Stubble-speared the new-mown sward,
Every morn shall lead thee through
Fresh baptisms of the dew;
Every evening from thy feet
Shall the cool wind kiss the heat;
All too soon these feet must hide
In the prison cells of pride,
Lose the freedom of the sod,
Like a colt's for work be shod,
Made to tread the mills of toil,
Up and down in ceaseless moil;
Happy if their track be found
Never on forbidden ground;
Happy if they sink not in
Quick and treacherous sands of sin,
Ah! that thou couldst know thy joy,
Ere it passes, barefoot boy!

Rock Me to Sleep

by Elizabeth Akers Allen (1832-1911)

Only the first two lines, but what a dream!

> Backward, turn backward, O time, in your flight,
> Make me a child again just for to-night!

Grandfather's Clock

by Henry Clay Work

Sounds so true you've got to believe it. At least make
believe you do.

> My grandfather's clock was too large for the shelf,
>   So it stood ninety years on the floor;
> It was taller by half than the old man himself,
>   Though it weighed not a pennyweight more.
> It was bought on the morn of the day that he was born
>   And was always his treasure and pride,
> But it stopped short—never to go again—
>   When the old man died.
>
> Ninety years without slumbering—
>   Tick, tick, tick, tick.
> His life seconds numbering—
>   Tick, tick, tick, tick.
> It stopped short—never to go again—
>   When the old man died.
>
> In watching its pendulum swing to and fro
>   Many hours had he spent while a boy;
> And in childhood and manhood the clock seemed to know
>   And to share both his grief and his joy,
> For it struck twenty-four when he entered the door
>   With a blooming and beautiful bride,
> But it stopped short—never to go again—
>   When the old man died.

My grandfather said of those he could hire,
    Not a servant so faithful he found,
For it wasted no time and had but one desire—
    At the close of each week to be wound.
And it kept in its place—not a frown upon its face,
    And its hands never hung by its side;
But it stopped short—never to go again—
    When the old man died.

It rang an alarm in the dead of night—
    An alarm that for years had been dumb.
And we know that his spirit was pluming for flight,
    That his hour for departure had come.
Still the clock kept the time with a soft and muffled chime
    As we silently stood by his side;
But it stopped short—never to go again—
    When the old man died.

Wanderlust
by Gerald Gould (1885-1916)

He's got it but good; no homebody
him. Prognosis: Incurable.

Beyond the East the sunrise, beyond the West the sea,
And East and West the wanderlust that will not let me be;
It works in me like madness, dear, to bid me say good-by!
For the seas call and the stars call, and oh, the call of the sky!

I know not where the white road runs, nor what the blue hills are,
But man can have the sun for friend, and for his guide a star;
And there's no end of voyaging when once the voice is heard,
For the river calls and the road calls, and oh, the call of a bird!

Yonder the long horizon lies, and there by night and day
The old ships draw to home again, the young ships sail away;
And come I may, but go I must, and if men ask you why,
You may put the blame on the stars and the sun and the white road
    and the sky!

Break, Break, Break
by Alfred Tennyson (1809-1892)
Obviously the break of a broken heart
from the loss of a dear one.

> Break, break, break,
>> On thy cold gray stones, O sea!
> And I would that my tongue could utter
>> The thoughts that arise in me.
>
> O well for the fisherman's boy,
>> That he shouts with his sister at play;
> O well for the sailor lad
>> That he sings in his boat on the bay!
>
> And the stately ships go on
>> To their haven under the hill;
> But O for the touch of a vanished hand,
>> And the sound of a voice that is still!
>
> Break, break, break,
>> At the foot of thy crags, O sea!
> But the tender grace of a day that is dead
>> Will never come back to me.

The Land of Beginning Again
by Louisa Fletcher
If we could live our life over. Wow!

> I wish that there were some wonderful place
>> Called the Land of Beginning Again,
> Where all our mistakes and all our heartaches
>> And all of our poor selfish grief
> Could be dropped like a shabby old coat at the door,
>> And never be put on again.

I wish we could come on it all unaware,
      Like the hunter who finds a lost trail;
And I wish that the one whom our blindness had done
      The greatest injustice of all
Could be at the gates like an old friend that waits
      For the comrade he's gladdest to hail.

We would find all the things we intended to do
      But forgot, and remembered too late,
Little praises unspoken, little promises broken,
      And all of the thousand and one
Little duties neglected that might have perfected
      The day for one less fortunate.

It wouldn't be possible not to be kind
      In the Land of Beginning Again;
And the ones we misjudged and the ones whom we grudged
      Their moments of victory here
Would find in the grasp of our loving handclasp
      More than penitent lips could explain.

For what had been hardest we'd know had been best,
      And what had seemed loss would be gain;
For there isn't a sting that will not take wing
      When we've faced it and laughed it away;
And I think that the laughter is most what we're after
      In the Land of Beginning Again.

So I wish that there were some wonderful place
      Called the Land of Beginning Again,
Where all our mistakes and all our heartaches
      And all of our poor selfish grief
Could be dropped like a shabby old coat at the door,
      And never be put on again.

Bill and Joe

by Oliver Wendell Holmes (1809-1894)

Sounds like Bill Success and Joe Failure cementing
their friendship at a class reunion. Very moving.

Come, dear old comrade, you and I
Will steal an hour from days gone by,
The shining days when life was new,
And all was bright with morning dew,
The lusty days of long ago,
When you were Bill and I was Joe:

Your name may flaunt a title trail,
Proud as a cockerel's rainbow tail;
And mine as brief appendix wear
As Tam O'Shanter's luckless mare;
To-day, old friend, remember still
That I am Joe and you are Bill.

You've won the great world's envied prize,
And grand you look in people's eyes,
With H O N and LL.D.
In big brave letters, fair to see,—
Your fist, old fellow! off they go!—
How are you, Bill? How are you, Joe?

You've worn the judge's ermined robe;
You've taught your name to half the globe;
You've sung mankind a deathless strain;
You've made the dead past live again:
The world may call you what it will,
But you and I are Joe and Bill.

The chaffing young folks stare and say,
"See those old buffers, bent and gray,—
They talk like fellows in their teens!
Mad, poor old boys? That's what it means,"—
And shake their heads; they little know
The throbbing hearts of Bill and Joe!—

How Bill forgets his hour of pride,
While Joe sits smiling at his side;
How Joe, in spite of time's disguise,
Finds the old schoolmate in his eyes,—
Those calm, stern eyes that melt and fill
As Joe looks fondly up at Bill.

Ah, pensive scholar, what is fame?
A fitful tongue of leaping flame;
A giddy whirlwind's fickle gust,
That lifts a pinch of mortal dust;
A few swift years, and who can show
Which dust was Bill and which was Joe?

The weary idol takes his stand,
Holds out his bruised and aching hand,
While gaping thousands come and go,—
How vain it seems, this empty show!
Till all at once his pulses thrill;—
'Tis poor old Joe's "God Bless you, Bill!"

And shall we breathe in happier spheres
The names that pleased our mortal ears;
In some sweet lull of harp and song,
For earth-born spirits none too long,
Just whispering of the world below
Where this was Bill and that was Joe?

No matter; while our home is here
No sounding name is half so dear;
When fades at length our lingering day,
Who cares what pompous tombstones say?
Read on the hearts that love us still,
Hic jacet[1] Joe. Hic jacet Bill.

[1] hic jacet: Latin for 'here lies'

The River of Life

by Thomas Campbell (1777-1844)

Most rivers flow fastest near their start! Why not
this one? We surely do miss more and more of
our old dear friends, as years slip by.

> The more we live, more brief appear
>   Our life's succeeding stages:
> A day to childhood seems a year,
>   And years the passing ages.
>
> The gladsome current of our youth,
>   Ere passion yet disorders,
> Steals, lingering like a river smooth
>   Along its grassy borders.
>
> But as the careworn cheek grows wan,
>   And sorrow's shafts fly thicker,
> Ye stars, that measure life to man,
>   Why seem your courses quicker?
>
> When joys have lost their bloom and breath,
>   And life itself is vapid,
> Why, as we reach the Falls of Death,
>   Feel we its tide more rapid?
>
> It may be strange—yet who would change
>   Time's course to slower speeding,
> When one by one our friends have gone
>   And left our bosoms bleeding?
>
> **Heaven gives our years of fading strength**
>   **Indemnifying fleetness;**
> **And those of youth, a seeming length,**
>   **Proportioned to their sweetness.**

Sometimes

by Thomas S. Jones, Jr.

Looking back to the future.

> Across the fields of yesterday
>   He sometimes comes to me,
> A little lad just back from play—
>   The lad I used to be.
>
> And yet he smiles so wistfully
>   Once he has crept within,
> I wonder if he hopes to see
>   The man I might have been.

One by One

by Adelaide Anne Procter (1825-1864)

A pleasant approach to life's duties, joys and
sorrows.

> One by one the sands are flowing,
>   One by one the moments fall;
> Some are coming, some are going;
>   Do not strive to grasp them all.
>
> One by one thy duties wait thee—
>   Let thy whole strength go to each,
> Let no future dreams elate thee,
>   Learn thou first what these can teach.
>
> One by one (bright gifts from heaven)
>   Joys are sent thee here below;
> Take them readily when given—
>   Ready, too, to let them go.
>
> One by one thy griefs shall meet thee;
>   Do not fear an armed band;
> One will fade as others greet thee—
>   Shadows passing through the land.

Do not look at life's long sorrow;
    See how small each moment's pain;
God will help thee for to-morrow,
    So each day begin again.

Every hour that fleets so slowly
    Has its task to do or bear;
Luminous the crown, and holy,
    When each gem is set with care.

Do not linger with regretting,
    Or for passing hours despond;
Nor, thy daily toil forgetting,
    Look too eagerly beyond.

Hours are golden links, God's token,
    Reaching heaven; but, one by one,
Take them, lest the chain be broken
    Ere the pilgrimage be done.

The Bells

by Edgar Allan Poe (1809-1849)

Poe, with his frequent manic-depressive moods, uses the various sounds of the Bells-Bells-Bells to take you from the most gentle tinkling bells of a winter sleigh ride, through the happy golden bells of a romantic wedding, to the clamor of a harsh alarm bell of some disaster, to finally slip into the solemn, melancholy bells of a funeral. The tintinnabulation of the bells, bells, bells throughout really gets the feeling of the occasion across. The more you read this, the more it gets to you.

I

Hear the sledges with the bells—
    Silver bells!
What a world of merriment their melody foretells!
    How they tinkle, tinkle, tinkle,
        In the icy air of night!
    While the stars that oversprinkle
    All the heavens, seem to twinkle
        With a crystalline delight;

Keeping time, time, time,
In a sort of Runic rhyme,
To the tintinnabulation that so musically wells
From the bells, bells, bells, bells,
Bells, bells, bells,—
From the jingling and the tinkling of the bells.

II

Hear the mellow wedding bells—
Golden bells!
What a world of happiness their harmony foretells
Through the balmy air of night
How they ring out their delight!
From the molten-golden notes,
And all in tune,
What a liquid ditty floats
To the turtle dove that listens, while she gloats
On the moon!
Oh, from out the sounding cells,
What a gush of euphony voluminously wells!
How it swells!
How it dwells
On the Future! how it tells
Of the rapture that impels
To the swinging and the ringing
Of the bells, bells, bells,
Of the bells, bells, bells, bells,
Bells, bells, bells,—
To the rhyming and the chiming of the bells!

III

Hear the loud alarum bells—
Brazen bells!
What a tale of terror now their turbulency tells!
In the startled ear of night
How they scream out their affright!
Too much horrified to speak
They can only shriek, shriek,
Out of tune,
In a clamorous appealing to the mercy of the fire,

In a mad expostulation with the deaf and frantic fire,
   Leaping higher, higher, higher,
   With a desperate desire,
  And a resolute endeavor,
  Now—now to sit or never,
 By the side of the pale-faced moon.
  Oh, the bells, bells, bells!
  What a tale their terror tells
   Of despair!
How they clang, and clash, and roar!
What a horror they outpour
On the bosom of the palpitating air!
  Yet the ear it fully knows,
   By the twanging,
   And the clanging,
  How the danger ebbs, and flows;
 Yet the ear distinctly tells,
   In the jangling,
   And the wrangling,
 How the danger sinks and swells,
By the sinking or the swelling in the anger of the bells—
   Of the bells—
 Of the bells, bells, bells, bells,
  Bells, bells, bells,—
In the clamor and the clangor of the bells!

    IV

 Hear the tolling of the bells—
   Iron bells!
What a world of solemn thought their monody compels!
  In the silence of the night,
  How we shiver with affright
At the melancholy menace of their tone!
  For every sound that floats
  From the rust within their throats
   Is a groan.
  And the people—ah, the people—
  They that dwell up in the steeple,
   All alone,
  And who tolling, tolling, tolling,

In that muffled monotone,
Feel a glory in so rolling
    On the human heart a stone—
They are neither man nor woman—
They are neither brute nor human—
        They are Ghouls:
    And their king it is who tolls;
    And he rolls, rolls, rolls,
        Rolls
    A paean from the bells!
And his merry bosom swells
With the paean of the bells!
And he dances, and he yells;
Keeping time, time, time,
In a sort of Runic rhyme,
    To the paean of the bells—
        Of the bells:
Keeping time, time, time,
In a sort of Runic rhyme,
    To the throbbing of the bells—
    Of the bells, bells, bells—
    To the sobbing of the bells;
Keeping time, time, time,
    As he knells, knells, knells,
In a happy Runic rhyme,
    To the rolling of the bells—
    Of the bells, bells, bells—
    To the tolling of the bells,
Of the bells, bells, bells, bells—
        Bells, bells, bells—
To the moaning and the groaning of the bells!

Life's a Game

by Unknown

A little play on cards.

> This life is but a game of cards,
> Which everyone must learn;
> Each shuffles, cuts and deals the deck,
> And then a trump does turn;
> Some show up a high card,
> While others make it low,
> And many turn no cards at all—
> In fact, they cannot show.
>
> When hearts are up we play for love,
> And pleasure rules the hour;
> Each day goes pleasantly along
> In sunshine's rosy bower.
> When diamonds chance to crown the pack,
> That's when men stake their gold,
> And thousands then are lost and won,
> By gamblers, young and old.
>
> When clubs are trump look out for war,
> On ocean and on land,
> For bloody deeds are often done
> When clubs are held in hand.
> At last turns up the darkened spade,
> Held by the toiling slave,
> And a spade will turn up trump at last
> And dig each player's grave.

A Bag of Tools

by R. L. Sharpe

Are you a stumbling blocker or a steppingstone builder?

Isn't it strange
That princes and kings,
And clowns that caper
In sawdust rings,
And common people
Like you and me
Are builders for eternity?

Each is given a bag of tools,
A shapeless mass,
A book of rules;
And each must make—
Ere life is flown—
A stumbling block
Or a steppingstone.

For Want of a Horseshoe Nail

Adapted From James Baldwin

This sounds like King Richard III's cry, "A horse, a horse, my kingdom for a horse," but his horse was killed in battle, not de-shoed.

For want of a nail, a shoe was lost,
For want of a shoe, a horse was lost,
For want of a horse, a battle was lost,
For want of a battle, a kingdom was lost,
    And all for the want of a horseshoe nail.

All the World's a Stage

(from As You Like It*)*
by William Shakespeare (1564-1616)

Poetry—no, but what a classic. Where do
you fit? I certainly envy the first five.

All the world's a stage,
And all the men and women merely players.
They have their exits and their entrances,
And one man in his time plays many parts,
His acts being seven ages. At first, the infant,
Mewling and puking in the nurse's arms.
Then the whining schoolboy, with his satchel
And shining morning face, creeping like a snail
Unwillingly to school. And then the lover,
Sighing like a furnace, with a woful ballad
Made to his mistress' eyebrow. Then a soldier,
Full of strange oaths and bearded like the pard,
Jealous in honour, sudden and quick in quarrel,
Seeking the bubble reputation
Even in the cannon's mouth. And then the justice,
In fair round belly with good capon lin'd,
With eyes severe and beard of formal cut,
Full of wise saws and modern instances;
And so he plays his part. The sixth age shifts
Into the lean and slipper'd pantaloon,
With spectacles on nose and pouch on side;
His youthful hose, well sav'd, a world too wide
For his shrunk shank, and his big manly voice,
Turning again toward childish treble, pipes
And whistles in his sound. Last scene of all,
That ends this strange eventful history,
Is second childishness and mere oblivion,
Sans teeth, sans eyes, sans taste, sans everything.

Some Time at Eve

by Lizzie Clark Hardy

A pleasant way to leave this "veil of tears."

Some time at eve when the tide is low,
        I shall slip my mooring and sail away,
With no response to the friendly hail
        Of kindred craft in the busy bay.
In the silent hush of the twilight pale,
        When the night stoops down to embrace the day
And the voices call in the water's flow—
Some time at eve when the tide is low,
        I shall slip my mooring and sail away.

Through the purpling shadows that darkly trail
        O'er the ebbing tide of the Unknown Sea,
I shall fare me away, with a dip of sail
And a ripple of waters to tell the tale
        Of a lonely voyager, sailing away
        To the Mystic Isles where at anchor lay
The crafts of those who have sailed before
O'er the Unknown Sea to the Unseen Shore.

A few who have watched me sail away
Will miss my craft from the busy bay;
        Some friendly barks that were anchored near,
        Some loving souls that my heart held dear,
        In silent sorrow will drop a tear—
But I shall have peacefully furled my sail
In moorings sheltered from storm or gale,
        And greeted the friends who have sailed before
        O'er the Unknown Sea to the Unseen Shore.

That's all folks.

I hope you enjoyed reading this book as much as I enjoyed putting it together. In closing, I think the following old Irish blessing best sums up my wishes for you one and all:

> May the road rise to meet you
> > May the wind be ever at your back,
> May the sun shine warm upon your face,
> > The rain fall soft upon your fields,
> And until we meet again,
> > May God hold you in the hollow of his hand.

God bless you,

Samuel N. Etheredge

P.S. I want to ask a very personal heartfelt favor—PLEASE don't put this book on a bookshelf and forget it. Instead, leave it on a desk or table where you can open it and get a quick lift or a laugh.

Thanks.

INDEX

FIRST LINE AND TITLE INDEX. TITLES ARE IN ITALICS.

A

A bunch of the boys were whooping it up in the Malamute saloon, 257

A feller isn't think' mean, 293

A fire-mist and a planet, 110

A horse can't pull while kicking, 67

A little more tired at the close of day, 422

A little red hen once found a grain of wheat, 31

A thing of beauty is a joy forever, 284

A wet sheet and a flowing sea, 291

A wise old owl lived in an oak, 55

Abou Ben Adhem, 106

Abou Ben Adhem(may his tribe increase!), 106

Across the fields of yesterday, 441

Again I hear that creaking step!, 211

Age is a quality of mind, 68

All the World's a Stage, 448

All the world's a stage, 448

All things bright and beautiful, 100

Always Finish, 179

America, 371

America for Me, 372

America, The Beautiful, 373

America's Answer, 403

Amid the cares of married life, 276

An ancient story I'll tell you anon, 232

An old man, going a lone highway, 142

And this is good old Boston, 251

Animal Fair, 7

Annabel Lee, 271

Are you almost disgusted with life, little man?, 32

Arrow and the Song, The, 16

As I was going to St. Ives, 34

Auld Lang Syne, 170

Ay, tear her tattered ensign down!, 387

B

Back of the beating hammer, 80

Backward, turn backward, O time, in your flight, 434

Bag of Tools, A, 447

Ballad of East and West, The, 361

Barbara Frietchie, 395

Barefoot Boy, The, 431

Battle of Blenheim, The, 359

Battle-Hymn of the Republic, 107

Be the Best of Whatever You Are, 59

Be True, 94

Behind him lay the gray Azores, 132

Bells, The, 442

Between the dark and the daylight, 15

Beyond the East the sunrise, beyond the West the sea, 435

Bill and Joe, 438

Birth of St. Patrick, The, 247

Bivouac of the Dead, The, 409

Blessing on the hand of women!, 39

Blessings on thee, little man, 431

Blind Men and the Elephant, The, 205

Blow, blow, thou winter wind, 168

Blue and the Gray, The, 392

Boots, 398

Bougainville, 411

Boy Reciter, The, 20

Boy Who Never Told a Lie, The, 19

Boy's Song, A, 18

Break, Break, Break, 436

Break, break, break, 436

I

Y

INDEX

AUTHORS AND TITLES